Major Events and Daily Lives

Readings on United States History Since 1865

SECOND EDITION

Major Events and Daily Lives

Readings on United States History Since 1865

EDITED BY Walter Miszczenko

College of Western Idaho

SAN DIEGO

Bassim Hamadeh, CEO and Publisher
Carrie Montoya, Manager, Revisions and Author Care
Kaela Martin, Project Editor
Christian Berk, Production Editor
Jess Estrella, Senior Graphic Designer
Alexa Lucido, Licensing Manager
Natalie Piccotti, Director of Marketing
Kassie Graves, Vice President of Editorial
Jamie Giganti, Director of Academic Publishing

Cover image copyright © 2012 Depositphotos/everett225.
Robert F. Sargent, "1944 Normandy LST ," https://commons.wikimedia.org/wiki/File:1944_Normandy LST_clean.jpg, 1944.
Copyright © 2016 Depositphotos/Gal Amar.
Evert F. Baumgardner, "Family Watching Television," https://commons.wikimedia.org/wiki/File%3A-Family_watching_television_1958.jpg, c. 1.
Lester Chadwick, "The rival pitchers; a story of college baseball," https://commons.wikimedia.org/wiki/File:The_rival_pitchers;_a_story_of_college_baseball_(1910)_(14753152755).jpg, 1910.
Frank Tousey, "An Old Scout. Young Wild West; or Saved by an Indian Princess," https://commons.wikimedia.org/wiki/File:Young_Wild_West_Missing.jpg, 1902.
Copyright © Lear 21 (CC by 2.0) at https://commons.wikimedia.org/wiki/File:West_and_East_Germans_at_the_Brandenburg_Gate_in_1989.jpg.
Janet McKenzie Hill/The Procter & Gamble Co., ""Almost As Necessary As The Cook"," https://commons.wikimedia.org/wiki/File%3AThe_Boston_Cooking_School_magazine_of_culinary_science_and_domestic_economics_(1908)_(14766643872).jpg, 1908
Glen Scott, " New Yorkers Listening to 1922 World Series by Radio," https://commons.wikimedia.org/wiki/File%3ANew_Yorkers_listening_to_1922_World_Series_by_radio.jpg, 1922.

Printed in the United States of America.

3970 Sorrento Valley Blvd., Ste. 500, San Diego, CA 92121

CONTENTS

PREFACE TO THE SECOND EDITION

I n the second edition of the book, *Major Events and Daily Lives*, I have made some changes. However, the basic structure of the book remains the same. The reader will find that some chapters have been dropped and new ones added. In selecting the readings for the second edition of the book I have sixteen chapters. The book opens with the article about the Wild West and how it has resulted in a myth popularized by Hollywood and pulp novels, while chapter 10 looks at the role comic books played in winning World War II, and chapters 15 and 16 look at managing the new Cold War between the United States and Russia.

Let me stress, students should not assume that this reader is a comprehensive text on American history. Rather, the aim is for students to get a wide spectrum of daily life that impacted the common people on an everyday life—yet these lives represent only a small fragment of the American experience. In short, these articles cover issues that impacted American lives during various times.

In the second edition, like the first, I found no need to do any extensive editing beyond selecting and arranging the articles to provide the substance, clarity, and balance appropriate to "readings" in American history. I have kept the brief introductory comments on the general features of each work, which are intended primarily as background information to students. In addition, I have added a question to each chapter for the student to consider.

While final responsibility for the selection of articles rest with me, I would like to give, as in the first edition, special thanks to my students at the College of Western Idaho. They have made this enterprise not only a duty but also a pleasure. I would like to single out and thank the assistance given to me by Kaela Martin, project editor at Cognella, and the assistance given to me by the rest of Cognella Staff, and last but not least, I would like to acknowledge the articles' authors, for without their permission to use their articles, this book would not be possible.

PART I

The Wild West

A Kansas Sod House in the 1890s. In the photo left to right: Ethel, Alpha, Roy, and Dewey.

CHAPTER 1

The Wild West and the Wrenching of the American Chronicle

By Stewart L. Udall

Editor's Introduction

The last frontier in the United States was the region west of the Mississippi River and east of California. In the early nineteenth century, Americans called this region the "Great American Desert." The first settlers to go out west were explorers, trappers, miners hoping to strike it rich, and outlaws. Local government was either nonexistent or ineffective in the region, which caused many citizens to form vigilante groups that took the law into their own hands; they did not always get the right man. In 1890 the U.S. Census Bureau announced the end of the American frontier. Thus, for most Americans, the "Wild West" was popularized by Hollywood and pulp novels. As a result, a myth emerged about the Wild West that persists to this day—a myth that, according to Stewart L. Udall, is dispelled by "records and reminiscences of settlers." In the following chapter, Udall writes that it was ordinary people, from the Native Americans to the pioneers, who settled and made the West—and not what was popularized by Hollywood and pulp novels.

Excerpts from

The Wild West and the Wrenching of the American Chronicle

By Stewart L. Udall

> "Despite all of the mythologizing, violent fatalities in the Old West tended to be rare rather than common."
> —Robert R. Dykstra

How wild was the West? One cannot put western violence into perspective without recognizing that, where firearms were concerned, there was a huge difference between the primitive weapons available in the Old West of the wagon settlers and the firepower of the guns civilians owned after the Civil War. In his great memoir, General Ulysses S. Grant observed that during the battles of the Mexican War, "at a distance of a few hundred yards a man might fire at you all day long without your finding out." The killing power of six-guns and rapid-fire rifles, which were not developed until the Civil War, along with increased social frictions that fostered lawless behavior, produced a much higher level of overall civilian violence in the postwar era than had existed previously in the West. How wild the West was depends on which West we are talking about—before or after the Civil War.

Violence and Nonviolence in the Old West

Impulses of self-preservation encouraged the lightly armed wagon families of the pre–Civil War era to use restraint in their encounters with Indians and other travelers on overland trails. These groups did not venture into the wild country as conquerors. They traveled as cautious companions who, first and last, wanted to avoid risks that would disrupt their journey to valleys where they hoped to arrive in time to plant crops and establish their homes.

Although the gold seekers' aims were starkly divergent from those of early pioneers bent on settlement, the hordes of single men bound for California's goldfields also had a selfish interest in avoiding delays. In their frantic race against time and one another, the forty-niners saw conflicts with Indians or with agrarian immigrants as distractions that could fatally delay their success in the goldfields.

The primitive weapons available in the antebellum period also contributed to the relative safety of travel on the first transcontinental trails. The immigrants wisely avoided conflicts with natives because the weapons most of them carried were cumbersome, hard to reload, single-shot hunting rifles. Lacking guns, Indian groups were constrained by the knowledge that their arrows, spears, and clubs could prevail only when they outnumbered or surprised their adversaries.

The spirit of caution induced by these realities produced a pattern of wary, sometimes even friendly, relations alongside most trails that prompted historian John D. Unruh Jr. to characterize the pre–Civil War period as a time of "essential safety" for travel. In his landmark study of overland migration, Unruh effectively undermined the legend that prewar westward migration was stained by high levels of violence between Indians and migrants. "The fatal trail confrontations that did occur were usually prompted by emigrant insults and disdain for Indian rights," Unruh pointed out, as we saw in chapter 3, concluding that the dangers of overland travel were "misrepresented by myth-makers' emphasis on Indian treachery."

During the two decades preceding the Civil War, the number of natives killed by immigrants (363, or an average of 18 per year) was comparable to the number of immigrants killed by natives (426, or an average of 21 per year). It was disease, not violence, that accounted for nine out of ten deaths on the trail. The results of his survey caused Unruh to doubt whether the mortality rate of the trails "much exceeded the average death rate among Americans resisting the call of the frontier to remain at home."

Such facts contradict the myth that prewar immigrants faced constant threats from armed Indian warriors. The responsibility for such persistent confusion rests with the legion of embellishers—beginning with William "Buffalo Bill" Cody's extravagant Wild West shows—who created the impression that post–Civil War firearms were not only available in earlier decades but also used with little provocation.

If a sharp line is drawn between these two distinctive periods—before and after the Civil War and the advent of the transcontinental railroads—we can see that most of the attacks on wagon trains took place *after* the war and that most forays by native warriors occurred on well-beaten commercial roads such as the Santa Fe Trail. The Winchester repeating rifle—the weapon that supposedly "won the West"—was not readily available until the early 1870s, and not until 1871 were metallic cartridge six-shooters first issued to U.S. soldiers. It is also revealing that nearly all the town marshals and outlaws who became American "legends" were only teenagers in the 1850s.

To present such facts is not to argue that the 1840s and 1850s were a pacific period in western history. Indeed, some violent episodes occurred even as civilization was catching up with the frontier. Although most of the prewar contacts between migrants and Plains Indians proved peaceful, in some areas deadly skirmishes erupted as settlers encroached on core areas of Indian homelands.

When natives and overlanders met trailside for the first time, their relations were not often strained by hostile attitudes. Nevertheless, the Old West lives on in the popular imagination as a turbulent, brawling region dominated by gunfighters, outlaws, Indian wars, and devil-may-care gold rushers. Acknowledging the power of these images, historian Richard White commented that most Americans are convinced that "the 19th century west was a perpetually violent and lawless place."

Technological developments in the aftermath of the Civil War both altered and ameliorated the economic and social conditions of western settlement. Most changes promoted order, but a few increased conflicts between individuals and groups. Railroads were the paramount agent of change, and they influenced the course of change in myriad ways. Although it took promoters nearly three decades to complete lines into all the main regions, significant development commenced as soon as tracks were extended westward from St. Paul, Omaha, Kansas City, and Fort Worth and delivered incoming migrants into unplowed heartlands.

Not only did new railheads provide access to national markets; machines they transported made the benefits of the rapidly evolving industrial age available to fledgling communities. And the prospect that branch lines could be built into remote areas encouraged eastern capitalists to contemplate bringing heavy machinery into wilderness settings and creating boomtowns in locations where minerals and lumber could be extracted and shipped to markets.

Along with acknowledgment of the great importance of railroads, the impression is often conveyed that nothing significant happened in western transportation in the pre-railroad period. But such interpretations ignore the use of waterways and the feats of wagon masters who harnessed the energy of horses, mules, and oxen. By the late 1850s, overland stages were carrying passengers and mail between the Mississippi River valley and San Francisco, and freighting companies on the Missouri River were shipping goods and machines brought upriver on steamboats to inland towns.

At the same time, settlers in the intermountain territories were using the energy of draft animals to transport produce over long distances to regional markets. Enterprising farmers, for example, used caravans of heavy wagons to deliver goods that sustained early mining camps in Montana, Idaho, Nevada, and Colorado. And all during the 1860s, the Mormons sent "church trains" to the Missouri River valley to bring thousands of European converts and cargoes of capital goods to Utah. What railroads did, then, was increase the intensity of this traffic and reach into areas where transport had previously been difficult.

Violence after the Civil War

"Personal violence certainly could reach extraordinary levels in the West, but it remained confined to very narrow social milieus." —Richard White

In the postwar period, disputes over land boundaries and grazing rights generated some deadly—though typically short-lived—conflicts in some regions of the West. In most instances, these were quarrels between individuals or families. The local clashes that resulted in the most casualties involved conflicts between mega-ranchers and small stockmen over free grass and water on unclaimed public lands. On a larger scale, the most violent disputes arose when the buffalo were exterminated and U.S. soldiers forced the Plains Indians from their traditional hunting grounds.

In most sections of the West, stockmen resolved range conflicts by compromise. However, in a few areas—notably central Texas—cattlemen armed their ranch-hands and disputes over property boundaries were resolved by ambushes or exchanges of gunfire. Thanks to pulp-fiction writers, some of these events entered the portals of western history as "wars."

Wyoming was another state where turf fights among cattlemen dominated a phase of its history. The open-range era in Wyoming began after the Sioux were defeated and affluent "British gentlemen" and other outside investors came west and assembled huge herds of cattle that grazed free of charge on millions of acres of public land. In short order, the Wyoming Stock Growers Association controlled the state government, and the governor trumpeted that the cattle business was "the most profitable business in the world."

In the freewheeling open-range environment that emerged, it was inevitable that deadly disputes would arise between large cattle outfits and small homesteaders. In 1891, for example, some of Wyoming's grandee ranchers hired twenty-two Texas gunmen and sent them to Johnson County to kill or "clean out" nesters (homesteaders) resisting the inroads of their herds. This incursion attracted national attention when the homesteaders fought back and captured the invading "army."

In the 1870s and 1880s, there were also homicidal disputes over grazing rights in Montana, in one Arizona county, in two New Mexico counties, and in two areas of western Nebraska. But unlike the case in Wyoming, these confrontations were local and had minimal effect on the social and political history of those states.

Certain feuds in Arizona and New Mexico have been sensationalized as "wars" by writers and magnified into events of lasting historical significance. Arizona's famous Tonto Basin War in the 1880s was actually a protracted old-fashioned feud between two families. This private quarrel produced a sequence of retaliatory ambush killings in a remote part of the state. The general public and the local sheriff learned little about the course of the feud. Yet, despite a sparsity of eyewitness accounts, author Earle Forrest won readers decades later by incorporating elements of drama in retelling the events and titling his book *Arizona's Dark and Bloody Ground.*

New Mexico's even more notorious feud gained notoriety as the Lincoln County War. In truth, it was nothing more than a series of shoot-outs between cowboys hired by competing mercantile companies in a thinly populated area 200 miles south of Santa Fe. The feud resulted in a few deaths but had no effect whatsoever on the lives of ordinary folk in the rest of the state.

Thanks to legends fashioned by filmmakers, boomtowns and the myths featuring Wyatt Earp and his fellow travelers have entered Hollywood's Elysian fields as a defining metaphor of western history for most Americans. To be sure, there were isolated violence-prone boomtowns in the Old West, but these quickie communities were atypical of western towns. Many of them mushroomed in secluded places, but even there gunplay was episodic and short-lived.

This truth applies with equal force to Dodge City and the famous cow towns of Kansas and to the early mining towns that flourished for a season or two in mountainous parts of the West. The most violent places were magnets for footloose single men who fought boredom with copious quantities of liquor. Order arrived late in the boomtowns, where there were few jails and more than half the businesses were saloons.

Outlaws such as William Bonney (originally Henry Bonney or possibly Henry McCarty)—more popularly known as Billy the Kid—typically lived and died in the outback and were rescued from oblivion by writers of pulp fiction. No aspect of western history has been so inflated and overdramatized as the activities of these legendary figures. Those who insist that robbers such as Jesse James were widely admired in some circles as American Robin Hoods too easily ignore the high value attached to law and order in communities where the great bulk of westerners resided.

Western history has been demeaned and distorted by writers who insinuate that the region as a whole suffered through "renegade years" and aver that the streets of some towns flowed with blood nightly. Such interpretations ignore the fact that outlaws laid low most of the time and focused their raids not on struggling, cash-poor villages but on larger communities with thriving banks and mercantile establishments.

Conventional accounts of the Old West's vigilance committees also need critical scrutiny. Profound differences emerge when one analyzes the motives of the disparate groups that marched under the vigilante banner. Some, led by prominent community leaders, encompassed well-meaning efforts to establish a semblance of order. Others were made up of ignorant individuals motivated by racial or ethnic animosities who sought to kill or subjugate those who they believed posed threats to their economic interests; still other committees appeared more or less spontaneously in response to local homicides. Formed in anger, the vigilance committees were usually headed by prominent citizens who took the law into their own hands. They apprehended individuals who were thought to have committed a capital crime, conducted peremptory trials, and carried out their verdicts by hanging. Many forays by these proponents of street justice involved murders in which evidence of wrongdoing was strong and law enforcement institutions were weak or nonexistent. In most instances, only one or two individuals were captured and condemned.

Favorable publicity about discipline imposed by two early citizen posses lent respectability to such activities. In 1851, a vigilance campaign led by prominent San Francisco businessmen produced a public event wherein four miscreants were hanged and twenty other putative lawbreakers were put on ships bound for foreign ports. In 1864, during a single month in Montana, outraged vigilance committees hanged twenty-five suspected "road agents" who had preyed on miners in the goldfields near Virginia City.

The mobs that killed and oppressed members of minority groups in some parts of the West were driven by baser motives. The organizers of these homicidal forays were not seeking to curb criminal activities. They wanted to crush the livelihood and the rights of "foreigners" and outcast groups. In northern California's Round Valley, for example, raiding parties of white men killed natives and expelled them from their homelands. Later, in Los Angeles, Seattle, and Tacoma, deadly riots were mounted against Chinese immigrants by agitators who coveted their jobs and businesses. Perhaps the most devastating of these pogroms occurred in Rock Springs, Wyoming, when fifty-one Chinese coal miners were massacred and several hundred were forced to flee.

But the most abhorrent use of deadly force by civilians in the postwar period was a prolonged private lynching party operating in the Missouri Breaks area of Montana. This hunt for supposed wrongdoers cannot be described as a vigilante

movement, for it was not a response to local criminal activity. Rather, it was organized by grandees of Montana's cattle industry with the aim of wiping out small
ranchers and farmers, who, they contended, were stealing their horses and cattle.

The expedition was organized by Granville Stuart, a cattle baron who put more
than 100 "nesters" and small ranchers on a death list. Stuart's two-year effort began
in 1882, at the end of Montana's frontier era. Montana was not a raw frontier when
this killing spree occurred; it was already linked to eastern cities by a railroad,
Butte was booming as the nation's new copper capital, and the state boasted a
penitentiary and a respectable system of justice.

With lordly contempt for the law, Stuart and the cattle kings met secretly, created
a code of punishment for their "kingdom," decreed the theft of a horse or calf a
capital offense, and ordered their hired hands to hang the individuals they had
blacklisted and burn their homes. The serial lynchings, performed by marauders
who called themselves "Stuart's Stranglers," should, of course, have been greeted
with abhorrence but instead were presented to Montanans as a triumph that brought
law and order to their commonwealth. When Montana gained statehood a few
years later, Stuart was even lionized as a noble founder, and the foul deeds of his
men were later commemorated by murals in the new capitol.

An analysis of civilian violence yields these insights about the postwar West:

- If areas where considerable personal violence occurred are plotted on a map,
  they appear as mere pimples. Social historian Robert R. Dykstra not only
  lamented "the evolution of the sturdy pioneer into the Marlboro Man" but also
  commented that the overwhelming number of communities in the postwar
  West were probably as law-abiding as similar towns in the farm states of the
  Midwest.
- Instances of personal violence waxed where social controls were weak or
  nonexistent and waned as soon as communities enacted laws and hired
  officers to enforce them.
- Human impulses toward violence were tempered in towns where mutual
  cooperation was traditional and face-to-face contacts were a feature of
  everyday life.
- Disorder was anathema to agrarians trying to wrest a living from the land
  and to frontier businessmen, who needed stable social conditions to prosper.

Religious faith was the sheet anchor in most frontier towns. Whether one
studies the lives of Bohemian settlers in Nebraska, Scandinavian Lutherans in
the Dakotas, Mennonites in Kansas, Germans in western Texas, Mormons in
Utah, Spanish Catholics in New Mexico, Presbyterians in Oregon, or the Irish

immigrants who poured into Butte, Montana, it becomes clear that amity was prized and churchmen usually succeeded in dampening frictions or resolving disputes in their communities.

* * *

The Wild West Masquerade

For more than a century, writers, artists, and film writers fashioned a mishmash of myths that came together in the form of the Wild West, an image implanted in modern memory as the exciting story of American westering. Overwhelmed by the legends of these mythmakers, the settling of the Old West slouched into history as a dramatic story of Indians attacking wagon trains and heroic U.S. cavalrymen coming to the rescue, excited gold rushers and gunslinging outlaws, and fearless sheriffs bringing order to lawless towns.

The Wild West avalanche began in 1883 when William Cody, a consummate showman who called himself Buffalo Bill, mounted a cowboys-and-Indians road show that lasted for three decades and drew huge audiences in the American East and in Europe. The pageants Cody presented were so simple and dramatic that they became the prism through which millions of Americans viewed this receding chapter of their history.

Born in 1846, Cody spent his boyhood on a farm in Iowa during the period when the treks of the wagon pioneers were cresting. Cody's theatrical career as a western Everyman was launched in 1869 when Edward Z. C. Judson, a greenhorn pulp-fiction writer who used the pseudonym Ned Buntline, encountered him in Nebraska, listened to his braggadocio, and wrote "Buffalo Bill, The King of Border Men" for a New York magazine.

Attired in flamboyant frontier costumes, Cody drifted east to convert his celebrity status into cash. His colorful tales and his talents as a thespian attracted backers. They helped him craft melodramas for New York audiences based on his purported exploits as an Indian fighter. Encouraged by what he learned in the theatrical world, on returning to Nebraska Cody staged cowboys-and-Indians pageants for local celebrations. These were so successful that he thought a touring company would be a hit in eastern cities.

Using the same techniques that made P. T. Barnum the master impresario of the nineteenth century, Bill Cody acquired investors, and in the summer of 1883 he reserved a special train and put his first Wild West show on the road. Advertised on gaudy posters as "America's National Entertainment," his vaudeville acts drew huge crowds in open-air arenas.

The performances featured tableaus of horsemanship, glimpses of native cultures, and a shooting exhibition that made markswoman Annie Oakley a household name. The finale, headlined as a scene in which "Howling Savages Pursue a Defenseless Stage Coach," was a mock battle in which an attack of bloodthirsty Indians was thwarted by rough-riding cowboys armed with six-guns.

As an impresario, Cody excelled as a casting director. Some of the Indians he recruited had participated in the famous fight with Custer, and he insisted they carry their weapons and don their warbonnets. To demonstrate that the savages truly had been subdued, in 1885 Buffalo Bill hired Sitting Bull to join his tour in full regalia. The legendary Sioux war chief rode in the parades on a beautiful gray horse and held court in a tipi, where he signed autographs for awestruck visitors.

As a promoter, "Colonel" Cody did not miss a trick. To burnish his fame, he hired a ghostwriter, who produced a flow of 121 "Buffalo Bill novels" that kept him in the limelight as a symbol of the fading frontier. His popularity and profits inspired imitation, and at one point more than fifty competing traveling shows were crisscrossing the country. By changing his scenarios, Cody kept his circuslike variety shows on the road for more than three decades. His pageants instilled a simple, vivid message: the West was a region where violence was an everyday experience, where hostile savages resisted the advance of pioneers, where guns prevailed over arrows and spears, and where the empire of the United States of America was enlarged by the feats of fearless cavalrymen.

With an assist from Owen Wister and Zane Grey, two extremely popular eastern novelists, by the time Cody's last show closed in 1917 his theatrical extravaganzas were accepted as the true story of western settlement. As historian Anne M. Butler reminds us, Bill Cody became "the national caretaker for western authenticity [and] almost single-handedly pushed [his] western notions into the modern scenario and made them accessible to the general public."

The whites-versus-Indians battles staged by Buffalo Bill involved fights between faceless groups. The novels of Wister and Grey provided a face—a gunfighting, justice-seeking cowboy—and a simple plot that evolved into the western, the twentieth century's most successful film formula. Moviemakers subsequently molded their protagonist into a heroic figure whose deeds made it possible to bring civilization into the American West.

Wister was a Philadelphia lawyer who spent a few summers on Wyoming ranches in the closing days of the frontier era. Grey, a young dentist from upstate New York, was so enchanted when he first saw the West in 1905 that he moved there. He became the most widely read author of his generation—15 million copies of his cowboy romances were purchased by avid readers. The works of Wister and Grey made meager contributions to American literature, but the scenarios in the fictions became cornerstones of the emerging edifice known as the Wild West.

As literary heirs of the Buffalo Bill tradition, Wister and Grey exhibited little interest in the experiences of actual settlers. The quiet struggles of men and women building homes, farms, and communities in frontier settings did not appeal to their imaginations. Needing exciting action to sell their books, they portrayed the West as a male bastion of badmen, skulking Indians, and fearless cowboys whose guns protected the lives and property of their neighbors.

Wild West stories and characters were made to order for the entrepreneurs who flocked to Hollywood to develop moving pictures that would appeal to mass audiences. Scenarios featuring cowboys, horses, and guns were a natural for the first generation of filmmakers. Thus, it was no accident that Hollywood's first identifiable star would be William S. Hart, a stern, taciturn, straight-shooting cowboy. The theatrical sons of Bill Hart—progeny running a gamut from director John Ford to actor Clint Eastwood—created a genre that became a distinctive feature of American culture. Their gaudy images captured a masquerade of legends that obscured the real West.

A raft of fascinating questions are raised by the psychological process by which this new form of entertainment produced such a result. How, for example, did fictions presented to mass audiences win acceptance as capsules of actual history? Why did westerns, with their stereotyped plots and foreseeable endings, mesmerize Americans for decades? Did myths about western settlement eclipse facts in viewers' minds because the virtues and moral triumphs of the cowboy heroes were so satisfying? Or did other influences, such as the West's stunning landscapes, combine to infiltrate Wild West values and themes into the mainstream of the nation's culture?

Explanations may vary, but in reality the phenomenal appeal of westerns—and the brainwashing accomplished by their myths—was widened with the advent of television. For much of the 1950s, eight out of ten prime-time television shows were serialized westerns based on variations of the Wyatt Earp "epic," and Hollywood's studios were grinding out a new cowboy movie almost every week. This myth-making caper was put in perspective by William Kittredge, head of the University of Montana's creative writing program, when he described it as "art designed for the widest possible audience, all of America and the world overseas, and as such it isn't about anybody really, and it's not centered anywhere actual."

After a half-century of screenings, the clichés depicted in westerns had acquired such authenticity that theaters became de facto classrooms where celluloid legends were transformed into historical facts. Only a few western historians challenged Holly-wood's mythmakers, and they found themselves spitting into stiff breezes whipped up by Hollywood's wind machines. Here is Larry McMurtry's description of the barrier these debunkers faced: "The romance of the West is so powerful you can't really swim against the current. Whatever truth about the West is printed, the legend is always more potent."

When Robert Dykstra presented the findings of his meticulous study of violence in the West to a Sun Valley symposium titled "Western Movies: Myths and Images," Henry King, director of a "classic" western, *The Gunfighter*, delighted the audience by rebuking "the professor" and denigrating his facts. Efforts by historians to put western violence in perspective encountered opposition not only from moviemakers but also from members of their own profession who glorified gunfighters as seminal figures of western history.

Epilogue

Wild West myths have obscured the overall story of western settlement. Nearly a century elapsed, for example, after the last of the Indian "wars" before artists and writers began presenting the Indian version of their encounters with the invading whites. This turning point came with the publication of Alvin Josephy Jr.'s *The Patriot Chiefs* (1961), Vine Deloria Jr.'s *Custer Died for Your Sins* (1969), and Dee Brown's *Bury My Heart at Wounded Knee* (1971) and the presentation of the first "pro-Indian" American film, *Little Big Man* (1970).

Had the images of the ersatz West not been so deeply implanted in the minds of Americans, an awakening might have been brought about by the words of children of pioneers—writers such as Willa Cather, Ole Rölvaag, Mari Sandoz, John Steinbeck, Wallace Stegner, and A. B. Guthrie—who created evocative accounts of the everyday lives of actual settlers that, in effect, accuse the filmmakers and their minions of hijacking western history.

One does not find routine accounts of gunfights or scenes of Main Street violence in the works of these artists. Willa Cather set a tone for these authors in her stories of the everyday lives of Nebraska farm families in *O Pioneers!* (1913) and *My Ántonia* (1918). Rölvaag struck a similar note in his novel *Giants in the Earth* (1927), which depicts the triumphs and travails of Norwegian immigrant farmers on the plains of the Dakotas. However, the voices of these writers were whisperings amid the ongoing cascade of dreamworks called westerns.

The most reliable and evocative facts about the real West can be found in the records and reminiscences of settlers. The myth-makers have inflated the significance of a few dramatic episodes, but the skin of western history is manifest in the artless letters, diaries, and journals of men and women who were actors in this epic. In recent decades, social historians have been enlarging the story of settlement by means of books and articles based on documents bequeathed by pioneer families to state historical societies and university libraries.

Details in letters written to relatives back home often combine to produce mosaics of the experiences of families and communities. Collectively, such communications constitute authentic folklore that deflates the balloons of Wild West writers. The reports of fatalities that recur in these letters typically concern not victims of gun violence but accounts of the quiet violence inflicted on communities by drought and disease, which sometimes decimated whole families.

Another balloon-deflator can be seen in the proceedings of such organizations as the Oregon Pioneer Association and the Society of California Pioneers. The annual gatherings of these settlers were dedicated to preserving respect for the achievements of the wagon pioneers. Their meetings rarely focused on Indian fights or altercations with outlaws but instead highlighted the experiences of emigrants who ventured across daunting terrain to create homes in virgin lands. Speakers recounted the trail days of Trekkers and the spirit of cooperation that enabled groups of emigrants to overcome obstacles that arose on their journeys.

More often than not, the reminiscences and the candid letters written to home folk concentrate on the communal sharing and caring that flourished on the trails and afterward. These pioneers did not see themselves as conquerors of the West, and one finds no trace of Manifest Destiny arrogance in their narratives. Listen to the summation offered by Montana's William Kittredge:

> If you start reading around in the journals and diaries and letters from the early West, mostly written by women, you will find quite a different story from those written for publication in the East. For instance, you will hardly ever find a holy gunfighter come from the wilderness to right the troubles of society.

The guileless testimony pioneers proffered to posterity provides an irreplaceable baseline of facts for those who want an accurate picture of the saga of western settlement. If this backdrop is kept in place, it debunks, all by itself, the simplistic stories that have been the stock-in-trade of the Wild West mythologists and their followers.

[Udall, Stewart L.] "The Wild West and the Wrenching of the American Chronicle." [In] *The Forgotten Founders: Rethinking the History of the Old West*, 165–175, 182–189. Copyright © 2002 by Island Press. Reprinted with permission.

Suggested Readings

The hard-line argument that the West was a place where gunfighters were prevalent and "the threat of gunplay was pervasive" is presented in works of senior western historian Richard Maxwell Brown.

One finds a counter-thesis in the writings of cultural historian Richard Slotkin. In *Gunfighter Nation* and other volumes, Slotkin examines the baleful influence of western films on American culture and on American glorification of violence.

In an effort to slow the mesmerizing influence of Hollywood's juggernaut, in the 1960s two forthright historians, Robert R. Dykstra and W. Eugene Hollon, separately demonstrated how western history was being mangled by the media. Dykstra's *Cattle Towns* debunked the myth that Dodge City and other central Kansas locations that served as railheads for Texas drovers experienced virtually continuous handgun violence. See also his incisive essay titled "Field Notes."

Hollon conducted the first general survey of this subject, and in *Frontier Violence* he demonstrates that, overall, there was more violence in American cities during the nineteenth century than in frontier communities. Hollon's thesis was buttressed the same year by Richard Bartlett in *The New Country*.

A scholar who has an uncommon feel for the frontier and for the lives people lived in this environment is Elliott West. All of his western history books are first-rate.

Bartlett, Richard A. *The New Country: A Social History of the American Frontier, 1776–1890.* New York: Oxford University Press, 1974.

Dykstra, Robert R. *The Cattle Towns.* New York: Knopf, 1968.

———. "Field Notes: Overdosing on Dodge City." *Western Historical Quarterly* (winter 1996): 505.

Hollon, W. Eugene. *Frontier Violence: Another Look.* New York: Oxford University Press, 1974.

Slotkin, Richard. *Gunfighter Nation: The Myth of the Frontier in Twentieth-Century America.* New York: Atheneum, 1992.

West, Elliott. *The Contested Plains: Indians, Goldseekers, and the Rush to Colorado.* Lawrence: University Press of Kansas, 1998.

———. *The Way to the West: Essays on the Central Plains.* Albuquerque: University of New Mexico Press, 1995.

Notes

165   "Despite all of the mythologizing": Robert R. Dykstra, "Field Notes: Overdosing on Dodge City," *Western Historical Quarterly* (winter 1996): 505.

166–67   "essential safety"; "fatal trail confrontations ... usually prompted by emigrant insults": These and other quotations are from John D. Unruh Jr., *The Plains Across: The Overland Emigrants and the Trans-Mississippi West, 1840–60* (Urbana: University of Illinois Press, 1979), 185, 379 et seq., 386, 408.

168   "a perpetually violent and lawless place": Richard White, *"It's Your Misfortune and None of My Own": A New History of the American West* (Norman: University of Oklahoma Press, 1991), 329.

169   "Personal violence ... confined to very narrow social milieus": Ibid., 332.

174   "Marlboro man": Robert R. Dykstra, "Field Notes: Overdosing on Dodge City," *Western Historical Quarterly* (winter 1996): 511.

184   Cody as "national caretaker for western authenticity": Anne M. Butler, in *The Oxford History of the American West,* ed. Clyde A. Milner II, Carol A. O'Connor, and Martha A. Sandweiss (New York: Oxford University Press, 1994), 781.

186   "art designed for the widest possible audience": William Kittredge, in Stewart L. Udall, Patricia Nelson Limerick, and Charles F. Wilkinson, *Beyond the Mythic West* (Salt Lake City: Peregrine Smith Books, in association with the Western Governor's Association, 1990), 138.

188–89   "If you start reading around": Ibid., 147.

QUESTION TO CONSIDER

- After reading Udall's article, how violent was the "Wild West"?

Cover page of a wild west dime novel.

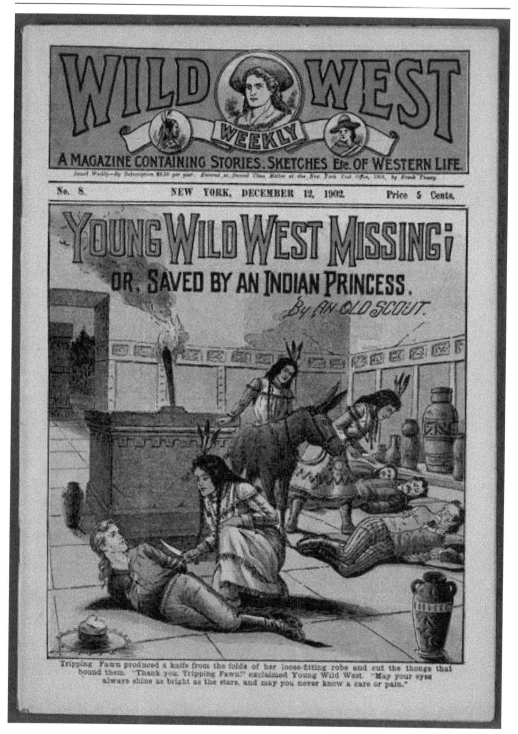

CHAPTER 2

Wild, Wild Women

By Joyce Roach

Editor's Introduction

How were women portrayed in the wild west dime novels? When it came to dime novels, which first came out around the start of the Civil War, they were reasonably priced, roughly 100 pages long, and distributed in numerical series at newstands or dry goods stores.These dime novels were regarded as low-grade fiction which the average American could afford.

The characters portrayed in these novels fell in love, got married, and sporadically killed each other and ocassionally themselves. In her article, Joyce Roach looks at heroines and how they were portrayed in dime novels.

Wild, Wild Women

By Joyce Roach

T he desperadoes are gaining fast.

"Leave me, Ted," she cried. "They will kill you if they get you, and you can escape on Sultan, which can outrun any of their horses."

Ted looked at her and laughed.

"I guess not," he called back. "Keep it up, we'll win yet."[1]

Naturally Ted does not leave her, and the couple get out of their predicament. This happy conclusion, however, is brought about by Stella, the "girl pard" of Ted Strong, not by the bumbling hero. Stella knows a solution when she sees one and Ted is sitting on it—Sultan, the stallion. When Ted is shot out of the saddle and left hanging thereon by the skin of his chaps, Stella approaches the "superb Sultan" who has never worked up a head of steam, catches him by the bridle and suggests to him that he ought to whoa. Sultan, like most dime novel stallions, understands Stella's every word, and allows the heroine to leap from her own mount after which, "as Ted reeled and was about to fall, she sprang into his saddle, caught him, and dashed away to safety." This 1906 adventure from *Rough Rider Weekly* entitled "King of the Wild West's Nerve; or, Stella in the Saddle" is a typical portrayal of what frontier heroines had become since 1860 when Beadle and Adams started issuing their versions of adventure in the form of dime novels.

There were other inexpensive weeklies before the firm of Beadle and Adams began to produce and there were cheap novels about people in all walks of life. As historians Joe Frantz and Julian Ernest Choate point out, "the cowboy, like America waiting on Isabella, needed only a sponsor to make his presence felt throughout the nation."[2] One of the sponsors turned out to be dime novels.

Before 1880, heroines seemed to exist solely to give the hero something to rescue. The women were not necessarily cowgirls but they were western types and often the reader made no distinction between the two. Certainly the cowgirl owed something to the behavior of her frontier sisters and predecessors, and the situations frontierswomen got into involved the same perils any cowgirl might face. In the early novels, the ladies manage to get themselves into one compromising situation after another and one wonders how that can be, considering that their study day and night was to protect their purity. Indian attack, for example, was one menace the ladies wished to avoid at all costs. Every reader knew, perhaps hoped, that a "fate worse than death" awaited the heroine at the hands of Indians, but with the authors, it was only a threat. The Indians of most dime novels were in great awe of maidenhood. They might dangle the victim over the coals, tie her to a stake, or devise other interesting tortures, but, as Edmund Pearson points out, "their honor was as safe as if they were in a convent. Indians were, all of them, gentlemen."[3]

Other dangers such as desperadoes, famine, flood, prairie fire, and disease were shared by all western heroines, but most of the ladies were of the helpless, fainting, fragile variety found in the tales of Cooper. Henry Nash Smith in *Virgin Land* sets 1880 as a general date when the western heroines began to change from genteel creatures placed around the scenery for rescuing, into active, vigorous women who, with pistol, whip, battleax and anything else they could lay hand to, were able not only to defend their own purity but also to snatch the hero out of sticky situations.

The transformation of heroines from passive objects to active ones began with the introduction into the action of Indian girls who could ride and shoot. Next followed the ancient device of disguising heroines in men's clothes. The disguised heroines often committed acts of violence, usually for revenge. Finally the heroine assumed all the skills and functions of a western hero. By 1878, with the appearance of Edward L. Wheeler's Hurricane Nell in *Bob Woolf, the Border Ruffian; or, The Girl Dead-Shot,* the heroine began to act like something out of a Wild West show. Nell can ride, shoot, rope, and yell like a man. She ropes a wild mustang, then rescues the hero (a Philadelphia lawyer) from the Indians by grabbing him around the waist and assisting him atop the back of the wild horse she has roped for him. She kills three of the enemy with as many shots from her rifle.[4] Nell is a girl among girls, and she is joined in similar exploits by Wild Edna, Calamity Jane and others.[5] Henry Nash Smith concludes that the heroine, when "freed from the trammels of gentility, developed at last into an Amazon who was distinguished from the hero solely by the physical fact of her sex."[6]

Douglas Branch believes that the "greatest writers of Dime Novels have not been pale young men from Connecticut, but men who had known the frontier."[7] Some writers who did not know the frontier, however, still wrote good novels. Perhaps it is safe to say that the authors knew *about* the frontier, if not from personal experience, at least from newspapers, travel journals, or, beginning very close to 1880, from Wild West shows and rodeo. Except for Calamity Jane, characters usually were not based on real people, but some were at least reminiscent of real people. Smith chalks up the outrageous behavior of heroines to an increase in and love for sensationalism.[8] While that is, no doubt, partly true, there are some heroines who bear enough resemblance to real people to cause one to wonder. A few examples will suffice: Rowdy Kate of *Apollo Bill, The Trail Tornado, or, Rowdy*

Kate From Right Bower, written in 1882, announces in a typical southwestern boast, "I'm a regular old double distilled typhoon, you bet." There was actually a Rowdy Kate in the 1870s. She was a dance hall girl, among other things, and she probably was thought of as a double-distilled typhoon.[9] Katrina Hartstein of *The Jaguar Queen; or, The Outlaws of the Sierra Madre,* written in 1872, goes about with seven pet jaguars on a leash and is the leader of a gang.[10] Annie Sokalski, who around the mid 1860s, accompanied her soldier-husband to his duty posts, was herself accompanied by thirteen trained hunting dogs which she kept on leash. She had the personality to control not only the dogs but a good many other people with whom she came in contact. Annie's riding habit, made of wolfskin and trimmed with wolf tails was topped off with a fur hat. She spent a good many hours at target practice, was a deadly shot, and could ride better than some of the cavalry.[11] Such a personality could have inspired a Jaguar Queen, and Frederick Whittaker, who created her, had been in the army.[12] The previously mentioned Hurricane Nell shows up in the Pike's Peak area dressed like a man.[13] Mountain Charley, who was actually Mrs. E. J. Guerin, joined miners at Pike's Peak dressed like, and passing for, a man in 1859. She published her autobiography in 1861—in plenty of time for a dime novel writer to have heard of her.[14] Iola of *A Hard Crowd, or Gentleman Sam's Sister* was "capable of shooting down instantly a man who accosted her in the street."[15] Any number of women previously described, such as Sally Skull, or the South Texas woman who blew a man's head off when he got fresh, could pass for Iola. C. P. Westermeier, in *Trailing the Cowboy,* quotes from six newspapers dating from 1877 to 1885 about cowgirls and cattlewomen, any of whom could have passed for a dime novel heroine.[16]

Many of the sensational women of dime novels fit the classification of "girl sports." Sports are usually beautiful women who dress in mannish fashion. They can perform all the manly feats with gun, whip and knife. They take their liquor straight and often swear expertly. Sports almost never get the hero's romantic attention, although they save the hero in time for him to fall into the arms of some other woman.

There were real-life Sports, among them Calamity Jane, who could have served as models. Mary E. Sawyer, known in Arizona as Mollie Monroe, had all the qualifications of a Sport. In the 1890s Mollie was known, according to the *Phoenix Herald,* as "the girl cowboy who in her day, would ride anything with four feet, chew more tobacco and swear harder than any man in Arizona."[17] *The San Francisco Mail of May 27,* 1877, reported that:

It was customary with Mollie to accompany all the leading scouts against the common foe, the Apache. Dressed in the uniform of the country of that day—buckskin pants, the usual appendages of beads and fringes, broad-brimmed hat, armed with a Henry rifle, two six-shooters, and a bowie knife, she was ready for the fray. And when it came down to a good square Indian fight, Mollie was there, as many a one of the Apaches found to his cost.

Mollie always had her purse open for those down on their luck, and she attended the sick like a "visiting angel." Supposedly unrequited love drove Mollie from her home to the wilds of Arizona.

Mollie was declared insane in 1877 and committed to the Clark and Langdon Sanitorium at Stockton, California. When a reporter visited her there, Mollie told him that "she was the meanest thing on earth, and intended to be so until she was turned out and allowed to do as she pleased."[18]

In *The Barranca Wolf, or, The Beautiful Decoy, A Romance of the Texas Border* by Joseph E. Badger, Jr., Lola is the Sport. She is dressed in white doeskin with leggings to match. She wears a cap of fur adorned with eagle feathers "such as the Kiowa wear." The dark-eyed brunette is pretty to look at as she sits her piebald mustang "savage style." Her rifle is balanced across her Mexican saddle and "other weapons gleamed from the belt that encircled her round, compact waist."[19]

Although Lola's father has taught her to hate men and to lure them into the Barranca for the purpose of foul play, she falls for Ned, the hero. Ned is promised and Lola dies defending him, but not before she asks Ned to marry her. Sports lack a certain tact when it comes to getting what they want, and they hardly ever get it, even when they are dying.

In *The Detective Queen; or, The Denver Doll's Devices* by E. L. Wheeler, the heroine is a Sport and a humdinger. She wears a "plumed slouch hat of snowy white" over her brown curls. Her figure of "symmetry and grace" is clothed in "an elegant suit of gray" with which she wears patent leather top-boots, a diamond studded "biled" shirt, and a sash about her waist—a costume "at once dashing and characteristic of the wild roving existence she led." Wheeler insisted that the Doll was a respectable woman sworn to break up a roadagent gang with the assistance of her helpers—a Negro, a Dutchman and a Chinese man.

The Doll is a formidable card player and one game features a duel with guns loaded with salt and pepper. Typical of Sports she declares, "I take but precious little stock in men,"[20] but the reader must take into account that the phrase is uttered before a suitable male wanders into the story.

Another of Wheeler's tales, *The Girl Sport; or Jumbo Joe's Disguise* features Leadville Lil. Lil takes her whiskey straight and smokes cigarettes while wearing a suit of "flawless fitting white duck," patent leather slippers, a diamond pin and a gold watch. Upon entering a bar armed with revolver and rifle, Lil puts up a kiss as her entry fee in a poker game.

There is another sporty type in the same story. Her name is Sadie. Sadie gets the hero, Joe, in her clutches and declares that she will have him tortured if he doesn't marry her. That rips it with Joe and he responds:

> Were death to stare me in the face in a hundred horrible shapes,
> I would welcome it rather than ally myself to a woman who
> takes the burden of matchmaking upon her own shoulders.[21]

Joe can afford to make smart remarks because Lil is waiting in the wings to rescue him. In the end Lil and Sadie fight and Sadie gets hers, not from Lil, but from Joe who shoots her. In an unexpected twist Lil turns out to be an heiress, a fact which does much to excuse her sporting ways, and she gets to marry the hero.

E. L. Wheeler's most famous Sport, Calamity Jane, is given detailed treatment in *Deadwood Dick on Deck; or, Calamity Jane, The Heroine of Whoop-Up*. When someone asks if Jane is a hard case, someone else explains that she is merely a daredevil. Some say a man deserted her and she took up a roving life to hunt him down. Others tell that she married a brute and ran away from him. Jane has a pretty but hard face. She wears buckskin pants "met at the knee by fancifully beaded leggins," dainty slippers, a velvet vest, and a boiled shirt. Her jacket is of velvet and her Spanish broad-brimmed hat is "slouched upon one side of a regally beautiful head."

Jane wears one revolver around her waist and carries a rifle strapped to her back. She rides a black pony richly equipped in Mexican style. When asked why she dresses like a man, Jane replies,

> I don't allow ye ken beat men's togs much fer handy locomo-
> tion an' so forth, an' then, ye see, I'm as big a gun among the
> men as any of 'em.[22]

In *Deadwood Dick in Leadville; or, A Strange Stroke for Liberty*, Jane saves a man's life in a crooked card game. When she draws her gun, everyone knows she means business. No one even dares look at Jane too long for fear it may anger her.

She boasts that she enjoys a good fight and never shoots at the same target twice. Jane refers to ammunition as "condensed death."[23]

George Waldo Browne's *The Tiger of Taos; or, Wild Kate, Dandy Rock's Angel* features the exploits of a Sport who feels that she is shunned by society because of her father's reputation as a horse thief. It apparently has not occurred to her that the shunning may be because she totes a rifle and a pair of revolvers and lives up to the name of Wild Kate.

Kate is not beautiful, but she has other things to recommend her. She is "attired in a fancifully trimmed and frilled suit of border gray, encircled at the waist by a belt of buckskin, which was nearly reached by dark chestnut waves of silken hair falling down over her shoulders." Riding a "strangely-spotted mustang" Kate saves the heroine, Alice, and the hero more than once.[24]

Most dime novel heroines fall into the general category of frontier women. They are not necessarily cowgirls. Their lives may be involved in any number of western activities—shooting, swearing, popping a whip, wielding a battleax, fist fighting, pounding leather, and dressing up like men—and their activities influenced what people believed about pioneer females. There were two heroines, however, who rode the dime novel range from 1900 until the 1920s and who were genuine cowgirls.

Arietta Murdock, created by Cornelius Shea, first appeared in 1902 in the *Wild West Weekly*. She is rescued from the Sioux by Young Wild West and his stallion, Spitfire. West is a doer of good out on the prairies—that is, he tries to be the doer, but with Arietta around he sometimes becomes the doee.

Arietta is described as a golden-haired blonde, and that should be a clue that she is going to have all the fun. Her father, Sam Murdock, is the postmaster of Weston in the Black Hills. She is a native of Wyoming and she shoots, not like the best cowboy shot, but "with the skill of the average cowboy or man of the border," and she rides vicious broncs too, provided they have been ridden at least once before. She is, then, for a woman, a cut above the average man, but just a shade under the hero. In "Rawhide Ralph; or, The Worst Cowboy in Texas" (the title refers to the villain, not the hero) of the August 14, 1908, issue of *Wild West Weekly,* Arietta shows what she is made of. While Wild and company are off somewhere, Arietta and two other lady friends decide to take a ride to see the neighbors. One of the other women is Eloise Gardner, the sweetheart of one of West's bunch. Reminiscent of some Wild West cowgirls, Eloise was once a circus performer. Although her occupation may appear a strange one for a western heroine, it indicates that Shea knew what was going on in the arena. Florence Hughes Randolph, for example, got into Wild West shows after being in the circus.

Once out on the prairie the girls discover a burned-out ranch, and guess, with astonishing accuracy, that "Rawhide Ralph" has done it. At that moment Rawhide himself rides up. Arietta knows from the condition of the villain's face that it has been in contact with young Wild West's fists. Rawhide is not feeling kindly toward West, and, seeing Arietta, he plots revenge. The girls try to ride away, but, unfortunately, only the heroes get to ride stallions, and, being poorly mounted, they are caught. Rawhide has sense enough to take the girls' weapons. They are, after all, western girls and the rifles hanging beside their saddles aren't just for decoration.

Fiendishly, Rawhide proposes marriage to Arietta, and he prepares for a mock ceremony. The other two women are allowed to go, and as the gang's attention is drawn to the doorway, Arietta pulls a revolver which was hidden in her buckskin jacket. In keeping with the code of other real-life heroines before her, Arietta, without hesitation, points her gun at Johnny Cole, one of the gang, and does not merely wing him, but blows him to kingdom come. In a second she is mounted and joins the other girls as young Wild West, just a shade late, rides to the rescue. J. Edward Leithead, writing for *Dime Novel Round-Up*, points out that Arietta's killing of Cole marks her as different from most western heroines:

> No hesitation, no girlish squeamishness about shooting to kill when she had to, no conscience—stricken aftermath, which marked Arietta as so different from pallid heroines of Western fiction who, even though fighting for their lives or in a good cause, seldom more than wounded a human target if they hit him at all or didn't down his horse instead. In Arietta Murdock, Cornelius Shea presented the type of girl who helped to win the West.[25]

Arietta is displayed on about eighty percent of the covers of *Wild West Weekly* and her name appears often in subtides. She rescues the hero with regularity by such feats as hurling dynamite, leaping chasms, shooting her revolver, riding for the posse, producing Indian amulets and charms, and stealing guns or horses from the outlaws.

Another series featuring a cowgirl heroine was the *Rough Rider Weekly*. Many of the stories were written by Ned Taylor, the pen name of St. George Rathbone. The series about the range and range life was probably launched to compete with *Wild West Weekly,* and in spite of what was considered better writing than appeared in the *Weekly,* lasted only 175 issues.[26]

Ted Strong, owner of a ranch in the Black Hills of Dakota, spends his time doing cowboy things with his group, the Rough Riders of Black Mountain Ranch. Ted was once a sergeant with Teddy Roosevelt's group; hence the name, Rough Riders.

There is realism in such stories as "Ted Strong's Wild West Show; or The Making of an Indian Chief" which features a rodeo contest between the boys of Black Mountain and the waddies of Sunset Ranch, in which incidentally, the hero loses. Ted saves the girl spectators by shooting a steer which charges the stands in an act reminiscent of Will Rogers' roping feat at a rodeo which brought him to prominence. Many of the performers of the 101 Ranch are even mentioned by name.[27] On a similar theme the *Wild West Weekly referred* to West's group as being caught in World War I.[28] The 101 group actually did get caught at the beginning of the war and their stock was impounded.[29] It would appear from such allusions that both series were well-acquainted with what went on in rodeo and Wild West shows and borrowed freely from both.

In *King of the Wild West's Haunt; or Stella's Escape From Sacrifice,* the heroine is introduced into the series. Stella is known in Texas as "Queen of the Range." She has been raised on her father's Sierra Blanca Ranch near El Paso, and when she is orphaned, the Rough Riders adopt her as their girl "pard," short for partner.[30] A Mrs. Graham accompanies Stella everywhere as her chaperone except when Stella rides out hell-bent for danger. Shooting and riding, Stella has no time for hanky-panky, anyway.

Stella is also a blonde. Her costume of white Stetson, bolero jacket, white leggings and red skirt embellished with a gun strapped on her hip, is reminiscent of costumes featured on Wild West posters.

In *King of the Wild West's Nerve; or, Stella in the Saddle* which introduced this chapter, are all the elements of a typical Rough Rider story. The tale begins in the San Simon meadows, where Captain Henry Foraker and Don Luis Fernando are in contention for land and cows. The meadow actually was a place frequented by Mexican and American outlaws, indicating that Ned Taylor was up on his history of the region.[31] Don Luis not only has his eye on Foraker's cattle but also on Foraker's beautiful and bountifully endowed daughter, Bonito. Bonito is a combination of her Spanish mama and her Puritan, Nordic papa—fire and ice. She has learned the social graces from convent schooling and the skills of riding, hunting and shooting from life with father on the range. The señorita is daddy's girl, and from him she inherits her love of the land. Bonito is large for her age, whatever age that is, "tall for a woman of the Southwest," and muscular from all that riding. In other words, another Amazon. Don Luis wishes to gain Bonito's hand in marriage along with her daddy's cattle. When the Forakers decline, Don Luis gets nasty, and his villainous behavior prompts the Forakers to summon Ted Strong. Wherever Ted goes, Stella is never far behind.

Bonito and Stella become instant, bosom friends. They must form an instant friendship because the book is not long enough to allow things to progress at normal speed. While Ted is out looking for trouble, the girls decide to take a ride to look at the cattle which remind Stella of the good old days on Daddy's ranch in Texas. That the ladies mount up and take an innocent ride is a giveaway that, while the hero is hunting trouble, the girls will not only find it first but get in it with both feet. Don Luis captures them (oh, if only those heroines could get hold of a stallion to ride!) but not before Stella has a chance to cut Don Luis down verbally by calling him a "dirty greaser." Such language may not have been unkind or in bad taste in 1906, but it was dangerous. Eventually Ted appears on his horse, Sultan, and the sound the animal makes is "pitty, pitty." When Ted cannot locate the girls at home, something wonderful happens:

> Something told Ted that the girls were in danger. It was that wonderful intuition of which he was possessed. It had never failed him yet, and he relied upon it as much as he did his senses of sight hearing and smell.[32]

The reader can only conclude that Ted certainly needs all the help he can get. The girls are treated to an unnecessary rescue. They could have managed it themselves, but Ted arrived prematurely.

Girl "pards" in literature, if dime novels count as literature, are not necessarily a new type, but they are an interesting variation on an Amazonian theme which predates Shakespeare's Hippolyta of *A Midsummer Night's Dream*. "Pards" are not like gun molls, who hang around to decorate the scenery or offer physical consolation to the boss. They are not like women such as Belle Starr who acted as a kind of gang boss. Although "pards" are definitely masculine in their abilities and sometimes even in their manner, they have a healthy interest in the opposite sex. While "pards" often wear men's clothes, they do not fall into the category of women who try to pass as men, and they are not to be confused with the rougher girl "sports." They are rather, as their name implies, partners of the cowboy, able to do almost everything he does, sharing equally the danger and the daring, and needing only occasional concessions to their femininity. It does not appear likely that the dime novelists were following any literary traditions, but rather based the female characters on actions, or what they thought were the actions, of real western women.

Girl "pards," although their roles become highly refined and they bear little resemblance to dime novel predecessors, show up in later literature. Several early writers of western stories mention partner-types. Wilson M. Hudson, in his study of Andy Adams, tells about a novel entitled *Tom,* after the heroine's nickname, which Adams never published. The story concerns a woman who can ride, shoot, herd cattle, and wrangle horses like a man. She marries the hero, Bob, in the end.[33] *The Virginian's* Molly, who does not at first understand the code of the West, shows signs of developing into a partner near the end of Owen Wister's novel. Emerson Hough's *North of 36* contains a genuine pard, although she seems a bungling one. Taisie Lockhart, possessing all the qualities which make a lovable and helpful pard, cannot seem to stay in the saddle once out on the trail. She keeps losing a trunk filled with valuable land scrip, falls in the river, and, it seems to me, cramps the cowboy's style in language and behavior. She is a pard who somehow gets off on the wrong foot, but apparently that is the way Hough wished it. Mattie Ross of *True Grit is* certainly one of the best pards and Charles Portis writes so convincingly of her that readers forget that the author's work is a parody of western dime novel. There was even an old dime novel series called the *True Grit* series.[34] The heroine of *Cut Ballou,* born during a thunderstorm and aided in her cause by all sorts of frontier types, is another "pard" of the dime novel variety.

The portrayal of western women and cowgirls in dime novels as Amazons is far from the truth. Dime novel authors generally stress that their heroines are large women, or the ladies' actions suggest that they must be bigger than average. Nearly all of the heroines surveyed by Henry Nash Smith are described in Amazonian terms and most are above average height, although no one ever specifies what the average is. Lola of *The Burruncu Wolf* is "tall for a woman, several inches above the medium height. ..."[35] The Denver Doll and Wild Kate are above medium height. Calamity Jane is only medium height but she performs as if she were *much* taller! Arietta and Stella are likewise quite capable of tall feats.

For whatever reason the actions of the heroines are depicted on a grand scale—sensationalism or an awareness of real western women's behavior—it is probably easy to imagine that only a large woman could accomplish such manly acts. However, a survey of women in Wild West shows, for instance, shows that most of them were not even average height. Annie Oakley and Lucille Mulhall were barely five feet in height. Of Mabel Strickland, Tad Lucas, Fox Hastings and Ruth Roach—all top names—none was over five feet three inches. Florence Hughes Randolph was only four feet six inches.

There were probably some larger women but one would be inclined to think that the horse was the great image builder and that seeing women on horseback performing ranch feats added to their stature. Observing women participating as pickup men and hazers—chores which Lucille Mulhall, particularly, often performed—must have caused writers to think of them as giants who like Stella Fosdick could hold the hero on her saddle.

Still another reason for portraying women as Amazons may have been that the actions in dime novels, according to Charles M. Harvey, "were physical, and they were told in language that made pictures in the mind."[36] Perhaps it took large women to create big mental impressions.

Dime novels perhaps even more than Wild West shows and rodeo helped to popularize notions about western cowgirls, and while it is difficult to approach the study of dime literature with anything but levity, the novels are a valuable tool for historians. William A. Settle, Jr., indicates that because of the glorifying and idealizing of the frontier, the West "entered for the first time into the consciousness of a large number of Americans."[37] Merle Curti writing for *Tale Review* found that the dime novels reflected "a much wider range of attitudes and ideas than the ballad or folk song," and were "the nearest thing we have had in this country to … a literature written for the great masses of people and actually read by them."[38]

The novels gave not only a picture of the Wild West, but, in the actions of the heroes and heroines, encouraged self reliance. Says Harvey: "Manliness and womanliness among the readers were cultivated by these little books, not by homilies, but by example." If we can believe Harvey, even the "taste and tone of the life of the generation which grew up with these tales were improved by them."[39]

Notes

1. Ned Taylor, *Rough Rider Weekly*, "King of the Wild West's Nerve; or, Stella in the Saddle" (New York: Street and Smith, 1906), 27.

2. Joe Frantz and Julian Ernest Choate, Jr., *The American* Cowboy (Norman: University of Oklahoma Press, 1955), 145.

3. Edmund Pearson, *Dime Novels, or, Following an Old Trail in Popular Literature* (Boston: Little, Brown and Co., 1929), 37.

4. Henry Nash Smith, *Virgin Land* (New York: Vintage Books, paperback, 1950), 129–31.

5. Titles of only a few dime novels such as *Ang'l of the Range; Backwoods Belle; Baleful Beauty of Brimstone; The Beautiful Amazon of Hidden Valley; Belle of the Border; Bessie the Stock Tender's Daughter; Blackfoot Queen; Border Huntress; Camille the Card Queen; Chip, the Girl Sport; Dainty Dot of Gold Gulch; Daisy Dare, the Sport from Denver; The Fair Huntress of the South-West; Fandango Queen; Frontier Angel; Flower of the Prairie; Girl Mustang Rider; Hunted Maid of Taos; Jack, the Girl Shot;*

Keetsea, the Queen of the Plains; Lillie, the Reckless Rider; Mad Madge, the Outlaw Queen; Masked Woman of the Colorado Canyon; Outlaw Queen; Rose of Wyoming; Stella Delorme's Comanche Lover, and *Wilda the Brand-Burner's Daughter* indicate to what extent women were involved in the action. Titles taken at random from list of titles in Albert Johannsen, *The House of Beadle and Adams and Its Dime and Nickel Novel* (Norman: University of Oklahoma Press, 1950).

6. Smith, *Virgin Land,* 134.

7. Douglas Branch, *The Cowboy and His Interpreters* (New York: Cooper Square Publishers, Inc., 1961), 181.

8. Smith, *Virgin Land,* 134.

9. Waldo E. Koop, letter to author, Tucson, Arizona, June 26, 1972. Mr. Koop, an authority on Rowdy Joe Lowe and Rowdy Kate found that Kate was very ladylike in most of her actions. She probably suffered from Rowdy Joe's reputation more than from her own.

10. Smith, *Virgin Land,* 129.

11. Brown, *The Gentle Tamers,* 59–65.

12. Johanssen, *House of Beadle and Adams,* 301.

13. Smith, *Virgin Land,* 131.

14. Mrs. E. J. Guerin, *Mountain Charley or The Adventures of Mrs. E. J. Guerin, Who Was Thirteen Tears in Male Attire,* eds. Fred Mazzula and William Kostka (New York: Ballantine Books, 1971), vii–xi. A first edition is in the DeGolyer Library, Dallas, Texas.

15. Smith, *Virgin Land,* 130.

16. Westermeier, *Trailing the Cowboy,* 323–27.

17. Quoted in "Arizona's Mollie Monroe Calamity's Counterpart," *Tucson Daily Citizen* (Friday, October 19, 1973).

18. "Our California Letter," *The Weekly Arizona Miner* (Prescott, Arizona) (January 30, 1880). For more about Mollie see also the Hayden File, Arizona Pioneer Historical Society Library, Tucson, Arizona.

19. Joseph E. Badger, Jr., *The Barranca Wolf; or, The Beautiful Decoy, A Romance of the Texas Border* (New York: Beadle and Adams), July 3, 1883, Half Dime Library, No. 310, 2.

20. E. L. Wheeler, *The Detective Queen; or, Denver Doll's Devices* (New York: M. J. Ivers and Co.), March 14, 1900, Deadwood Dick Library, 3.

21. Wheeler, *The Girl Sport; or, Jumbo Joe's Disguise* (New York: M. J Ivers and Co.), March 7, 1900, 4–7, 23.

22. Wheeler, *Deadwood Dick on Deck; or, Calamity Jane, The Heroine of Whoop-Up* (New York: M. J. Ivers and Company), June 21, 1899, 2–4, 24.

23. Wheeler, *Deadwood Dick in Leadville; or, A Strange Stroke for Liberty* (New York: M. J. Ivers and Company), August 16, 1899, 9–22.

24. George Waldo Browne, *The Tiger of Taos; or, Wild Kate, Dandy Rock's Angel* (New York: Beadle and Adams), June 17, 1879, Half Dime Library, 3–5.

25. J. Edward Leithead, "Arietta: Heroine of Wild West Trails," *Dime Novel Round-Up* (April 15, 1963), 32–36.

26. Leithead, "Ted Strong and His Rough Riders," Dime Novel Round-Up (June 15, 1961), 66–67.

27. Leithead, "Arietta," 33.

28. Leithead, "Ted Strong and His Rough Riders," 77.

29. Russell, *The Wild West,* 83.

30. Leithead, "Ted Strong," 78.

31. Frank Lockwood, *Pioneer Days in Arizona* (New York: 1932), 282.

32. Taylor, King of *Wild West's Nerve,* 2–24.

33. Wilson M. Hudson, Andy Adams: *Storyteller and Novelist of the Great Plains* (Austin: Steck Vaughn, 1970), 29.

34. True Grit Series was introduced by Henry T. Coates and Company in 1902. Information from Denis R. Rogers, "A Publication Pattern," *Dime Novel Round-Up* (September, 1972), 81.

35. Badger, *The Barranca Wolf,* 8.

36. Charles M. Harvey, "The Dime Novel in American Life," *Atlantic Monthly* (July 1907), 44.

37. William A. Settle, "The Dime Novel as an Historian's tool," *Dime Novel Round-Up* (September 1970), 95.

38. Merle Curti, "Dime Novels and the American Tradition," *Tale Review* (Summer, 1937), 761.

39. Harvey, "Dime Novel in American Life," p. 43.

Bibliography

BOOKS

Branch, Douglas. *The Cowboy and, His Interpreters.* New York: Cooper Square Publishers, 1961.

Brown, Dee. *The Gentle Tamers.* Lincoln: University of Nebraska Press, 1968.

Frantz, Joe and Julian Ernest Choate, Jr. *The American Cowboy.* Norman: University of Oklahoma Press, 1956.

Guerin, Mrs. E. J. *Mountain Charley or The Adventures of Mrs. E. J. Guerin, Who Was Thirteen Tears in Male Attire,* ed. Fred Mazzula and William Kostka. New York: Ballantine Books, 1971.

Hudson, Wilson M. *Andy Adams: Storyteller and Novelist of the Great Plains.* Austin: Steck Vaughn, 1970.

Lockwood, Frank. *Pioneer Days in Arizona.* New York: Macmillan, 1932.

Russell, Don. *The Wild West.* Fort Worth: Amon Carter Museum of Western Art, 1970.

Smith, Henry Nash. *Virgin Land.* New York: Vintage Books, 1950.

Westermeier, C. P. *Trailing the Cowboy.* Caldwell: Caxton Printers, 1950.

DIME NOVELS

Badger, Joseph E., Jr. *The Barranca Wolf; or, The Beautiful Decoy, A Romance of the Texas Border.* Half Dime Library. New York: Beadle and Adams, July 3, 1883.

Brown, George Waldo. *The Tiger of Taos; or, Wild Kate, Dandy Rock's Angel.* Half Dime Library. New York: Beadle and Adams, June 17, 1879.

Curti, Merle. "Dime Novels and the American Tradition," *Tale Review,* Summer, 1937.

Harvey, Charles M. "The Dime Novel in American Life," *Atlantic Monthly,* July 1907.

Johannsen, Albert. *The House of Beadle and Adams and Its Dime and Nickel Novel.* Norman: University of Oklahoma Press, 1950.

Leithead, J. Edward. "Arietta: Heroine of Wild West Trails," *Dime Novel Round-Up,* April 15, 1963.

———. "Ted Strong and His Rough Riders," *Dime Novel Round-Up,* June 15, 1961.

Pearson, Edmund. *Dime Novels; or, Following an Old Trail in Popular Literature.* Boston: Little, Brown and Co., 1929.

Denis R. Rogers, "A Publication Pattern," *Dime Novel Round-Up.* September, 1972.

Settle, William A. "The Dime Novel as a Historian's Tool," *Dime Novel Round-up*, September, 1970.

Taylor, Ned. *Rough Rider Weekly*. "King of the Wild West's Nerve; or, Stella in the Saddle." New York: Street and Smith, 1906.

Wheeler, E. L. *Deadwood Dick on Deck; or, Calamity Jane, The Heroine of Whoop-Up*. New York: M. J. Ivers, June 21, 1889.

———. *Deadwood Dick in Leadville; or, a Strange Stroke for Liberty*. New York: M. J. Ivers, August 16, 1889.

———. *The Detective Queen; or Denver Doll's Devices*. New York: M. J. Ivers, March 4, 1900.

———. *The Girl Sport; or, Jumbo Joe's Disguise*. New York: M. J. Ivers, March 7, 1900.

LETTERS
Koop, Waldo. Letter to the author. Tucson, Arizona, 1972.

NEWSPAPERS
Tucson Daily Citizen. "Mollie Monroe Calamity's Counterpart," October 19, 1973.
The Weekly Arizona Miner. "Our California Letter," January 30, 1880.

QUESTION TO CONSIDER

- How does Joyce Roach portray women of the "Wild West?"

PART II

Leisure and Labor, 1890

The lady of the house preparing a meal for the family.

CHAPTER 3

A Woman's Work Is Never Done

By Katherine L. Turner

....

Editor's Introduction

In the second half of the nineteenth century, cooking was strongly identified with women. The woman of the house got up long before anyone in the family. She would complete some chores before starting breakfast. If living in the country—during this period our nation was rural—a woman would not only do housework but was also expected to help her husband. She would have to feed the chickens, milk the cows, tend to the garden. She may be needed at various times during the year on a regular basis. One today just has no idea how much work a woman did in the home. In the following chapter, Turner looks at why "a woman's work is never done."

A Woman's Work Is Never Done

Cooking, Class, and Women's Work

By Katherine L. Turner

Providing food for a working-class family required cooperation from everyone, whether through wages, marketing, producing food through garden and livestock chores, acquiring cooking tools, or bringing in extra income by keeping boarders or a family business. However, cooking was inextricably linked to women's identities. In popular thought and culture, cooking defined the identities of women, especially married women, who were expected to provide physical as well as emotional nurture for their families. As a central feature of femininity, cooking was seen as a test of moral character as well. Good women cooked well and were happy to do it; bad women complained or shirked their duty. Reformers who studied working-class foodways from the 1880s through the 1910s in an attempt to help poor families eat and live better saw cooking through a heavily gendered and moral perspective. This perspective colored the questions they asked and the evidence they collected, as well as the solutions they offered to the problem of food.

Any question about cooking was also a question about women's role in society. Did housework—women's work—"count" as real economic activity, or should it be kept separate from economy and commerce and considered strictly an act of love? In an industrial society, should women's work change with the times, or should it stick to the time-tested, old-fashioned techniques? Women's work, like men's, was increasingly done outside the home. Could cooking could ever leave the house entirely and be taken over by collective enterprise or industry, as had butchering, soap making, weaving, and other preindustrial arts? Could the traditional family survive if this most basic of nurturing tasks was removed from the home? As the old adage said, a woman's work was never done. What, then, was a woman without work to do? What would happen to women's character if they were freed from this exhausting, rewarding, demanding, and inherently "womanly" work? Alternately, could women ever be truly modern if they continued to cook? Could women ever achieve full citizenship and a place in public life without getting off the treadmill of preparing and serving three meals a day?

Ultimately, these questions about cooking and gender were also inseparable from questions about class. From the perspective of those who offered solutions to

Figure 3.1 Women's social identity was heavily tied to feeding, from breastfeeding and beyond. This Chicago mother was visited and photographed by the Infant Welfare Committee sometime between 1910 and 1920. Here tools for cooking, feeding, childcare, washing, and other household tasks are jumbled closely together in a small space. Breastfeeding Chicago 1910–20 Infant Welfare #9 ICHI 03852. Chicago History Museum.

the problems of poverty, working-class women seemed to have a special obligation to be "good women," that is, to perform their role by devoting all their time and energy to proper housewifery. Reformers sensed the great importance of women's traditional work in the working-class household. They knew that women's work was important, but their understanding revolved around virtue rather than economy.

The Economic Value of "Women's Work"

Women's work in the household has often not been counted as "real work" because it is unpaid and because there are so many cultural and emotional wrappings around it. Yet some historians and economists have recognized what working-class people already knew: housework had major economic value and was vital to a family's survival. In her research on antebellum working-class women, Jeanne Boydston calculates the value of women's labor, including cooking, cleaning, laundry, the production of clothes, scavenging, gardening, and child care, and finds that women added more to the family economy than they took out, and more, in fact, than they could ever earn in wages. "A wife working without pay at home may have been more valuable to the family maintenance than a wife working for pay—inside or outside the home," she suggests.[1] Women's labor continued to be essential to family survival into the twentieth century, especially in times and places when married women rarely worked for wages. Historian Ewa Morawska estimates that the immigrant women of Johnstown, Pennsylvania, who kept boarders and produced much of their family's food, added about twenty dollars a month to their family's income, the equivalent of two-thirds to three-fourths of their husbands' earnings in the mill in the years before World War I.[2] The 1918 Department of Labor study used a multipage survey form to accurately capture family income and expenditure patterns. There were six categories for family income: earnings, board and lodgings, net from gardens and chickens, gifts of money, food, and clothing, net from rents and interest, and fuel picked up. Some married women contributed cash earnings from wages, but many more families included calculated income (in cash or in kind) from the "women's work" of keeping boarders, raising food, and scavenging for fuel.

Scott Nearing, a radical economist of the early twentieth century, recognized the great economic importance of women's household work at a time when many other economists did not. He wrote that, especially for low-income families, "If the family is not to suffer, the mother must be a woman of rare ability. She must know how to make her own and her children's clothing; she must be physically able to do all of the household work, including the washing. And she must know enough to purchase with her allowance food that has the proper nutritive value." He concluded that a man who was employed to perform this level of skilled management work in a factory would be highly paid, but poor women had to do it to ensure family survival.[3] Nearing was concerned that most low-income women were poorly educated for these complex and vital tasks.

In times of economic depression or family crisis women worked even harder, and many took on again labor such as laundry and cleaning that they might otherwise have paid for. Historian Lois Rita Hembold found that during the Great Depression, "when cash income declined, housewives replaced purchasing with subsistence production. Whether they planted gardens, canned food, remade old clothing, made do with less heat, or moved into poorer housing which required extra effort to keep clean and comfortable, women worked harder."[4] A study of South Bend, Indiana, in the 1930s found that families were "less likely to rely on financial strategies such as using up their savings, taking out loans, going into debt for unpaid bills, or cashing in insurance policies. Rather, they depended on additional work from women as their first line of defense."[5]

The nature of industrial capitalism demanded hard work from women. Marxist historians as well as Socialists like Nearing argued that women's labor at home, including cooking and other kinds of housework, was a necessary complement to men's wage work under industrial capitalism. Men could not truly support themselves and their families on their wages without a wife to "reproduce" their labor. Women produced food, washed the laundry, and maintained the household so that men could return to work day after day. Men's wages could be artificially low because women's unpaid work at home made up the deficit in the cost of living. The cultural association of women with cooking thus supported the economic structure. Women had to do the work of cooking (and cleaning, and food production) in order to reproduce their family's labor, and to ensure family survival when wages were low.[6] It was impossible for working-class families to survive without women's work.

Although Marxists pointed to a close connection between men's wage work and women's work at home, most people in the nineteenth century tended to think of them as separate worlds. Wage work outside of the home was defined as "masculine" (although clearly many women worked for wages). The home and all its tasks were defined as "feminine," reinforcing the idea that cooking was the natural task of woman (although men still participated in some home food production tasks and other housework). The gendered division of labor had not always been so inflexible. Household work had been increasingly feminized over the course of the nineteenth century. Historian Ruth Schwarz Cowan writes that in the colonial period, "the work processes of cooking required the labor of people of both sexes; cooking itself may have been defined as women's work (which it was), but cooking could not be done without prior preparation of tools and foodstuffs, and a good deal of that prior preparation was, as it happens, defined as men's work."[7] That is, men built the fireplace and chopped the firewood and made the iron pots and raised the wheat that women cooked. But during the nineteenth century, "in almost every aspect of household work, industrialization served to eliminate the work that men (and children) had once been assigned to do, while at the same time leaving the work of women either untouched or even augmented."[8] Men were released from household work to wage work; women remained behind with their traditional tasks, which were lightened but not materially changed by urban amenities.

The ideology of "separate spheres"—the belief that men belonged in commerce and women belonged in household work—converted this economic reality into the defining characteristics of masculinity and femininity. The ideology was most powerful among middle-class women, whose husbands usually worked outside the home in business, managerial, or professional work. Barred from the professions and socially discouraged from wage work, these women were most in need of an identity. Although their housework was lighter than it had been in the past, and they could employ servants (in a period of low wages, even lower-middle-class families could hire some), housework and the judicious management of the household was still a palpable contribution to the family economy.

In fact, women of all classes were never truly isolated from the market. Farm women took a keen interest in selling their eggs, milk, and other farm produce, and their "egg money" was often vital to family survival. Married working-class women took on wage work even while doing their own housework by taking in laundry, sewing garments or assembling small items by the piece, keeping boarders, or selling cooked food. Middle-class women who were pinched for money could take on more genteel work, such as teaching or fine sewing. Millions of women in the middle and working classes played an active part in their husbands' businesses, or ran businesses themselves.[9]

However, the idea of the existence of separate spheres was a powerful one, and it shaped the way that people, and especially middle-class women, wrote and talked about housework. Men belonged in the world of politics, capitalism, and commerce; women belonged in an opposing world of children, home, and love where commerce should not enter. To abandon one's proper sphere suggested immorality. A woman who neglected her housework or paid others to do it was as immoral as a man who neglected his business and loafed all day. For example, women whose families chose to live in boardinghouses, which included room and board (and allowed freedom from housework) were lambasted as "selfish, lazy, extravagant, and poorly trained in the art of domestic management"; boarding represented "wifely insubordination."[10] But, in a display of the disconnect between ideology and practice, millions of families lived in boardinghouses for short or long periods despite the attending moral pressure.

Middle-class and educated women in the late nineteenth century spent a lot of time thinking and writing about the meaning of their primary function in the home, and their thoughts influenced the public discourse on cooking. The most prominent writers on the subject sought to glorify housework, not eliminate it. Catherine Beecher, one of the earliest and best-known writers on domestic economy and housework in the nineteenth century, devoted her career to raising the status of housework by emphasizing its skilled nature and its social importance. Though unmarried, childless, and never a homeowner herself, she spent her life teaching and writing about the home arts and praising domesticity from the perspective of married, middle-class American mothers.

Beecher believed that because housekeeping was considered low-status "drudgery," women were inclined to neglect it, causing illness through bad food and unhealthy homes. Rather than being elevated by entering the public sphere and having political power outside the home, she argued that women should derive social and (indirect) political power through the traditional female tasks of housekeeping. Beecher combined practical advice and plans for more efficient and sanitary kitchen and home plans with reflections on the uplifting nature of housework. Housekeeping wasn't drudgery; it was work of the highest social importance, sanctified by moral power. As historian Nicole Tonkovich points out, to Beecher, the simple act of making bread demonstrated a mastery of household science (through an understanding of the mechanism of raising), artistry (because making bread well was difficult but rewarding), Christian devotion (because bread provided symbolic sustenance, as at the Last Supper), and patriotism (because bread provided strength for citizens of the republic). And, since Beecher's imagined audience would supervise servants rather than knead the bread themselves, teaching a servant how to make bread properly was described as an act of education and loving charity.[11] Done well, housekeeping could improve the nation's health, happiness, and spirituality, and it was much easier when done systematically.

Beecher never wavered from the perspective of middle-class women, who expected servants to do much of the heavy housework. Beecher imagined the mistress's role as that of a benevolent and well-informed supervisor. Although she did argue that servants should be treated and paid well, she frequently slipped into the use of stereotypes, describing the clumsy, oafish "Biddies," or Irish immigrant servants, who were supposedly difficult to train and oblivious to aesthetic niceties. Unlike later Progressive reformers, she seemed to have little interest in the domestic problems of poor and working-class women, who had no relief from the heaviest housework (and, in fact, often worked a double shift, doing paid housework or other work on top of fulfilling their own family responsibilities).[12] Further, working-class women had little opportunity to lighten their work by remodeling the kitchen or moving into a better-designed home, like the ones she recommended.

Later writers on housework were inspired by Beecher's practical suggestions for a more systematic and rational approach to the work. Home economists like Ellen Richards (who created the field and spent her life advocating for the place of women in university sciences) sought to bring science and efficiency to housework, not only in order to make it both easier and more rewarding for housewives, but also to provide opportunities in the sciences for professional women. The home economists promoted a more public, secular version of Beecher's vision. Better-kept homes meant a healthier, happier nation, with less disease, better-raised children, more nutritious food, and a more rewarding public role for women.[13]

Neither Beecher nor the home economists, however, challenged the idea that cooking was women's work. They sought to make it a more rewarding job with better results, and argued that it was so important a job as to warrant higher social status for women, but they never suggested that women stop cooking or find alternatives. In fact, their project to uplift housework magnified its moral importance. Writers on housework who followed Beecher were uncomfortable with what they saw as working-class attempts to shirk housekeeping duties like cooking. Such important work must be studied and perfected, not left to commerce.

Some social theorists around the turn of the twentieth century did, however, suggest that cooking and other forms of household production were better turned out of the house altogether and addressed as collective enterprises. Some Socialist thinkers, more radical than either Beecher or the home economists, argued that women needed to be freed from housework, either by community-based voluntary cooperation or by commercial services, in order to pursue careers outside the home. Their intellectual forerunners in America were the Fourierists and other utopian groups, who gathered together to create ideal communities by reimagining men's and women's social roles and the nature of their work. Unlike Beecher, Socialist thinkers didn't consider housework particularly uplifting or rewarding, but rather as a set of dull but necessary tasks critical to social survival. Socialists wanted to use the tools of modern mass production to relieve women from the backbreaking, endless, and inefficient labor of home food production. Marxist Socialists advocated cooperation, arguing that women's oppression was linked to the institution of private property, and that they could only be freed when all property (and all housework) was made collective.[14] A writer for the *Chicago Daily Socialist* in 1906 made a connection between Socialist goals and the improvement of women's condition. In a Socialist society food would be prepared centrally, freeing women from drudgery. Responding to the claim that socialism would "break up the home" (and refuting those who saw women's household labor as "natural"), the writer asked, "If your bread was made by a system that takes thirty seconds to make and bake a loaf, as is now done in large establishments, instead of your wife broiling all day over a hot stove to bake six loaves, would that break up the home?"[15]

Socialists disagreed among themselves on many subjects, but in general they shared the "producerist" belief that labor was the source of all wealth, and therefore all labor was important. Only a few Socialist thinkers expanded this definition to encompass even the unpaid home labor of women.[16] Socialist women were also more likely to perceive that women's labor, both inside and outside the home, was a necessary part of the "reproduction" of proletariat labor, vital to the continued oppression of industrial capitalism. They saw very plainly that cooking was subject to the same exploitation and inequality as any other sort of capitalist labor.[17] The Socialist critique of food and cooking stood out from those of all the other reformers and activists who were interested in food because only Socialists saw food as a purely material issue. Nearly everyone else viewed cooking through a prism of gender and morality that obscured the nature of cooking as labor.

A wide variety of activists, more or less radical, took up the call for cooperative housekeeping in the late nineteenth and early twentieth centuries. Historian Dolores Hayden labels these activists "material feminists." Many of them embraced Socialist theories as well as related ideas like the Nationalism espoused by followers of Edward Bellamy and his plan for a peaceful revolution and an egalitarian society.[18] Charlotte Perkins Gilman was the best known of those who advocated centralized, commercial services to replace housework. Instead of individual women toiling over individual stoves in poorly designed individual kitchens, families could simply pay to have their meals prepared in a professional kitchen by trained cooks, delivered hot and fresh, and the dirty dishes whisked away afterward. But Gilman was most concerned with freeing middle- and upper-class women from "drudgery" and was glad to shift it onto low-paid but efficient professional cooks and servants.[19] Other reformers seized on the idea that nutritious food could best be prepared centrally and sold at low cost to working-class women. The New England Kitchen's organizers sought both to offer good-quality "quick food" like soup, mush, and boiled beef as an alternative to saloon lunches and cheap pies, and to "educate the palates" of their customers by teaching them to prefer what the reformers considered simpler, more wholesome food. These reformers accepted the idea that the function of cooking might leave the home in an industrial society; indeed, they thought that mass-produced food would be more efficient and more sanitary than home cooking. The founders of the New England Kitchen merely wanted to make sure the food was healthy, affordable, unadulterated, and "honest" in a way that commercial pies could not be. Others, especially the home economists who began working for the food industry, testing and endorsing new food products, thought that public opinion (along with careful supervision by trained home economists) would soon produce commercial food that was better and cheaper than home cooking for everyone.[20]

The Progressive reformers of the early twentieth century drew ideas from both home economists and Socialists. Although the term encompasses a sprawling and complex movement, the Progressives were unified by their interest in the connection between the home and the wider society. Michael McGerr argues that the Progressive project to remake people and their environments in the mold of the middle class was even more central to the movement than the better-known campaign to control corporate power.[21] Progressives held complicated ideas about the connections between women and food. Although they often advocated a greater role for women outside the home and insisted that the public was responsible for the private matter of food, reformers still evinced a particular concern for the moral perils surrounding home cooking.

McGerr points out that Progressives showed compassion for the poor, and that their emphasis on the power of the environment refocused blame from the individual to the society.[22] Indeed, after 1900 many Progressives devoted their careers to publicizing and correcting the material conditions in homes and neighborhoods that made good cooking difficult, like a lack of clean running water, filthy conditions, and contaminated food.[23] They sought to address problems associated with food with methods such as tenement reform, journalism, school lunch programs, cooking classes, and home visits. But, although their methods were progressive, focused on correcting the home environment, their language betrayed a lingering tendency to equate cooking with morality. To an extent, Progressive reformers understood and sympathized with the problems of cramped kitchens, poor utilities, and long work hours, but, ultimately, cooking was too closely linked to gender performance and virtue to let women off the hook.[24]

Housework and Virtue

For many of those who studied the food problems of the poor, cooking seemed to express virtue, and virtue seemed especially important for poor women to maintain. Cooking, the heavenly ordained task of women, was considered their primary contribution to their family's health, and to neglect or reject cooking was seen as a sinful shirking of responsibility and an indication of bad character. Even wealthy and middle-class women, who were never expected to do all the heavy work of cooking, were criticized if they left their cooks unsupervised and untrained. The many poor and working-class women who bought their way out of the job with baker's bread, delicatessen food, or other kinds of prepared food came under heavy criticism. Attempts to lighten the load of cooking by buying prepared food or paying for cooking services were interpreted, by both men and other women, as evidence of bad moral character. In Harlem around 1910, in a middle-class preacher's family in which the mother did heroic amounts of cooking, it was considered "a disgrace to bring in bread from a store, and, for that matter, anything that was already baked."[25] As late as the 1940s a Chicago housewife captured the social stigma of purchasing bakers' bread: "Women who go running out to the bakeshops are lazy no-goods who don't care anything about the health of their families."[26] Similarly, married working women who relied on cooked food from the delicatessen were called lazy, frivolous, or bad managers. By contrast, the labor of cooking was often portrayed as a virtue.

The humble lunch pail often functioned as a symbol of a loving wife's care and affection for her husband, demonstrated through skillful cooking and a neat, tidy presentation. Working-class men, if they did not work near a saloon or cheap restaurant or couldn't afford to buy lunch, took lunch pails to work each day. Lunch pails (also called dinner pails), which were made of a light metal, such as tin, had covers and were sometimes divided into two or more interior compartments stacked in layers. A "three-story pail" would have a bottom section for tea or other liquid, a middle section for sandwiches, and a top section for pie.[27] Sometimes there were small separate tins that fit inside to hold condiments or wet items. Other lunch pails were simple covered buckets, which could double as "growlers" to carry beer home from the saloon. Lunch pails were usually filled with sandwiches of some kind, eggs, fruit, and cake or pie. Cookbook author Mary Hinman Abel suggested packing a lunch pail for a winter's day with "bread, cold boiled pork, cold baked beans with mustard and vinegar, doughnuts, apple pie, cold coffee."[28] The lunch pail was so ubiquitous that it could function as a political statement. In 1900 President McKinley's reelection campaign slogan promised workers a "full dinner pail."[29]

In journalism and fiction the lunch pail was a symbol of home, and of a wife or mother's devotion. In the early twentieth century Progressive journalist Margaret Byington, who wrote about steelworkers' wives in Pittsburgh, was impressed with their hard work and resourcefulness. She described how each would "take great pains" with her husband's lunch-pail meal "to make it appetizing, especially by adding preserves in a little cup in the corner of the bucket. They try to give the man what he likes the most."[30] A tragic story published in the Socialist *Daily People* in 1911 told a pathetic tale of a worker killed on the job. His neat appearance, with clean and patched clothing, and his carefully packed lunch indicated his devoted wife (now widow) at home: "Here is his lunch basket. Who'll take it home to the woman who patched those overalls? Let's see what she put in this morning. A bottle of coffee first; a napkin of snowy white; one egg, two thick sandwiches—that is to say, the slices of bread were thick, the meat was very thin—and a piece of home-made apple pie. That's all."[31] Although the family could not afford thick slices of meat, still the lunch pail expressed his wife's virtue. The napkin was kept as clean as his clothes, and its whiteness suggested her pure moral character. The pie was homemade instead of purchased at the store, reflecting her willingness to work hard at home rather than pay someone else to cook for her. The wife's dedication highlighted the tragedy of her husband's needless death.

Another wife, this one entirely fictional, assented to the loving duty of making lunches only gradually. A 1910 story in the *Craftsman* (a journal dedicated to the Arts and Crafts movement that also praised the dignity of honest labor) told the story of a young department store salesgirl who marries a clerk, hoping to rise into gentility. However, when her husband loses his desk job and cheerfully takes a laborer's job "in the yards" (the stockyard or the rail yard), she is crushed. She particularly resents his new habit of carrying a lunch pail (instead of buying his lunch), which she regards as a degrading mark of manual labor. She refuses to make his lunch, forcing him to fill his pail with his own "thick, clumsy" sandwiches. Eventually, she regains respect for her husband and demonstrates it by surprising him with a well-packed lunch she makes herself. The lunch pail was a symbol of working-class life, but also of a wife's pride in her husband.[32] Only a complaining, selfish woman would refuse to perform the wifely duty of packing a nice lunch.

That women's home cooking carried heavy moral weight can also be glimpsed in the Progressive reformers' general distaste for "handouts," like those offered at charity soup kitchens. By 1900, some reformers argued that the old tradition of feeding the poor at soup kitchens bred "generation after generation" of paupers. A charity publication claimed that by handing out soup, "mendicancy is bred; vagrancy is encouraged; entire neighborhoods are degraded and pauperized."[33] Handing out food for free, they argued, caused these moral and social problems. If women didn't cook, the whole neighborhood went to pot, so to speak. The new, more modern style of philanthropy took the form not of charity handouts, but rather enabling (and, indeed, requiring) women to cook for themselves. Ironically, although settlement workers and home economists were themselves engaged in carving out new fields of endeavor for women in public life, they repeatedly argued that most women must devote all their time and energy to being better housekeepers, for the good of the family, for the good of society, and for their own good. The future of the industrial city depended on housewives' hard work and self-discipline.

School lunch programs became another battlefield for conflicts about women's home cooking. Until the early twentieth century, schools did not generally offer lunches. Children either brought a lunch, went home for food, went without, or bought inexpensive snacks on or near the school premises from vendors who offered candy, pastries, and other items, usually made from cheap materials.[34] Progressive reformers, interested in the diet of the poor and newly aware of the importance of nutritious food for growing children, were dismayed that children survived on nasty, nonnutritive, and possibly adulterated sweets sold by suspicious-looking, unregulated vendors.[35]

Around the turn of the twentieth century, social settlements in poor neighborhoods began to tackle the school lunch problem as a way simultaneously to help children and to educate families about nutrition. The Starr Centre settlement house in Philadelphia is a good example of the types of programs that sprang up in major cities such as Boston, New York, and Chicago. Beginning in 1894, the Starr Centre offered "penny lunches," prepared by settlement house workers or volunteers and sold to children on school grounds. The penny lunches offered a variety of foods at one penny for each serving. Children could thus put together a meal with any amount of money they had, aided by some gentle nutritional guidance by the volunteers. In 1909 the menus included graham wafers, pretzels, milk biscuits, coffee cakes, tea buns, a variety of fresh and stewed fruit, shredded wheat biscuit, milk, cocoa, hominy, rice pudding, bean soup, and meat sandwich.[36] (The options betrayed the early nutritionists' fondness for carbohydrates as a cheap source of nutrition.)

The penny lunch program had a dual purpose: to alleviate children's hunger immediately at small cost without providing a morally degrading free lunch, and to teach nutrition and good food choices by example. The 1908 Starr Centre annual report proudly announced that, as a result of the "habits of neatness and cleanliness enforced by our helpers," "the recess is more quiet; there are fewer quarrels; and a perceptively less amount of surreptitious cigarette smoking, as well-fed boys do not crave cigarettes as hungry ones do."[37] The Starr Centre also sent an investigator to the homes of children who consistently had little or no money for lunch, or who seemed half-starved. The investigator sought to learn whether children were underfed "because of poverty, ignorance, or neglect."[38] Mother's "ignorance"—of the right foods to choose and the right ways to cook them—seemed as likely as poverty or neglect to cause underfeeding.

The center's penny lunch program was successful, as were school lunch programs elsewhere. Giving children a few cents for lunch was no doubt easier for parents than packing a lunch or preparing a hot one; the competitors who had sold children snacks were casual peddlers who could not or would not defend their commercial turf; and the food sold (especially the buns, biscuits, and cakes) seems to have been similar enough to students' usual fare to be accepted by the children. So the penny lunch program thrived. In several cities, settlement school lunch programs evolved into hot lunches organized and funded by the school district. This was an instance in which reformers offered institutional cooking to replace the lack of home cooking and as an alternative to the unregulated commercial alternatives.

By 1911, however, organizers at the Starr Centre had developed a nagging uncertainty about the lunch program. "Does [the program] remove a responsibility from the home which could be kept where it belongs?" the trustees asked in their annual report. "If so, it is mistaken philanthropy."[39] No matter how much the penny lunches might contribute to children's health, they still should not stand in the way of the mother's fundamental responsibility to provide nutrition for her family. To have mothers actively tend to their children's nutrition was the ultimate goal; moving that responsibility out of the home was only a temporary solution. Eliminating or minimizing home cooking might contribute to the breakdown of family life.

At the same time that the Starr Centre philanthropists began to feel uncomfortable with offering mothers a pass from cooking, pioneering home economist Ellen Richards was struggling with the place of cooking in an industrial society. As in so much else in her pathbreaking life, she stood at the forefront of a shift away from the old-fashioned domesticity of Catherine Beecher. Richards strongly believed that there was a right and a wrong way to cook. The New England Kitchen she helped develop offered cooked food as both a solution to inadequate kitchens and a template for the right kind of cooking. She was one of the creators of the home economics movement, which sought to bring science, efficiency, and thereby legitimacy to housework. Richards dismissed the idea that housework was naturally "uplifting," as Beecher had argued. As she wrote in 1900, all of the personally rewarding productive tasks had been removed from the home by industrialization, leaving only cooking and cleaning, which were much less than satisfying. "What is cooked one hour is eaten the next; the cleaning of one day must be repeated the next, and the hopelessness of it all has sunk into women's souls. It is like sweeping back the sea or digging the sand in face of the wind—nothing to show for it."[40]

Richards recognized that many middle-class women had eliminated cooking and other housework from their lives by living in boardinghouses or hotels. She thoroughly disapproved of this development but conceded that, ultimately, cooking at home could be at least partly replaced by mass-produced food for middle-class people. Since we already accept other mass-produced goods, she argued, "Why cannot bread made by the yard and pies by the hundred, be in like manner accepted?" In fact, she looked forward to the cleaner and more efficient production of food: "When housekeeping is reorganized on a business basis the present waste and drudgery and dirt in the house-kitchen will be abolished, and along with the soap-making will go the soup- and bread-making—the heavy kettles and greasy dishes. The cleaning of fowls, the trimming of vegetables will be done out of the house." In 1900 she envisioned "the home of 1920," in which the kitchen would be connected by pneumatic tubes to a supply station that would distribute prepared foods.[41]

However, Richards revealed a lingering distaste for consumerism and the place of commerce in household work. She believed that the home was the basis of civilization, and thus she felt it should remain a place of moral and personal development. Cooking at home, though heavy, repetitive work, was educational, and women's labor was the glue that held together their families. "In sociological work is it not considered a great step when a family is persuaded to gather as a unit about the table instead of each taking from the bakeshop or the cupboard that which will serve to keep body and soul together?"[42] Women must understand the work of cooking as a test of management skills, and the act of dining together as a school for children's social and moral development. Although cooking and eating outside the home might be more efficient, Richards argued, it was not always worth the loss in moral education.

If cooking was discipline, then "consuming" cooking (by buying cooked or convenience food) was a dangerous extravagance. By the early twentieth century the United States had completed its transformation into a consumer culture, one in which most people bought everything they used, and in which possessions as much as family, work, race, or religion defined individuals and groups. Critics of consumerism often charged that the ability to buy household services rather than doing the work degraded virtue, especially among the women on whose labor the household most depended. Richards wrote with vehemence about the self-indulgence and profligacy caused by consumption. She believed that to buy household services instead of doing the work turned the home from "a nursery of good citizens" to "a place of selfish ease, of freedom amounting to license, a receiving all and giving nothing."[43] According to Richards, "luxuries" like consumer goods, abundant food, and labor-saving devices had turned the home into a place of selfishness and wastefulness instead of a place where citizens learned to be frugal and sober. Richards was torn between the efficiency of bread baked by the yard and the unpleasant spectacle of bakery food (with its old connotations of lazy, selfish women) replacing the family meal. Home economists in later years, like Christine Frederick, would wholeheartedly embrace consumption and work closely with food manufacturers to promote easier cooking and housekeeping for everyone. The efficient mass-prepared food to which Richards looked with wariness was the wave of the future for working-class and middle-class women alike.

Maintaining Boundaries:
Women and Domestic Spaces

To people who believed that cooking expressed moral character, the organization of working-class kitchens could be troubling indeed. Richards's discomfort with commerce in the home was not unique. To late nineteenth-century middle-class Americans, a well-ordered home indicated a well-ordered family.[44] The social world (indicated by the parlor) should be entirely separate from the work spaces (the kitchen). Like their husbands, middle-class women were supervisors, not manual laborers. The lady of the home oversaw maids, cooks, laundresses, and others who did the difficult, dirty, and heavy work in specific workrooms (the kitchen and the basement or cellar). Meanwhile, she instructed her children, maintained the family's social networks, and did light, attractive handwork in the parlor, dining room, and bedrooms.[45]

Even more importantly, the world of the family was to be a refuge from the public world, and therefore entirely free from any suggestion of commerce. In homes that employed servants, this meant that hired workers must be kept separate from family members. A model home designed in 1897 featured a kitchen that was "in every way separated from the main part of the house by two doors. ... The servants also go directly to their rooms by the back stairway without at any time entering the main parts of the house."[46] In a well-designed middle-class home, housework was almost invisible.

Naturally, in many families that considered themselves middle class, there was not quite enough money to effect a complete separation between worker and supervisor. Most middle-class women did some of the cooking and other heavy tasks themselves (and a fair proportion did almost all of it), and the work spaces may have been in extremely close proximity to the social spaces. But "respectable" women at least tried to keep them separate.[47] They sought to have their home free from cooking odors when guests arrived in order to preserve the division between work and social areas. They also tried to hire maids who would be unobtrusive and "know their place," so that the wage-earning members of the household would be properly distanced from the family. Even a woman who "did her own work" (a euphemism for lacking a servant) would try to cover up the evidence of it when company came, so that her work as housekeeper would be distinct from her identity as mistress of the home. In an 1871 novel, a woman and her daughter are forced to fire their maid and begin doing their own cooking. In order to maintain the appearance of gentility, they put the cookstove in the dining room, tucked behind a green screen. The resulting "art kitchen" was kept sparkling clean and pleasant.

Because they worked to keep everything perfectly tidy, no odors or smoke betrayed their embarrassing and inappropriate labor to the guests.[48]

Because women were the embodiment of the home, a disorderly home reflected badly on them personally. A woman who let her housekeeping spill over into the home's public spaces, without regard for boundaries, was considered lazy and slatternly.[49] When middle-class observers looked at working-class homes as they attempted to solve social problems like poverty, they were bothered by the lack of clearly established boundaries between work and leisure, between commerce and family life, and between individual family members' private lives. The crowded multiuse rooms of workers' housing seemed to carry moral consequences. In an 1896 dietary study, nutritionists W. O. Atwater and Charles Woods described the home of a very poor family.

> The bedrooms were so small that there was only room for the bed. Two of the children slept on mattresses on the floor of the front room. There were set tubs and a sink in the kitchen. The kitchen served as a dining room. The table was not set and the family did not sit down together to eat their meals. There were no regular meals, the table serving more as a lunch counter where each one went and helped himself. No meal was prepared at noon.[50]

This report focused on the lack of clearly defined sleeping and eating areas and an orderly family schedule. There was no spatial distinction between the family's working, eating, and sleeping areas, and the family lacked set meal times. Improper spaces resulted in improper behavior. The implication was that family life would necessarily be degenerate in a home where activities were not clearly organized and where spaces were so jumbled. The disorder showed most clearly in the family's eating habits, where commerce had been allowed to creep into the sacred family sphere. "The oldest daughter contributed to a 'common spread' with her shopmates, and the children were given 5 cents each per day with which they bought cakes and fruits at the open stands on the street."[51] The mother didn't pack lunches; instead, the father ate at his restaurant job and the children purchased prepared food outside the home. The family's kitchen was even compared to a commercial lunch counter. According to Atwater and Woods, "The great trouble here, as in most of the cases studied, is in the lack of management."[52] It was not the family's essential poverty, or the need for all members to work for wages, or the cramped conditions in their rented rooms that was the problem. The problem was the mother's mismanagement, which was manifested by disordered spaces and the reliance on consumption rather than production.

According to the nutritionists, this kind of family disorder could be cured through improvements in the family's living space and through the mother's renewed attention to her "proper" tasks. An update written some months after the initial dietary survey reported that the family's situation had initially gotten worse. The mother became too sick to work, and much of the furniture was pawned. But then their lives began to improve, starting with a new apartment. The mother got a job as a tenement housekeeper (cleaning the halls and common areas of the building they lived in) and in exchange paid reduced rent on a better apartment (with the same number of rooms, but sunnier).[53] The major change was in the mother's work patterns, as she now gave more time to homemaking. According to the update, "The family have improved in their way of living. The table is now set with a white cloth and the family sit down together. ... When it is necessary for the girls to carry a lunch the mother prepares it for them, and it costs less than a third of what it would otherwise."[54] The table suggested a clearly defined dining area, and the white cloth was emblematic of the mother's new ability to keep a clean house. The mother cooked regular meals and packed lunches (presumably on top of her duties cleaning the tenement house) instead of allowing her family to promiscuously and wastefully pay for someone else's labor to cook meals. Although it is impossible to tell exactly how the mother herself felt about these changes, she seemed to have embraced the chance to keep a tidier house and to use her own labor to provide better food for her family. She, too, liked the idea of a white cloth and a family meal, even if it came at the cost of more labor. From the nutritionists' perspective, a disorderly family had become orderly simply through an improved separation of spaces and the "correct" use of the mother's time.

Cooking was certainly heavily gendered—but it was also perceived through the lens of class. From the perspective of upper-class observers trying to offer solutions to the problem of food and poverty, working-class women needed to adhere even more strongly to their traditional feminine role. Richards, the settlement-house workers, and the nutritionists unconsciously held the working class to middle-class standards of behavior in regards to women's roles. To them, if working-class women could be more like middle-class women—managers as well as workers, able to devote all their time to housewifery, and committed to separating domestic and commercial life—then they would enjoy the undoubtedly more comfortable, stable life of the upper class.

When femininity was defined in middle-class terms, working-class women could not but fail to be truly feminine. Buying food rather than cooking it, allowing their husbands and children to buy food, performing their cooking tasks half-heartedly or without love, and failing to keep commerce out of the home were seen as grave errors by reformers around the turn of the twentieth century. Yet most of these same reformers seemed intent on rejecting the economic importance of housework. Though they sensed that cooking was vital to family survival, they explained its importance through concepts of womanliness and virtue rather than economics.

We know much less about how working-class women understood their own lives and identities because so much of the information available about them was recorded by outsiders. Yet it seems clear that, despite criticism from reformers, working-class women—as they sought to show love through cooking but also juggled wage work with housework, cooked sometimes and bought prepared food sometimes—were the wave of the future, more so than the middle-class women who controlled the mainstream discourse about housework. For their part, working-class women continued doing what they needed to do for their own and their family's survival whether it met the middle-class criteria of "womanly virtue" or not.

Intense reform efforts centered on home cooking began to fade in the 1920s, although working-class people continued to struggle to make ends meet in that decade and beyond. The home economics movement that had begun in the late nineteenth century to rationalize home work had shifted much of its energy to supporting the food industry. Home economists parlayed their degrees and expertise into jobs with food processors, helping to develop, test, and promote new processes and packages of food. Rather than encourage women to produce plain, nourishing food at home, home economists now urged them to take advantage of industrial shortcuts, try new products and new recipes, and otherwise consume the fruits of the industry. Christine Frederick, who wrote a guide for advertisers called *Selling Mrs. Consumer*, exemplified the new direction of home economists.[55] The "bread by the yard" that Richards envisioned did come about, as bakery bread finally edged out homemade bread for everyone, not just the working class. At the same time, her critique of consumption faded and was replaced by other voices that cheerfully endorsed new products as "modern," not extravagant or sinful. Home economists talked less about virtue and more about how to maximize the household budget with careful buying rather than careful cooking.[56] The shift from morality to consumption foreshadowed the immense expansion of the food industry and its effects on all Americans in the remainder of the twentieth century.

Notes

1. Jeanne Boydston, "To Earn Her Daily Bread: Housework and Antebellum Working-Class Subsistence," *Radical History Review* 35 (1986): 19; Elizabeth Blackmar, *Manhattan for Rent, 1785–1850* (Ithaca, NY: Cornell University Press, 1989).

2. Ewa Morawska, *For Bread with Butter: The Life-Worlds of East Central Europeans in Johnstown, Pennsylvania, 1890–1940* (Cambridge: Cambridge University Press, 1985), 130.

3. Scott Nearing, *Financing the Wage-Earner's Family: A Survey of the Facts Bearing on Income and Expenditures in the Families of American Wage-Earners* (New York: B. W. Huebsch, 1914), 85.

4. Lois Rita Helmbold, "Beyond the Family Economy: Black and White Working-Class Women during the Great Depression," *Feminist Studies* 13, no. 3 (Fall 1987): 629–55.

5. Ibid.

6. Bonnie Fox, ed., *Hidden in the Household: Women's Domestic Labour under Capitalism* (Toronto: The Women's Press, 1980).

7. Ruth Schwarz Cowan, *More Work for Mother: The Ironies of Household Technology from the Open Hearth to the Microwave* (New York: Basic Books, 1983), 24.

8. Ibid., 63–64.

9. Gamber's work on dressmakers and boardinghouse keepers illustrates the many ways nineteenth-century women engaged in business. See also Gamber, *The Female Economy: The Millinery and Dressmaking Trades, 1860–1930* (Urbana: University of Illinois Press, 1997).

10. Wendy Gamber, *The Boardinghouse in Nineteenth-Century America* (Baltimore, MD: Johns Hopkins University Press, 2007), 117, 122.

11. Nicole Tonkovich, foreword to *The American Woman's Home* by Catherine E. Beecher and Harriet Beecher Stowe (Hartford, CT: Harriet Beecher Stowe Center; Rutgers University Press, 2002).

12. Ibid.

13. Sarah Stage and Virginia B. Vincenti, eds., *Rethinking Home Economics: Women and the History of a Profession* (Ithaca, NY: Cornell University Press, 1997).

14. Sally M. Miller, "Social Democratic Millennium: Visions of Gender," in *Expectations for the Millennium: American Socialist Visions of the Future,* ed. Peter H. Buckingham (Westport, CT: Greenwood Press, 2002), 60.

15. *Chicago Daily Socialist,* November 26, 1906 (emphasis in the original).

16. On Socialist critiques of domestic life, see also Francis Robert Schor, *Utopianism and Radicalism in a Reforming America* (Westport, CT: Greenwood Press, 1997), especially chapters 1 and 2.

17. Kate Weigand, *Red Feminism: American Communism and the Making of Women's Liberation* (Baltimore, MD: Johns Hopkins University Press, 2001), 28.

18. Dolores Hayden, *The Grand Domestic Revolution: A History of Feminist Design for American Homes, Neighborhoods, and Cities* (Cambridge, MA: MIT Press, 1981), chapters 2 and 10.

19. Miller, "Social Democratic Millennium," 59; Mark W. Van Wienen, "A Rose by Any Other Name: Charlotte Perkins Stetson (Gilman) and the Case for American Reform Socialism," *American Quarterly* 55, no. 4 (December 2003): 603–34. Van Wienen points out that although Gilman repudiated much of her Socialist activity during the 1930s, she lectured and published frequently on reform socialism during the 1890s, when she was Charlotte Perkins Stetson. Gilman advocated "gradualist" or "reform" socialism (as opposed to "revolutionary" socialism) at least through the 1890s; she was involved with Nationalism, Populism, and Fabianism, and promoted centralized, commercial services to replace housework.

20. Laura Shapiro, *Perfection Salad: Women and Cooking at the Turn of the Century* (New York: Farrar, Straus and Giroux, 1986), 210.

21. Michael McGerr, *A Fierce Discontent: The Rise and Fall of the Progressive Movement in America, 1870–1920* (New York: Free Press, 2003), 79.

22. Ibid., 79.

23. Suellen Hoy, *Chasing Dirt: The American Pursuit of Cleanliness* (New York: Oxford University Press, 1995), 102.

24. Linda Gordon identifies a similar situation, in which inadequate knowledge of context promoted moralistic judgments in the case of welfare for single mothers in *Pitied but Not Entitled: Single Mothers and the History of Welfare* (Cambridge, MA: Harvard University Press, 1994).

25. Frederick Douglass Opie, *Hog and Hominy: Soul Food from Africa to America* (New York: Columbia University Press, 2008), 58.

26. Robert J. Casey, *Chicago Medium Rare* (Indianapolis: Bobbs-Merrill, 1949), 107; cited in William D. Panschar, *Baking in America: Economic Development. Volume I* (Evanston, IL: Northwestern University Press, 1956), 96.

27. "The Full Dinner Pail," *Daily People* (New York), July 21 1900.

28. Mary Hinman Abel, *Practical Sanitary and Economic Cooking Adapted to Persons of Moderate and Small Means* (Rochester, NY: American Public Health Association, 1890), 177.

29. This campaign promise was roundly rejected by the Socialist newspaper the *Daily People*: "The dinner pail is obsolete. It is an anachronism, a memory of the halcyon days when you could get three dollars for ten hours work, and for three dollars you could get three square meals, one of which was carried in the pail. The average laborer to-day carries his dinner in a paper bag in his pocket, or else in a small box. He does not have enough to make a pail necessary." Furthermore, the author protested the idealization of the dinner pail: "At the very best, the fact that a man must eat a cold, tasteless meal, and one that becomes clammy from its confinement in a tin pail, should arouse the working class." "The Full Dinner Pail."

30. Margaret F. Byington, *Homestead: The Households of a Mill Town* (reprint, Pittsburgh: University Center for International Studies, University of Pittsburgh, 1974), 64.

31. "News for Somebody's Wife," *Daily People* (New York), August 13, 1911.

32. Lucille Baldwin van Slyke, "The Dinner Pail: A Story," *Craftsman* 18, no. 3 (June 1910): 335–46.

33. "Philadelphia Free Soup," *Charities Review* 10, no. 2 (April 1900): 52.

34. Mary Hinman Abel and Ellen Richards, *The Story of the New England Kitchen: Part II: A Study in Social Economics* (Boston: Press of Rockwell and Churchill, 1893), 162.

35. One of the early focuses of the pure food reform movement, frequently discussed in the popular press, was the synthetic dyes used to color cheap candy and ice cream. Journalists liked to portray ragged slum children spending their pennies on unnaturally colored, unhealthy, and probably poisonous confections. See "The Nation's Annual Candy Bill," *New York Times,* January 2, 1910; "Stuff One Gets in Candy. Sulphurous Acid, Glue, and Shellac Some of It," *Daily People* (New York), February 21, 1910.

36. Annual Report, the Starr Centre, 1909, p. 19; Annual Reports collection, box 84, folder "Starr Centre," Urban Archives, Paley Library, Temple University. The graham

wafers, pretzels, coffee cakes, stewed prunes, rice pudding, hominy, and bean soup were noted as "very popular."

37. Ibid.

38. Ibid., 20.

39. Ibid. McGerr finds a few other Progressives grappling with the worry that well-meaning public institutions could supplant, rather than support, the home. *Fierce Discontent,* 115.

40. Ellen H. Richards, "Housekeeping in the Twentieth Century," *American Kitchen Magazine* 12, no. 6 (March 1900): 204.

41. Ellen H. Richards, ed., *The Cost of Living as Modified by Sanitary Science* (New York: J. Wiley, 1913), 85; Richards, "Housekeeping in the Twentieth Century," 204.

42. Richards, *The Cost of Living,* 83.

43. Ibid., 25–26.

44. Katherine C. Grier's *Culture and Comfort: Parlor Making and Middle-Class Identity, 1850–1930* (Washington, DC: Smithsonian Institution Press, 1988) remains the best discussion of the manifold cultural implications of middle-class homes and furnishings, especially in the parlor. See especially the introduction on the symbolism of home furnishing.

45. Harvey Green, *The Light of the Home: An Intimate View of the Lives of Women in Victorian America* (New York: Pantheon Books, 1983), 59.

46. Walter Keith, "A Model $2000 House," *Ladies' Home Journal,* March 1897, 25.

47. Clifford E. Clark Jr., "The Vision of the Dining Room: Plan Book Dreams and Middle-Class Realities," in *Dining in America, 1850–1900,* ed. Kathryn Grover (Amherst: University of Massachusetts Press; Rochester: Margaret Woodbury Strong Museum, 1987), 162–63.

48. Priscilla J. Brewer, *From Fireplace to Cookstove: Technology and the Domestic Ideal in America* (Syracuse, NY: Syracuse University Press, 2000), 194–95.

49. Plante, Ellen M. *The American Kitchen 1700 to the Present* (New York: Facts on File, 1995), 117.

50. W. O. Atwater and Charles D. Woods, "Dietary Studies in New York City in 1895 and 1896," USDA Office of Experiment Stations, Bulletin No. 46 (Washington, DC: Government Printing Office, 1898), 26.

51. Ibid.

52. Ibid., 28.

53. The improvement in the family's standard of living suggests that the new rooms were larger, but this information is not directly stated in the report.

54. Atwater and Woods, "Dietary Studies," 28.

55. Christine Frederick, *Selling Mrs. Consumer* (New York: Business Bourse, 1929).

56. Shapiro, *Perfection Salad,* chapter 8.

Bibliography

ARCHIVAL COLLECTIONS

Urban Archives, Paley Library, Temple University.

Abel, Mary Hinman. *Practical Sanitary and Economic Cooking Adapted to Persons of Moderate and Small Means.* Rochester, NY: American Public Health Association, 1890.

Abel, Mary Hinman, and Ellen Richards. *The Story of the New England Kitchen: Part II: A Study in Social Economics.* Boston: Press of Rockwell and Churchill, 1893.

Atwater, W. O., and Charles. D. Woods. "Dietary Studies in New York City in 1895 and 1896." USDA Office of Experiment Stations, Bulletin No. 46. Washington, DC: Government Printing Office, 1898.

Byington, Margaret F. *Homestead: The Households of a Mill Town.* 1910. Reprint, Pittsburgh: University Center for International Studies, University of Pittsburgh, 1974.

Frederick, Christine. *Selling Mrs. Consumer.* New York: Business Bourse, 1929.

"The Full Dinner Pail." *Daily People* (New York), July 21, 1900.

Keith, Walter. "A Model $2000 House." *Ladies' Home Journal,* March 1897.

"The Nation's Annual Candy Bill." *New York Times,* January 2, 1910.

Nearing, Scott. *Financing the Wage-Earner's Family: A Survey of the Facts Bearing on Income and Expenditures in the Families of American Wage-Earners.* New York: B. W. Huebsch, 1914.

"News for Somebody's Wife." *Daily People* (New York), August 13, 1911.

"Philadelphia Free Soup." *Charities Review* 10, no. 2 (April 1900): 52.

Richards, Ellen H., ed. *The Cost of Living as Modified by Sanitary Science.* New York: J. Wiley, 1913.

———. "Housekeeping in the Twentieth Century." *American Kitchen Magazine* 12, no. 6 (March 1900).

"Stuff One Gets in Candy. Sulphurous Acid, Glue, and Shellac Some of It." *Daily People* (New York), February 21, 1910.

Van Slyke, Lucille Baldwin. "The Dinner Pail: A Story." *Craftsman* 18, no. 3 (June 1910): 335–46.

SECONDARY SOURCES

Beecher, Catharine E., and Harriet Beecher Stowe. *The American Woman's Home.* ed. Nicole Tonkovich. Hartford, CT: Harriet Beecher Stowe Center; Rutgers University Press, 2002.

Blackmar, Elizabeth. *Manhattan for Rent, 1785–1850.* Ithaca, NY: Cornell University Press, 1989.

Boydston, Jeanne. "To Earn Her Daily Bread: Housework and Antebellum Working-Class Subsistence." *Radical History Review* 35 (1986): 7–25.

Brewer, Priscilla J. *From Fireplace to Cookstove: Technology and the Domestic Ideal in America.* Syracuse, NY: Syracuse University Press, 2000.

Clark Jr., Clifford E. "The Vision of the Dining Room: Plan Book Dreams and Middle-Class Realities." In *Dining in America, 1850–1900,* ed. Kathryn Grover. Amherst: University of Massachusetts Press; Rochester: Margaret Woodbury Strong Museum, 1987.

Cowan, Ruth Schwartz. *More Work for Mother: The Ironies of Household Technology from the Open Hearth to the Microwave.* New York: Basic Books, 1983.

Fox, Bonnie, ed. *Hidden in the Household: Women's Domestic Labour under Capitalism.* Toronto: Women's Press, 1980.

Gamber, Wendy. *The Boardinghouse in Nineteenth-Century America.* Baltimore, MD: Johns Hopkins University Press, 2007.

———. *The Female Economy: The Millinery and Dressmaking Trades, 1860–1930.* Urbana: University of Illinois Press, 1997.

Gordon, Linda. *Pitied but Not Entitled: Single Mothers and the History of Welfare.* Cambridge, MA: Harvard University Press, 1994.

Green, Harvey. *The Light of the Home: An Intimate View of the Lives of Women in Victorian America.* New York: Pantheon Books, 1983.

Grier, Katherine C. *Culture and Comfort: Parlor Making and Middle-Class Identity, 1850–1930.* Washington, DC: Smithsonian Institution Press, 1988.

Helmbold, Lois Rita. "Beyond the Family Economy: Black and White Working-Class Women during the Great Depression." *Feminist Studies* 13, no. 3 (Fall 1987).

Hoy, Suellen. *Chasing Dirt: The American Pursuit of Cleanliness.* New York: Oxford University Press, 1995.

McGerr, Michael. *A Fierce Discontent: The Rise and Fall of the Progressive Movement in America, 1870–1920.* New York: Free Press, 2003.

Miller, Sally M. "Social Democratic Millennium: Visions of Gender." In *Expectations for the Millennium: American Socialist Visions of the Future,* ed. Peter H. Buckingham. Westport, CT: Greenwood Press, 2002.

Morawska, Ewa. *For Bread with Butter: The Life-Worlds of East Central Europeans in Johnstown, Pennsylvania, 1890–1940*. Cambridge: Cambridge University Press, 1985.

Opie, Frederick Douglass. *Hog and Hominy: Soul Food from Africa to America*. New York: Columbia University Press, 2008.

Panschar, William G. *Baking in America: Economic Development. Volume I*. Evanston, IL: Northwestern University Press, 1956.

Plante, Ellen M. *The American Kitchen 1700 to the Present*. New York: Facts on File, 1995.

Shapiro, Laura. *Perfection Salad: Women and Cooking at the Turn of the Century*. New York: Farrar, Straus and Giroux, 1986.

Stage, Sarah, and Virginia B. Vincenti, eds. *Rethinking Home Economics: Women and the History of a Profession*. Ithaca, NY: Cornell University Press, 1997.

Van Wienen, Mark W. "A Rose by Any Other Name: Charlotte Perkins Stetson (Gilman) and the Case for American Reform Socialism." *American Quarterly* 55, no. 4 (December 2003): 603–34.

QUESTION TO CONSIDER

- What did Katherine L. Turner mean by "a woman's work is never done?"

A 1910 painting of college baseball.

CHAPTER 4

The Legend of the Lively Ball

By Robert H. Schaefer

Editor's Introduction

In the early days of baseball, the center of a ball would consist of anything from a walnut to a rock with yarn or string wrapped around it to make a ball. The ball of string often was encased in leather. There was no standardized ball, since each player made them to his own specifications. Thus, the team that supplied the balls had an advantage over the opposing team.

By the 1850s, baseball had become more organized and rules began to be applied, which changed over time. Read Robert H. Schaefer's article on the transformation of the "ball" used in America's popular sport.

The Legend of the Lively Ball

By Robert H. Schaefer

What makes the fielders run so fast?
The lively ball, the lively ball.
What makes the Boston Club run last?
The lively ball, the lively ball.
What makes the pitchers pant and blow?
What makes the hit column grow?
What makes the swatter the whole show?
Why nothing but the lively ball.
What makes the fielder's tongue hang out?
The lively ball, the lively ball.
What makes the rooters rave and shout?
The lively ball, the lively ball.
What makes our suppers all so late,
The patient weary housewife wait
Until the clock shows half-past eight?
Why nothing but the lively ball.
—"The Lively Ball," by Roe; *The Sporting News*, June 15, 1911

Two of our national pastime's most famous legends involve lively baseballs: (1) In 1911 the A.J. Reach Company introduced a ball with a new cork center which inadvertently made the ball livelier, and (2) the Dead Ball Era ended in 1920 due to the surreptitious introduction of the so-called rabbit ball.

Is there any truth in either of these legends?

In order to place them in their proper perspective we must first review the history of "dead" and "lively" balls. It may be surprising to modern fans, but the lively-ball controversy dates all the way back to the 1850s and '60s. In those early days pioneers such as Daniel Adams, John Van Horn, and Harvey Ross meticulously handcrafted each individual baseball.

Handcrafted Baseballs

Daniel Lucius Adams, a physician, was one of the original members of the New York Knickerbockers. In memoir published in *The Sporting News* on February 29, 1896, Dr. Adams related that in the late 1840s he personally made all the baseballs used by most of the clubs in the New York City area. Adams had volunteered to furnish baseballs as a courtesy to the clubs because "no one could be found to make or cover a ball." He, at some point aided by an unnamed Scotch saddler, provided this service for six or seven years. With a pronounced scarcity of baseballs, it was no wonder the clubs demanded that a single ball survive the entire match. Constructing baseballs was strictly a sideline for Dr. Adams, but he significantly advanced the state of the new art.

In 1859, John Van Horn, a player on the Baltic Base Ball Club of Brooklyn, was recruited by his club to craft baseballs on a paid basis. A shoemaker by trade, he worked and resided in lower Manhattan, near Houston Street. As early as 1854 his little shop was located at number 33, Second Avenue, and it remained at this address for more than twenty years. Initially, Van Horn produced only fifty to sixty balls a year, completely alone, one ball at a time. The labor-intensive process limited the volume of balls that could be fabricated by an individual. Nonetheless, the Van Horn ball proved successful and its reputation grew rapidly. By the early 1860s the Van Horn ball had captured the majority of the considerable New York trade.

Van Horn made the cores of his baseballs by cutting old rubber shoe soles into strips and forming them into crude spheres which weighed as much as four ounces. (The Ross dead ball, on the other hand, was said to contain less two ounces of rubber.) This mass of rubber was then heated so that it melted and fused together. He next wrapped the rubber sphere with cotton yarn until it was the proper size, and then stitched on a leather cover. Sheepskin was the material of choice for covers until c. 1870 when it was replaced with the much more durable horsehide. The finished ball was about ten inches in circumference and weighed more than six ounces. Although Van Horn was a highly skilled craftsman, no two balls were exactly identical. This variability problem was compounded by the fact that the technique of fusing rubber strips to form a core produced an irregular and unpredictable degree of liveliness from one ball to the next. This difficulty was not overcome until the late 1860s when a method for molding a spherical rubber core was devised.

Because a ball with a core of rubber that weighed four ounces exhibited a remarkable degree of liveliness, it was known as an "elastic" ball. Elastic balls presented a dreadful hazard to the barehanded players of the 19th century.

In addition to the danger of dislocated fingers and broken bones, the specter of death lurked behind every lively ball. On July 9, 1870, the New York *Clipper* reported: "Two young people have been killed outright from being struck on the head with one of these elastic rubber balls—one in Chicago from a swiftly thrown ball, and the other in Dover, New Hampshire, from a batted ball."

Later the same year this report of frequent injuries attributed to the lively ball appeared in the *Clipper*: "...within our vicinity players on our club nines have sustained injuries in the form of blackened eyes, bruised faces, broken fingers, split hands and endless smaller injuries received from efforts to stop or catch swiftly batted or thrown rubber balls."

The First Dead Ball

Reacting to the dangers of the elastic ball, the quantity of rubber used in its center was gradually reduced, deadening the ball and making it safer. A New York toy and novelty maker, Alex Waugh, achieved the ultimate "dead ball" when he crafted a baseball without using any rubber in its core. Waugh announced his rubberless dead ball in 1868. All the leading ball manufacturers quickly copied the concept and the new dead ball proved very popular. Although it was successful in making the game safer for the players, it also made the game duller for the spectators as hitting declined.

Following many years of experimentation, during which time the ball was gradually reduced in size and mass, a weight of 5 to 5¼ ounces and a circumference of 9 to 9¼ inches was finally determined to give the best satisfaction. These physical dimensions and their variation tolerances were established in 1872 and have not changed since. The issue of the ball's liveliness remained an open question, however, as the 1872 specification in no way addressed the quantity of rubber to be used. In fact, a requirement that the ball meet approved resiliency standards was not added to the Rule Book until 1951. Any ball that satisfied the physical dimensions of 1872 qualified as a "regulation" ball, irrespective of the type (or quantity) of material used as its core.

Albert G. Spalding founded his sporting goods firm in 1876. He secured the privilege of supplying the National League with its official ball despite the fact that he did not own a facility for manufacturing baseballs. He solved this problem by contracting with a renowned ball manufacturer—Louis H. Mahn, of Jamaica Plains, Massachusetts—to supply the balls. The League ball was in fact the Mahn Double Cover Number 1, patented in 1872, but with the name Spalding prominently stamped in bold letters on its cover.

Spalding's victory in capturing the rights to supply the National League with its official ball was limited, however, because use of the Spalding ball in all League games was not mandatory. The home team retained the right to choose the ball of its preference. This was an important strategic consideration; if the visiting nine was made up of light-hitting muffins, the home team likely would select a "regulation" lively ball—in other words, one that satisfied the League-mandated dimensional specifications, but that contained an ounce or two of rubber in its center. This type of ball provided for heavy hitting, with the expectation that the home nine would out-slug the light-hitting visitors. Conversely, if the visiting nine were composed of famous sluggers, the home team would certainly opt for the rubber-less Spalding ball.

Figure 4.1 Baseballs with cork-cushioned (left) and rubber centers.

The First Official Lively Ball

In 1877 the National League mandated that its official ball have a molded rubber core that contained exactly one ounce of pure India rubber. Further, the League eliminated the home team's option of selecting the ball to be used in the game, mandating the exclusive use of the Spalding ball. These new rules successfully standardized the ball used in all League games. Once more, Spalding turned to Louis Mahn for the production of his new League ball. Mahn designed and constructed a ball to meet the new specifications, and it was identified as the Mahn ball No. 3.

Factory-Produced Baseballs

When the game of baseball first entered the sporting scene, balls were handmade, one at a time, by the same craftsman from start to finish. By the late 1850s the burgeoning demand for baseballs could not be satisfied by an artisan laboring in solitude; methods of mass production had to be devised. In 1858 Mr. Harrison

Harwood established the firm of Harwood & Sons in Natick, Massachusetts, and in a large three-story building opened the first facility dedicated to the mass manufacture of baseballs. (Incidentally, this structure still stands today. In 1985 it was renovated and converted into an apartment complex—The Baseball Factory Condominium.)

Thirteen years after Harwood established his factory, *The New York Times* unequivocally stated that the town of Natick was the greatest baseball manufactory in the world. The newspaper reported that Harwood & Sons, "the oldest established manufacturers of base balls in America," filled single orders as large as 6,000 balls at a time. Individual craftsmen, no matter how talented, simply could not meet this overwhelming demand. Factories similar to Harwood's sprang up, principally in the Nassau Street area of New York, which the *Times* characterized as "the Nation's grand emporium of base ball." Despite ball-making being a labor-intensive process, the factories were able to produce huge quantities of baseballs. By 1871 the *Times* speculated that the United States would "bat to pieces" as many as a half a million baseballs.

Figure 4.2 Ryan's Dead ball was the first to be mandated for game use, 1873.

A ball factory was able to achieve a high level of output due to a careful division of labor and task specialization. The division of labor made each worker responsible for only a single step in the balls' construction. When this step was completed, the emerging ball was passed along to the next specialist. For example, the covers were cut from hides in one room using a steel, hourglass-shaped template and a wooden mallet, then sent on to another location where the holes necessary for stitching them together were punched. The prepared covers were then sent to the sewing room, where women using saddler's needles and thread stitched the covers' halves together. The woolen yarn was wrapped and compacted to form a core by yet another specialist.

The worker formed the ball's core by stripping the yarn off the wall-mounted pulley, then shaped and compacted it in his hands. When he judged it about right, he placed the embryonic core into an iron hemisphere, about the size of a teacup, which was mounted atop the wooden pedestal before him. Using the iron hemisphere as a mold, he then further compacted the core by whacking it with a wooden mallet, rotating it, and then whacking it some more, winding on additional yarn as needed. The process of building up the ball's core is a vivid illustration of why liberal variation tolerances—a full quarter-ounce in weight and a full quarter-inch in circumference—were absolutely essential in the days of handmade baseballs.

Baseball Embraces the Machine Age

In the last half of the 19th century a phenomenon swept through western civilization known as the Industrial Revolution. Machinery replaced tedious and repetitive manual tasks in manufacturing processes. Automation came to the baseball-manufacturing industry in 1889, when a man from Delaware, Samuel Brown, patented a machine for balling yarn in perfectly spherical form for the purpose of manufacturing baseballs. Brown's patent was granted on September 4, 1889, and was immediately assigned to Ben Shibe and A. J. Reach. This gave the firm of A. J. Reach & Co. a huge advantage; it not only allowed them to increase production, but it also allowed for greater uniformity and precision in the finished products.

Marvelously, the tension of the yarn wound on the core could be regulated by adjusting settings on the winding machine. Surely, there was a period of trials at the factory while they determined the effects of systematically varying the tension controls on the new winding machine before they established the optimal conditions for full-scale production. The experimental process must have been an eye-opening experience for the A. J. Reach Co., as they discovered the wide-ranging potential the winding machine gave them in regulating the ball's liveliness. All of the ball's physical dimensions could easily be held within the liberal (and now obsolete) tolerances, with the rubber core maintained at exactly one ounce, and yet the ball's liveliness could be calibrated across a wide range of resiliency.

The Dead Ball Era

In the wake of the 1902 peace settlement, the two now-equal major leagues descended into a period of lackluster hitting and low-scoring games today known as the Dead Ball Era. The most prominent characteristic of this era was a ball that was utterly and completely without resiliency.

Another noteworthy facet of the Dead Ball Era was ballparks with gigantic dimensions. Some parks measured as much as 550 feet to the farthest fence, and the nearest fence in other parks was 360 feet away. No human being could possibly hit a ball out of most of those parks, no matter how elastic the ball in use. Indeed, the philosophy behind the vast expanses of the ballparks was to allow the outfielders to show off their skill in chasing and capturing long hits. On the other hand, if a long hit eluded a flychaser, the batter had to do his utmost to circle the bases. The blatant and insulting "home run trot" had yet to be demonstrated. Inside-the-park home runs and long three-baggers thrilled the cranks.

Hitting was additionally repressed during the Dead Ball Era by the legalization of "trick" pitches. Pitchers liberally applied an assortment of foreign substances, such as tobacco juice, saliva (sometimes enhanced by slippery elm), and licorice, to the ball. Some pitchers rubbed paraffin into the fabric of their pants leg prior to the game, then swiped the ball across the swatch of paraffin before throwing it to the batter. This action caused bits of paraffin to become lodged between the seams of the ball. Other pitchers scuffed up the ball's cover with a bit of emery cloth hidden on their person. The net effect of all these tricks was to alter the flight characteristics of the ball so that it behaved in an unusual and unpredictable manner during its path toward home plate.

How did the hitters try to deal with the spitball and other assorted trick pitches? Well, they just tried to get a piece of the ball. To increase their chances of getting the bat on the ball, they choked up on the bat's handle, in some cases as much as eight or ten inches. Instead of taking a full swing, they just slapped at the ball. Free-swinging sluggers were more likely to be bothered by the trick pitches than disciplined and scientific place-hitters like Willie Keeler. The style of choke-hitting used to combat the trick pitches may also have accounted for the paucity of extra-base hits during this era.

The combination of a dead ball, trick pitches, and vast playing fields led to the development of a style of play known variously as the Inside Game, Inside Baseball, or, sometimes, Scientific Baseball. The strategy of the Inside Game was based on the bunt, the hit and run, the sacrifice, and heady base running, all desperately structured to produce that rarest of commodities during those days: a single run. The Inside Game dominated the manager's thinking—from recruiting players with specific skills that complemented it, to designing and executing clever and innovative plays on the diamond. John McGraw of the Giants became one of the

Inside Game's chief proponents and was widely hailed as baseball's resident genius as his team enjoyed success after success.

The Cork-Center Ball of 1911

Since the earliest days of baseball, the ball-makers had sought to fabricate a ball that was capable of enduring the full nine innings. It was an elusive goal, and in 1909 Ben Shibe was still in the hunt. During the closing years of the 19th century, the molded rubber center proved unsatisfactory because, when the ball was struck with terrific force, the rubber would burst, deforming and distorting the ball, rendering it unfit for play. Instances of such deeds were documented in the newspapers of the day. These accounts confirm that famous sluggers such as Big Ed Delahanty and Nap Lajoie walloped the ball with sufficient force to destroy it. The problem of bursting balls was summarized in a report that appeared in *The Sporting Life* on May 14, 1910:

> For years the brightest minds of the great Reach factory have been working to solve the problem created by occasional cracking of the [balls'] rubber centers. Despite the use of the costliest and most perfect Para rubber the solid core occasionally broke under terrific strain. This eventually burst not only the multitude of yarn wrappings, but the horsehide cover as well. Perhaps only twenty or thirty a season—but enough to make Reach Company seek a superior substitute. ...

On June 18, 1909, Shibe patented a new ball with a cork center to deal with this problem. He stated in his patent application:

> The object of my invention is to produce a playing ball of said class having a resilient central core that is less yielding than has heretofore been made upon which the layers of yarn may be wound under greater tension, whereby greater compactness results, perfect concentric formation is attained, and a more durable and rigid structure secured and uniform resiliency acquired and maintained.

The patent application makes it clear that one of the benefits of the cork center was the ability to wind the yarn under greater tension, thus producing a higher level of resiliency. In other words, a livelier ball. Shibe was also emphatic in stating that the resulting ball would be more durable. Subsequently, patents for improvements to the corkcenter ball were issued to Shibe on August 31, 1909, and August 1, 1911.

Shibe's new design was calculated to extend the useful life of the ball by protecting the rubber with cork. The very first advertisement publicizing Reach's new corkcenter ball appeared in *The Sporting News* of May 12, 1910. It announced:

> Big Improvement Made in Base Balls
> A.J. Reach & Company Patents a Cork Core, supplanting the rubber center, and producing the finest ball ever known. More rigid and durable, will absolutely keep its shape.
> The Perfect Ball at Last.

A.J. Reach & Co. surreptitiously arranged to launch the cork-center ball in American League games during the latter half of the 1910 season. Later that fall, the company slipped it into several World Series games, unbeknownst to League officials or team owners. Well after the World Series had been concluded (on December 8, 1910), an advertisement appeared in *The Sporting News* that brazenly boasted:

> The Reach Ball
> The Cork Centered Ball
> Was the Official Ball
> of the World Series

The cork-center ball became the official American League ball for the 1911 season. There was an immediate outbreak of heavy hitting. A burning hue and cry arose accusing A. J. Reach & Co. of tampering with the ball. Reach officials insisted that the only change was the cork center. After only a few weeks of play in the 1911 season, this advertisement appeared in a national sporting publication on May 14.

It pointedly declared that the cork center was responsible for the noticeable increase in home runs, triples, doubles, and even singles. Similar ads appeared regularly throughout the 1911 season.

The National League immediately followed suit with a corkcenter ball of its own, one bearing the Spalding label. As we now know, the Spalding ball was made at the Reach factory in Philadelphia—on the same machines and by the same technicians that made the American League ball. The Spalding cork-center ball was announced in the September 1911 issue of *Base Ball Magazine*. This ball, the advertisement stated, was registered with the U.S. Patent Office, but no patent number or date was provided. Interestingly, the ad concluded with this statement: "Warranted to last a full game when used under ordinary conditions." Evidently, A. G. Spalding & Bros. thought they had found the baseball manufacturers' Holy Grail—an indestructible ball. However, there were no instructions for returning a ball that failed to last the full nine innings, nor was there anything resembling a promise to provide a dissatisfied customer with a free replacement for a failed ball.

Despite the unquestionable increase in hitting in 1911, with more extra-base hits, the style of play remained unchanged. The Inside Game prevailed, and managers continued to rely on the bunt, the hit and run, and the stolen base.

HAVE YOU NOTICED

THE NUMBER OF

HOME RUNS,

THREE BASE HITS,

TWO BASE HITS

AND SINGLES

that the batters in the American and all the other big leagues are making? They are all due to the big improvement in base ball.

THE PATENTED

CORK CENTER BASE BALL

Write for free illustrated catalog to

A. J. Reach Company, Philadelphia

Pacific Coast Branch: Phil B. Bekeart Co., San Francisco, Cal

Figure 4.3 The lively ball controversy in ad from May 1911.

Although the ball was clearly livelier, the fundamental strategy of the game was unaffected. Ty Cobb and his proselytes would have it no other way. The sensational aspects of the cork-center ball gradually faded as the season of 1912 unfolded. That year proved to be only slightly less amazing, in terms of hitting, than the previous one. For the remainder of the decade the hitting remained noticeably improved over what it had been during the depths of the Dead Ball Era. Nonetheless, there were no indications of an inclination to abandon, or even modify, the Inside Game.

The "Rabbit Ball" of 1920

In contrast to the 1911 season and its modified baseball, the season of 1920 opened without fanfare. Nothing aroused the suspicion of the fans; no announcements alerted them that something even more sensational than the cork-center ball of 1911 was to be set loose on the diamond. Babe Ruth had just been sold by the Boston Americans to the wealthy New York Yankees for a then-unimaginable sum of money. It was a foregone conclusion that Ruth would improve upon his home run record of 1919, as he now had the advantage of playing home games at the Polo Grounds, which were far friendlier to left-handed hitters than was Fenway Park. Ruth's record of 29 round trippers—with only nine at Fenway and 20 on the road—should have suggested to the game's observers that Ruth was about to usher in a new era of power-hitting.

Ruth blasted homer after homer playing in the Polo Grounds, reaching the astonishing total of 54 when the season ended. Ruth hit more home runs than did 14 major league *teams*. Only the cellar-dwelling Phillies, playing in the tiny Baker Bowl, managed to out-homer the Babe. George Sisler, who captured the American League batting championship with a robust .407 average, finished second to Ruth in individual home run honors. It was a distant second, as Ruth out-homered Gorgeous George by 35. Furthermore, five of Sisler's 19 homers were of the inside-the-park variety, whereas none of the Babe's failed to clear the fence.

Sportswriters of 1920 sought out veteran players to obtain their views about the surge in power-hitting. The most accomplished outfielder of his day, the legendary Tris Speaker, revealed that the new breed of offense forced him to abandon his habitual center-field post (which was a mere 20–30 feet behind second base) and play deeper. National League center fielder Edd Roush shared Speaker's view. Roush pointed out that previously, outfielders were stationed close enough to the infield so as to make throws directly to home plate; the outburst in heavy hitting spawned the now-familiar phenomenon of the relay man.

Famed sluggers Rogers Hornsby and Babe Ruth were adamant in their belief that there was no difference in the 1920 ball. Whether the ball was indeed livelier, or whether hitters simply wished to imitate Ruth's success by copying his home run swing, what is certain is that more baseballs flew over the fence than ever before. In addition to being a man with awesome strength, Ruth employed an uppercut swing that was deliberately designed to loft the ball over distant fences. Without this style of swing, the balls hit by Ruth would simply have been blistering line drives that stayed in the ballpark. Veteran sluggers such as Cy Williams, who had not previously been known as home run hitters, began to emulate Ruth's swing. And although their efforts paled in comparison to the Babe's, they too became famous as home run hitters.

The most popular explanation for the increased offense in 1920 is that the team owners conspired to increase the liveliness of the ball to neutralize the odorous aftermath of the 1919 World Series Black Sox scandal, and to compensate for an anticipated drop in attendance. About this time the phrase "rabbit ball" was introduced to baseball's vocabulary to account for the outbreak of heavy hitting. However, the team owners solemnly declared they had not tampered with the ball. The ball manufacturers denied having made any changes to the ball's liveliness. A feeble suggestion was put forth that the switch to Australian wool used to wrap the ball caused an increase in liveliness. This type of wool allegedly allowed the yarn to be wrapped tighter, thus creating a livelier ball.

Winding the ball tighter, as Doc Adams realized as early as the 1850s, does in fact produce a livelier ball. Could the manufacturers have taken advantage of this reality and surreptitiously manipulated the ball? A quality-control manager of the current ball maker, the Rawlings Company, claimed in 1990 that winding the ball tighter makes it impossible to meet the mandated specifications for weight and circumference. He argued that if a more tightly wound ball were constructed to the proper circumference it would be overweight, and, conversely, if a more tightly wound ball was of the correct weight it would be undersized.

This does not, however, account for the rather substantial dimensional tolerances that were in place at the time. Within those liberal limits—imperative back when baseballs were entirely handmade—the yarn could be wound to encompass a wide range of resiliency.

The Reach Revelation

Long after the Roaring Twenties had faded into history, Dick Cresap of the *Philadelphia Evening Bulletin* interviewed George A. Reach, former executive of A. J. Reach & Co. (published on May 9, 1949). Reach, then 81 years of age, was the son of the late Alfred Reach who had founded the company in the 1860s. During the course of the interview Reach made several startling admissions that finally and definitively revealed the truth and exploded all the myths. His words drastically alter our understanding of the Dead Ball Era and the advent of the "rabbit ball":

> No one knows more about the so-called rabbit ball than I. The other day a New York fellow wrote that the [rabbit] ball first appeared in the teens. He was as wrong as anyone could be. ... We used our newly-patented cork center ball for the first time in the 1910 World Series. ... The next year, 1911, the ball was the liveliest it ever has been. In fact, we had to tone it down. We were making infielders out of outfielders. ... The

peculiar thing about the cork-centered ball is that the new center had nothing to do with the ball's new habit of making the pitcher duck. ... The resiliency of the ball is governed by the way the wool yarn is wrapped around the core, rather than the texture of the core. ... It's best illustrated by a plain rubber band. Stretch it too tight and it breaks. Stretch it a little and it's too loose. Stretch it just right, and you get the greatest resiliency.

The reporter commented to Reach that hot stove league discussion in the 1920s compared the liveliness of the American League ball with the National League ball. The conventional wisdom was that the American League ball had much more "rabbit" in it. Reach responded: "That is so much rubbish. There was absolutely no difference in the ball until the late twenties when the cover on the National League ball was a little thicker and had extra stitches. The balls for both leagues were made on the same machines and wound exactly the same way."

Reach went on to confirm that the sole purpose of the switch from a rubber to a cork center was to increase durability. He implied that attributing the liveliness of the 1911 ball to its cork center was a smokescreen to mask the fact that they had deliberately enlivened the ball.

Conclusions

This seems to be the unvarnished truth—an acknowledgment of deception straight from the ball manufacturer. A.J. Reach & Company did, in fact, adjust the resiliency of the ball whenever they felt it needed juicing up or toning down—not just in 1911 and 1920, but virtually on a yearly basis. A careful observer will note marked annual variations in the level of offense over the years. Until George Reach debunked the legend of the cork-center ball, there was no plausible explanation for these variations. In retrospect, it is a shame that Reach wasn't more specific as to which years the ball was juiced up and in which years they killed the rabbit, as that would appreciably improve our understanding of individual hitters' year-to-year performances.

Remarkably, the technique described by Reach to regulate the ball's liveliness is the same understood by ball makers in the 1850s. The "lively cork-center ball" turns out to be just about the biggest myth in all of baseball history, second only to the fable of the Creation in Cooperstown. The deception perpetrated by A. J. Reach

& Company causes one to wonder about the current ball and its manufacturer, the Rawlings Co. Are they now using the same tricks?

Bibliography

Curran, W. 1990. *Big Sticks*.

——— 1985 *Mitts*.

Gilbert, T. 1996. *Dead Ball*.

Lane, F. 1925. *Batting*.

Levine, P. 1985. *A.G. Spalding and the Rise of Baseball*.

Lowry, P. 1986. *Green Cathedrals*.

McGraw, J. 1923. *My Thirty Years in Baseball*.

Nemec, D. 1994a. *The Beer and Whiskey League*.

——— 1994b. *The Official Rules of Baseball*.

Okkonen, M. 1992. *Baseball Memories 1900–1909*.

Sowell, M. 1992. *July 2, 1903*.

Spink, A. 2000. *The National Game*.

Wright, R. 1999. *A Tale of Two Leagues*.

QUESTION TO CONSIDER

- Explain the transformation of an early baseball.

PART III

Modern Times

The 1920s

New Yorkers listening to the 1922 World Series by radio.

CHAPTER 5

They Sway Millions as if by Some Magic Wand

The Advertising Industry Enters Radio in the Late 1920s

By Cynthia B. Meyers

....

Editor's Introduction

The end of World War I transformed the United States from a debtor nation to a creditor nation; thus, the 1920s were a time of booming American business. It was a time when radio waves carried news of city life into isolated farmhouses. It was, after all, the Roaring Twenties, and there was a revolution in communications. By the end of the 1920s, there were over 100 million radios in use in America. Radio sales jumped from $60 million in 1923 to more than $842 million by 1929. For an American family living in the mid-1920s, a typical radio set cost about $150. The popularity of radio did not go unnoticed by advertisers, who saw the opportunity to reach millions of Americans at one time. Hence, radio advertising changed the public service face of radio to one of private enterprise and profit. Consequently, radio advertising became big business by the late 1920s. Nevertheless, there were those who questioned the influence of radio on American society, but their voices were not heard, since at the time it was the in thing to have a radio. The following essay examines the impact of the advertising industry on radio in the 1920s.

They Sway Millions as if by Some Magic Wand

The Advertising Industry Enters Radio in the Late 1920s

By Cynthia B. Meyers

In the 1920s unending economic growth seemed possible, and the advertising industry appeared to be its motor; would radio technology help fuel further growth? By the end of the decade, advertising industry revenues reached a record $3.4 billion.[1] In claiming much credit for stimulating the booming economy, the advertising industry was perhaps a bit overconfident of its power over consumers. But in confronting the prospect of broadcast advertising, it expressed misgivings along with such confidence. While boosters promoted broadcasting as a better way to express business ideals and personalize selling than the voiceless medium of print, others dismissed it as a fad. To some admen, radio advertising remained mysterious; as *Fortune* magazine later pointed out, radio was a business of "sell[ing] time, an invisible commodity, to fictitious beings called corporations for the purpose of influencing an audience that no one can see."[2] Advocates of both the hard and soft sell expressed resistance, some citing radio advertising's ephemeral nature, others the risk of offending audiences. Nonetheless, advertising agencies began, in the late 1920s and early 1930s, to create internal radio departments for handling the new medium. Having entered radio, advertising agencies were forced to consider which print strategies could be translated to radio—and which could not.

Resistance to Radio: "Acute Inflammatory Radioitis"

Initially many admen resisted the new medium. NBC promoter E. P. H. James recalls that most agencies in the 1920s were "quite indifferent to radio."[3] The conservative trade journal *Printers' Ink*, in an editorial against radio advertising in 1922, complained that "[t]he family circle is not a public place, and advertising has no business intruding there unless it is invited."[4] Unlike print, consumed by a reader in silence, radio could be heard by anyone in range. The entire family would have to listen, and the young might be exposed to sexual innuendo, jazz, or other inappropriate material. But even if the program were "high-class entertainment," *Printers' Ink* further editorialized in 1923, listeners who have been "wheedled into listening to a selfish message will naturally be offended," because a high cultural experience will have been debased by advertising.

However, *Printers' Ink* revealed what was probably its chief motive in attacking radio when it warned that newspapers would stop publicizing radio programs "if the broadcasters are themselves going to enter into advertising competition with the newspapers."[5] Thus, concern over straining relations with their primary business collaborators, the print publishers, motivated some admen to protect their interests in the print media by openly criticizing radio. Furthermore, most of the advertising pages in *Printers' Ink* were sold to newspaper publishers, and thus the trade magazine sought to cater to its own largest advertisers.[6] Newspaper publishers alternately tried to quash or take over radio: In the press–radio "wars" of the early 1930s, the major print wire services, such as the Associated Press, refused to allow radio stations to subscribe to their news services. The penetration of radio into the news market, claimed the head of one newspaper trade association, "is seriously depreciating the value of the newspaper's chief asset in the minds of listeners." As late as 1933, some newspapers still refused to carry any radio program listings, arguing that listings were advertising, not news, and therefore should be paid for as such.[7]

But advertising agencies had other concerns about radio aside from their desire to maintain good relations with print publishers; they had also to consider the reputation of their profession. The historian Roland Marchand usefully divides the admen who sought to advance professionalism in advertising into two general groups, the "real pros" and those who viewed advertising as "uplift." Real pros believed advertising was only as good as the sales figures it generated. Seeking to shake its association with medicine show–style entertainment and bring it into the mainstream of conventional business practice, real pros represented advertising as both a business and a science; they favored quantifiable results and emphasized hard sell strategies, such as "reasons why" to buy a product, over soft sell strategies, such as the use of associations and emotions. Admen such as Albert Lasker and Claude Hopkins of the Chicago agency Lord & Thomas subscribed to many "real pro" beliefs. The "uplift" model of advertising, on the other hand, promulgated most famously by Bruce Barton of Batten Barton Durstine & Osborn, represented advertising as a form of education and a kind of public service and sought to associate it with high forms of culture. Many who believed in the uplift model looked to education, especially the formation of advertising curricula in higher education, as a route to respectability and professionalism.[8]

Radio presented problems for both factions. To begin with, in the early to mid-1920s radio appeared to be a passing fad, a pastime for amateurs and engineers.[9] Both real pros and uplifters feared that associating their clients with a fad of limited appeal could detract from the seriousness of their business. Furthermore, before standards improved with the establishment of the networks, uplifters wished to avoid juxtaposing commercial messages with local programs of variable quality, many of which relied on unpaid and amateur performers. The inconsistency of program quality and the outrageousness of fraudulent advertisers such as John Brinkley, who promoted goat glands as a cure for impotence until his station license was revoked, tainted radio as vulgar, especially for uplifters. Consequently, beginning with NBC's announcement in 1926 that it would improve programming,[10] the networks continually stressed their ability to elevate the quality of programming precisely in order to attract advertisers and agencies concerned with potentially damaging associations.

Real pros dismissed radio for its ephemeral nature: No one knew how many listeners received a broadcast commercial message; it left no mark or solid evidence of its existence.[11] The historian Alexander Russo notes that this was the central problem of broadcasting, generating anxiety for both broadcasters and advertisers.[12] Unlike print media circulation, for which the advertising and publishing industries had established "audited" figures overseen by the Audit Bureau of Circulations, radio's reach or penetration could not be measured.[13] Unlike film and theater, radio provided "no box office receipts, nor rising or falling subscriptions to measure the public's approval or indifference," as one agency pointed out.[14] Some argued that this lack of hard data did not mean radio advertising was ineffective; they compared radio to billboards or transit advertising, for which there were likewise no circulation measurements.[15] Some sought to measure listenership through fan mail and instigated promotions, contests, and giveaways to stimulate such mail. A high volume of mail could be used to persuade a potential sponsor of the size of radio audiences. John Sample, of the agency Blackett-Sample-Hummert, described the results of one premium offer made on the *Ma Perkins* radio program:

> Then we offered a package of zinnia seeds for a dime. We drew about 1,000,000 dimes. The letters covered the floor of an office. … I took Mr. Deupree and some other top [Procter & Gamble] people and I went in there and we walked around on top of all those letters. That's the first time P&G executives

had demonstrated to them the power of this relatively new advertising medium.[16]

Detractors, however, dismissed such mail because fans usually gushed about the program rather than the product sponsoring it. Most letters requesting offered premiums expressed no gratitude toward the sponsor such as might manifest itself in the purchase of the sponsor's product.[17] Real pros, then, distrusted this measure of radio circulation. As the radio director of J. Walter Thompson (JWT) admitted in a private staff meeting, mail volume was no true indication of a program's selling effectiveness.[18] By 1930, the Association of National Advertisers established the first "circulation" figures for radio broadcasts.[19] But though networks' circulation claims thus gradually grew more credible, many admen worried that radio provided "wasted coverage" because networks broadcast to markets in which their clients did not sell, thus incurring increased expense without increased sales.[20]

Some admen, including real pros, doubted the usefulness of "good will" advertising, arguing that good will advertising was simply not worth the expense of program production for most advertisers. Good will advertising would be useful only to advertisers more concerned with national corporate image than with product sales. Many admen therefore viewed advertisers' interest in radio as simply a case of "acute inflammatory radioitis," or the desire of corporate leaders to scratch the "publicity itch"—to seek glory, not sales.[21] Furthermore, the model of radio as a good will medium had obvious limits. As one dissenter at JWT pointed out, if two competitors each provided sponsored programs, such as Clicquot Club and Canada Dry for similar products, then which ginger ale company would reap good will from listeners? Would all that good will cancel itself out?[22]

Many of the uplifters, on the other hand, extolled radio as a good will medium. Many in the professional middle classes regarded radio as a vehicle of cultural uplift for the masses through educational and high cultural programming.[23] Corporations applying enlightened self-interest would, they felt, sponsor opera, theater, and educational talks aimed at raising the level of cultural discourse.[24] Many admen regarded radio as a kind of home theater, to be quietly appreciated with all the dignity and gravitas that accompanied the attending of opera. Direct advertising of packaged goods and the like could only jar and offend audiences with such expectations. The fear that direct advertising would undercut the medium's effectiveness lay behind the consistent emphasis on indirect selling within agencies throughout the 1920s. Radio, according to *Advertising & Selling* radio editor Edgar Felix, should be recognized as "a medium for winning good will and as a method of establishing a pleasant association with a trade or firm name."[25] Admen who believed this often reflected the views of their clients. For example, in an exchange with the B. F. Goodrich Company in 1925, the advertising manager of the Kolynos Co., later a significant radio advertiser, was asked the value of radio advertising. He responded, "We feel that direct advertising through the radio would be more likely to antagonize rather than produce sales, and that anything that is done should be put in the form of entertainment."[26] The Good-rich advertising manager concurred, concluding that the "value of this advertising is in the indirect effect it has on its listeners."[27] By 1929, an industry-sponsored survey indicated that just over half of radio listeners were "annoyed" by radio advertising.[28] Thus, as late as 1930, many in broadcasting and advertising remained certain that direct selling on radio would offend listeners.[29]

The debate over the viability of direct advertising on radio repeated to some extent a similar debate over whether radio should be "selling its editorial pages."[30] Following the print model, some admen argued that editorial and advertising functions on radio should be kept distinct, that advertisers should not be providing the editorial material—that is, the programs. In 1926 the advertising manager for General Electric, while enthusiastic about radio advertising, assumed that "[b]roadcasting will probably not be employed in direct selling until some plan is provided by which such advertising can be definitely segregated from all other programs."[31] An anonymous but "prominent" adman argued in the trade press that the conflation of editorial and advertising on radio by way of sponsored programs would eventually undermine the advertising effectiveness of the medium.[32] In 1928, a staff member at JWT argued that because "All radio 'space' is *editorial space*" and because advertising space cannot be "skipped or delayed until time suits its reading," advertisers risk earning "ill will" from listeners if the advertising is not "universally pleasing."[33] In print media, the publisher has the responsibility to attract readers with editorial material; advertisers buy the attention of those readers only by purchasing space adjacent to editorial material. Some admen argued that broadcasters should likewise provide content instead of "scattering the responsibility" for it among advertisers and their agencies.[34] They suggested that, to guarantee the medium's viability, the networks should take control over programming, leaving only brief periods, at intervals of a half hour or so, to the agencies and their advertisements.[35]

Radio advertising's detractors had other concerns about the value of the airwaves. By defining advertising as "salesmanship in print," admen sought to associate selling not with the patent-medicine trade but with the sober, calculated, and literate venue of print. Radio brought this association into question. As one adman claimed, "The longstanding definition of advertising, 'Salesmanship in print,' passed into the discard when radio made its debut."[36] Radio "is oral salesmanship instead of salesmanship in print."[37] The reliance on oral selling strategies raised uncomfortable associations with the carnival barker and the medicine show. Some admen cheerfully admitted that radio selling was not unlike the traveling medicine shows, in which the vendor would put on a show out of his wagon to attract crowds for sales of patent medicine. Robert Colwell of JWT conceded, "Get the crowd around, and then sell your wares. Good radio is just as simple as that."[38] More often, however, radio critics of the 1930s would use the medicine show analogy to criticize commercial broadcasting.[39]

Another objection, one that would affect debates over the role of the advertising industry in broadcasting well into the 1950s, was whether advertising men should be involved in entertainment. If advertising were to become a respected business enterprise, then involvement in show business would seriously undermine admen's insistence that they were professionals, or "consumption engineers," in Calkins's phrase. The entire discourse of progressive business practice was predicated on the application of scientific principles to shape predictable outcomes. Many admen seeking the imprimatur of business professionalism viewed show business as an unpredictable and risky enterprise, operating in a marginal and disreputable social sphere populated by hustlers and subject to the disruptive sexuality of fallen women. As George Faulkner of JWT explained, "[T]he word showman carries an undignified, cheap connotation. It has a vaguely Semitic, Barnumish, Broadway air to it."[40] How could respectable men of business enter show business and guarantee results for their advertising clients? Too many factors were difficult to control: the tempers of talent, the whims of popular taste, the risks of offending audiences, and other imponderables. The tension between the strategies of rational appeals and the strategies of the carnivalesque would shape the intra-industry debates throughout the history of advertising agency involvement in programming.

Advertising Agencies Found Radio Departments

Former WEAF staffer Mark Woods credits the William H. Rankin agency with being one of the first major agencies to "back this new medium."[41] Rankin's broadcast of actress Marion Davies promoting cosmetic company Mineralava on WEAF in 1922 was probably the first agency-produced sponsored program.[42] Pointing out that agencies had already experienced a change of function, from space brokers into marketing specialists, Edgar Felix urged agencies to consider radio as just one more function to add to an ever-increasing roster of services to provide clients.[43] However, many agencies signaled their reluctance to engage too deeply with radio by keeping their newly formed radio departments somewhat apart from other departments; and despite their increasing importance over the next two decades, many radio departments remained marginal. Many heads of agencies, such as Raymond Rubicam of Young & Rubicam, continued long into the radio era to view radio as "a necessary evil."[44] According to one observer, agencies "resented the new form."[45]

Nonetheless, agencies began to expand into radio and counter the competition for clients who needed programming. Agencies competed with "radio service bureaus," which were independent program producers. JWT radio executive Robert Simon dismissed these competitors as just "concert managers or broken-down actors or anybody who thought he could sell an idea."[46] The independent bureaus, as well as stations, "do not have many seasoned advertising men" to help advertisers.[47] Advertising agencies' competitive advantage was that they could put the advertiser's marketing needs foremost and apply their selling expertise. According to Roy Durstine, one of the founders of BBDO, "The showman isn't an advertising man," and thus advertisers needed agencies to protect them from these dubious show business figures.[48] Felix urged agencies to learn the broadcasting and entertainment businesses, not necessarily to become full-time "showmen" but to have a "most wholesome and constructive influence" on the broadcasting industry, as well as to intervene to save clients from the "self-appointed unauthorized middlemen" who sought to profit from clients' inexperience in show business.[49] The other major competitors to the agencies were the network programming departments. While network programming departments built programs and then looked for an advertiser to buy them, the advertising agencies' competitive advantage was that they began with the advertiser's needs and then located or developed programs to fit those needs.

As a rule, agencies did not have expertise in show business any more than the showmen had expertise in advertising. Ralph Hower, in his 1939 in-house history of the N. W. Ayer agency, notes that radio was "no special boon" to agencies because it "forced them into the entertainment business, a field in which they had no experience."[50] JWT's Colwell argued, however, that admen in radio therefore worked harder than showmen. The "average Broadway writer," for example, "takes his assignment with the attitude that he can dash it off with one hand." Admen were not only more modest about their expertise, they took the job more seriously.[51] Mark Woods later suggested that the involvement of agencies in radio helped promote programming innovation in the late 1920s because agencies convinced advertisers to spend more on programming—budgeting for star talent and the like—in order to attract larger audiences. Furthermore, Woods pointed out that, unlike other producers perhaps, the agencies were motivated to distinguish their clients' programs from other programs so as to establish their unique radio presence, thereby spurring more program "diversification."[52] With more hyperbole, the manager of the Erwin Wasey radio department suggested that advertising agencies were also "contributing to the daily contentment and culture of millions."[53]

Whether or not agencies believed they belonged in radio, they felt pressure from their clients to get into radio. In the privacy of a staff meeting, a JWT staffer asserted that advertisers wanted to be involved with radio because it was the "more or less suppressed desire of every capitalist to become involved in show business" without "the suggestion of something naughty that goes with the backing of a show on Broadway."[54] Chester Bowles, founder of Benton & Bowles, claimed that once agencies realized that "radio was no passing phenomenon" and that "they would have to take a more and more active part in the building of radio programs," agencies began to recruit personnel who might bring them show business expertise.[55] Thus, many agencies that had been go-betweens for sponsors and broadcasters eventually began producing programs for sponsors directly. By 1929, according to one count, 33 percent of one network's programs were produced by advertising agencies, 28 percent by the network itself, 20 percent by sponsors, and 19 percent by independent program packagers, or radio bureaus.[56] Network radio advertising revenues jumped from $3.9 million in 1927 to $19.2 million in 1929.[57]

As advertising agencies began to respond to clients' interest in radio, many newly created agency radio departments included at least one man with network or broadcast experience who could explain the ins and outs of the broadcasting "game." According to Mark Woods, NBC began loaning out some of its personnel to help agencies set up radio departments; agencies also began to recruit network personnel, offering them higher salaries, so NBC "lost a number of men to the advertising agencies."[58] Advertising agencies also recruited from CBS; for example, Ralph Wentworth and Norman Brokenshire left CBS in 1929 to join radio departments in agencies.[59] Many of the network men recruited by the agencies were time salesmen who knew how to sell broadcasting generally. These men were often joined at the agencies by someone who could specialize in program building, and by a "statistician" who could present data to clients on radio's effectiveness. The salesman would sell the idea of radio to clients, the program man would present program ideas, and the statistician would supply circulation (or listenership) data.[60]

N. W. Ayer, a well-established agency based in Philadelphia, became involved in radio as early as 1922 while serving its client AT&T, and by 1923 it was also helping produce *The Eveready Hour* for its client National Carbon Co. *The Eveready Hour* was probably the first sponsored program distributed to multiple stations simultaneously; a variety show, it featured the announcer Graham MacNamee and performers such as Will Rogers and Art Gillham, the "Whispering Pianist." N. W. Ayer, which had already claimed to have founded the first agency copy department, the first agency art department, and the first agency publicity department, now also claimed to have founded the first agency radio department.[61] N. W. Ayer leader H. A. Batten claimed for his agency nearly every innovation that occurred in early radio programming, including the first "drama-type program designed for broadcasting" in 1924, the first adaptation of a full-length novel in 1926, the first variety show in 1926, and the first "informal commercials" with Jack Benny in 1932.[62] Whatever the truth of these claims, they served to promote N. W. Ayer to potential clients, positioning the agency at the cutting edge of advertising practice.

National Carbon Co.'s incentive for sponsoring radio programming is obvious in a 1927 print advertisement (see Figure 5.1).[63] As manufacturer of Eveready radio batteries, National Carbon hoped to stimulate radio set and battery sales. Under the headline "Perfecting the gift of radio" and an illustration of a family enjoying gifts beside a Christmas tree, the text explains that "When you give the great gift of a radio set, remember that you are giving not merely a handsome, intricate and sensitive instrument, but you are also giving radio reception, radio enjoyment, radio itself." N. W. Ayer's ad copy thus emphasizes not just the technical quality of the product—radio batteries—but also the "enjoyment" of radio entertainment, the actual interest of radio listeners. Acknowledging that buyers seek radios that reliably provide entertainment, the text further explains that Eveready batteries are so dependable that they will provide "hours, days, weeks and months of use, of solid enjoyment of radio at its best." Integrated into the ad is a reminder: "Tuesday night is Eveready Hour Night," including a list of every radio station carrying the program. Along with the tag line "Radio is better with Battery Power," the ad concludes with the urgent reminder that "The air is full of things you shouldn't miss."

Although its client AT&T was the impetus for N. W. Ayer's initial involvement in radio, the agency culture at N. W. Ayer was not well suited for radio.[64] At least one agency leader, Wilfred Fry, disliked radio advertising.[65] The radio department was never well integrated into the rest of the agency and was dismissively called the "wireless department" by some.[66] N. W. Ayer's longtime relations with print media such as the *Saturday Evening Post* predisposed its leaders to consider radio as an adjunct. Even at the peak of radio revenues, in the late 1930s and early 1940s, N. W. Ayer leaders believed radio should be used only moderately and in tandem with other media.[67] N. W. Ayer therefore did not pursue radio accounts, and other agencies quickly took the lead, especially after the Philadelphia-based agency moved its broadcasting department from New York back to Philadelphia. New York had

Figure 5.1 Eveready: "Perfecting the gift of radio." (*The Literary Digest*, 17 December 1927, n.p.)

developed as the center for most radio production, and when given the choice of going "ninety miles to Philadelphia as opposed to going across the street to a New York agency," most broadcast advertisers found other agencies.[68] By 1932, in the estimation of competitor JWT's Robert Simon, N. W. Ayer's radio star had fallen. Its good reputation from producing *The Eveready Hour* had dissipated: "Since then, nothing important has emanated from the Ayer offices."[69]

The main competitor to the claim for first agency radio department was Batten Barton Durstine & Osborn. The Batten agency, before it merged with Barton

Durstine & Osborn (BDO) in 1928, had hired George Podeyn (formerly of WEAF) to run its radio department, and BDO had hired Arthur Pryor Jr., the son of a bandleader, for his putative skills in the music industry.[70] As early as 1925, BDO oversaw, but did not produce, radio manufacturer Atwater Kent's presentations of the Metropolitan Opera.[71] BBDO hedged its claim by saying it had established the "first complete radio department" in about 1926.[72] Among BBDO's hires after the merger in 1928 were an NBC executive, Herbert Foster, and a former WEAF programmer, Annette Bushman.[73] Radio's chief supporter at BBDO was Roy Durstine, a vocal proponent of agency involvement in the medium. Although one of its most important programs, the Atwater Kent program, was not produced by the agency, Durstine was convinced by client interest in radio that agencies should take a stronger role in programming.[74] In 1928, BBDO oversaw five programs in addition to the Atwater Kent program: *General Motors Family Party*, *Soconyland Sketches*, *National Home Hour*, *Happy Wonder Bakers*, and *The Armstrong Quakers*, all but the last broadcast on WEAF.[75] BBDO's radio department soon became a general selling point for the agency; having a radio department indicated a facility for forward thinking, modern technical know-how, and serious commitment to the cultural uplift of the masses. In a 1930 advertisement to the trade, BBDO boasted of a radio staff of twenty-three, "which is becoming as familiar with this new art as it is with any of the older forms of advertising."[76] BBDO also noted that, with three exceptions, "the creative work of writing, rehearsing and directing … is all ours."[77] By 1933, the trade magazine *Variety* described BBDO as "innovators of the big name and money star" programs for their institutional advertising clients, General Electric, General Motors, and Atwater Kent.[78]

Lord & Thomas, the large Chicago-based agency led by Albert Lasker, became involved in radio on behalf of one of its clients, RCA, parent company of NBC. However, because of its relationship with the network, Lord & Thomas left program production to NBC.[79] Lord & Thomas's most significant action in early radio was to pick up what would become the *Amos 'n' Andy* show, then locally syndicated out of Chicago, and put it on the NBC network in August 1929. The spectacular rise in sales for *Amos 'n' Andy*'s first sponsor, Pepsodent, helped establish national network programs as significant advertising vehicles.[80] *Amos 'n' Andy*, firmly based in minstrel traditions, featured white actors performing in aural blackface as versions of the minstrel characters Jim Crow and Zip Coon. Its explosive popularity single-handedly raised audience awareness of radio networks.[81] Although it was closer in format to today's situation comedies than soap operas, open-ended storylines about Amos and Andy's migration north, their efforts to run a business, and their romantic entanglements continued over weeks and months, keeping listeners returning for the latest developments. Reputedly, movie theaters piped in the weekly broadcast in order to retain their audiences. Although the two performers wrote the program, L&T supplied the brief advertising announcements—one minute at the opening and a short announcement at the end. Announcer Bill Hay read this 1932 commercial after the opening theme song—note how it reflects the hard sell tenets of L&T's Lasker: As we have told you repeatedly, Pepsodent Tooth Paste today contains a new and different cleansing and polishing material. We want to emphasize the fact that this cleansing and polishing material used in Pepsodent Tooth Paste is contained in no other tooth paste. That is very important. It is important to us, because Pepsodent laboratories spent eleven years in developing this remarkable material. It is important to the public, because no other cleansing and polishing material removes film from teeth as effectively as does this new discovery. What's more, this new material is twice as soft as that commonly used in tooth pastes. Therefore, it gives greater safety, greater protection to lovely teeth. Use Pepsodent Tooth Paste twice a day—See your dentist at least twice a year.[82]

The earmarks of reason-why advertising appear in the repetition of key points ("cleansing and polishing"), the claim of scientific progress ("Pepsodent laboratories"), use of superlatives ("new and different," "new discovery," "greater safety"), and multiple "reasons why" to buy the product.

By 1933, *Variety*'s assessment was that L&T's admen were "specialists in human-interest script serials," which also included *Clara, Lu 'n' Em* (1931–36) and *The Goldbergs* (1929–46).[83] The former, one of the very first radio serials and sponsored by Colgate-Palmolive, sold Super Suds dishwashing soap while the three title characters chatted and gossiped. *The Goldbergs*, like *Amos 'n' Andy*, was an ethnic humor situation comedy, in this case about a Jewish family in the Bronx, with continuing storylines written by their chief performers. Each program traced the struggles of immigrants (foreign and domestic) sympathetically, but through the strategy of illustrating their characters' "cultural incompetence" with accents, dialect, cultural confusion, and "fish out of water" situations, perhaps flattering the potential user of Super Suds or Pepsodent for a superior level of general know-how that might be applied to the choice of "scientifically proven" domestic products.[84]

By 1928, a number of other New York agencies had begun radio departments, including Lennen & Mitchell, Thomas & Logan, Young & Rubicam, Frank Seaman, Erwin Wasey, and Calkins & Holden.[85] Lennen & Mitchell's early programs featured stars such as Paul Whiteman and Fred Waring, well-known bandleaders.[86] Initially, Erwin Wasey's department operated almost independently of the rest of the agency. However, once the radio department was better integrated, according to JWT's Simon, "What followed was a regime that probably holds all records for literal-mindedness. It obeyed all rules, including imaginary ones. If a music program had been approved by a client, no deviation could be made under any circumstances. ... The agency allowed itself no latitude, no discretion." Simon's evaluation of the Erwin Wasey radio department by 1932 was that, though headed by "a bit of an aesthete," it still suffered from too much "adherence to routine" and "very little creative talent."[87] However self-serving Simon's critique of a competitor, his summary points up an important dilemma in early radio departments: to hew closely to client demands, or to develop independent expertise?

H. K. McCann, soon to become McCann-Erickson, would found a radio department, as would Campbell Ewald. In 1930, McCann's director of radio, Ruth Cornwall, asserted that radio should be regarded "as a supplementary medium" to print. The direct sales pitch should be made in print; on radio, only the advertiser's name and product should be mentioned.[88] One of McCann's first programs was for Chesebrough Manufacturing Co.'s Vaseline. In a series of sketches about small-town life, with a "simple, homely and old fashioned" atmosphere, characters integrated Vaseline into their conversations, introducing its various uses.[89] By 1933, McCann-Erickson oversaw programs for Standard Oil featuring the Marx Brothers and music stars.[90]

Young & Rubicam (Y&R), founded by defectors from N. W. Ayer, started its department in 1928 in order to sell a daytime radio program for women called *Radio Household Institute*.[91] The program consisted mostly of advice, tips, and recipes, many of which involved the sponsors' household products. This early instructional format would soon be jettisoned in favor of more entertaining formats for housewives, specifically serials. By the mid-1930s, Y&R had developed a major radio department, led by Hubbell Robinson, who would later run programming at CBS Television. Despite founder Raymond Rubicam's distaste for radio advertising, the radio department was an important innovator, developing a staff that wrote all of its programs and in which there was "a constant striving for novelty."[92] Y&R understood early the value of innovation and novelty for attracting audiences and developed its radio department to exploit that understanding.

J. Walter Thompson recruited former WEAF staffer William Ensign to help start its radio department in 1927. Gerard Chatfield and Roosevelt Clark also joined JWT from NBC in 1928.[93] Ensign, who came to JWT as a radio man, not an adman, had to build interest in radio not only among JWT's clients but among agency personnel as well. He wrote articles for the in-house news organ to promote radio use and in a staff meeting confessed that JWT's relative slowness to expand into radio might be his fault: "I probably have not been as aggressive as I should have been in trying to sell you gentlemen on the medium."[94] Ensign felt his closeness to radio, after his experience producing *Roxy and His Gang* at WEAF, might have blinded him to how others perceived it. *Roxy and His Gang* had been an extremely successful musical variety show featuring Samuel Rothafel, the entertainment impresario; its success informed his enthusiasm for radio, which clashed with the skepticism of other JWT departments, which viewed it as new competition for billing dollars. In 1928, explaining that radio was in all their interests, Ensign remarked, "It's not billings alone but the fact that I feel that some J.W.T. clients are missing a good thing in not being on the air."[95] JWT leader Stanley Resor then exhorted his staff to cooperate with Ensign and help him with client contacts. At this time, JWT had only one client on the air, Maxwell House coffee, but within a few years, it became one of the largest radio agencies. By early 1930, radio head John Reber reported that JWT oversaw thirty-one programs a week that were "successful from a business point of view."[96] JWT claimed 14 percent of the commercial radio "business" in 1932; by 1933, NBC recognized JWT as its "largest revenue producing agency."[97] By 1933, *Variety*'s analysis of agencies placed JWT near the top as "the flashy lads of the air" and "a staunch proponent of the use of stage and screen names and one of the most successful air merchandisers in the business."[98]

As advertising agencies became more involved with radio, their radio departments evolved. At first these departments were loosely structured and staffed, but gradually, as radio revenues increased, they expanded and professionalized. In a few years, more potential employees had had radio experience, and so the labor pool widened and deepened. An adman named M. Lewis Goodkind described this process as occurring in three phases.[99] First was the "delegated authority" stage, when agencies gradually took over more and more radio production tasks and, to run their radio departments, hurriedly hired anyone who claimed to know something about the medium, such as "the sponsor's nephew." During this phase, according to JWT's Simon, the radio department was often a "one-man" operation, run by announcers or "broken-down actors" or agency "relatives who had to have jobs, or for venerable employees who had never been good at anything."[100] The second phase was the "performer's vogue," when agencies looked to musicians and theatrical directors for guidance in running radio departments. The third and final phase was when an agency at last developed a fully professional radio staff. In the case of JWT, one of the first radio department heads was a musician named Henry Joslyn, who took over the radio department in 1929. When radio billings began to expand rapidly, Joslyn was replaced by former "new business" manager Reber, an account executive charged with finding new clients for JWT. His ability to "sell" (or sign) new clients won him the position of radio department head over competitors Joslyn and Aminta Cassares, who managed the women's division.[101] His appointment signaled the new importance of the radio department within the agency. Joslyn, the musician, and Cassares, the women's specialist, despite experience apparently relevant to radio programming, lost the contest to an executive who was able to prove he could deal with clients effectively. Reber went on to build one of the largest and most stable agency radio departments.

The advertising agencies that first entered radio usually fit one of two categories: the well established and the upstart. The former, such as BBDO, JWT, or N. W. Ayer, developed radio departments as an extra service in order to retain already existing clients. However, these agencies were also staffed with many conservative executives who did not necessarily trust radio advertising. While the establishment connections of these agencies helped bring more conventional advertisers into the untested medium, their underlying bias toward print media may have undermined their ability to innovate in the aural medium of radio. The latter, the upstart agency, such as Benton & Bowles, founded in 1929, turned to radio as a way of getting started in business and to attract clients away from agencies unwilling to manage their clients' radio needs. Benton & Bowles, unfettered by convention, changed radio practices in key ways. Another major radio agency, Blackett-Sample-Hummert, founded in 1927, focused most of its efforts on radio advertising, becoming one the single largest buyers of airtime during the 1930s. Whether an agency moved into radio for defensive or offensive competitive purposes, by the mid-1930s radio was acknowledged as a powerful advertising medium.

Translating Print Strategies to Radio: "They Sway Millions as If by Some Magic Wand"

As radio advertisers moved away from indirect advertising approaches, such as naming the program after the product, and toward direct advertising approaches that included product information, admen accustomed to print media struggled to adapt. Many print strategies were obviously inapplicable; there were no visual illustrations or typefaces in radio. Nonetheless, print-trained admen sought to translate what they could into the new medium. In a 1930 staff meeting, JWT staffer George Faulkner listed the challenges of radio: "1. Lack of visual aids. 2. Fleeting impression. 3. The human voice in place of type as medium. 4. Censorship barriers. 5. Need for showmanship."[102] The first issue, the lack of visual aids, stymied admen who distrusted a nonvisual approach to selling; one BBDO staffer worried that "the ear as a sense organ has never been educated as the eye has been."[103] JWT radio department head Reber argued, in contrast, that communication was in the first instance an oral experience and thus radio, by "speak[ing] to a lot of people at once," was "getting back to the first principle" of communication.[104] Unable to rely on well-known visual strategies, admen had to invent new aural strategies, such as sound effects, that would "educate the ear" to receive advertising messages.

The second problem, radio's "fleeting impression," was a result of its evanescence. Once the message was out on the air, it could not be recaptured, measured, repeated, or reviewed by listeners. Magazine readers were able to reread an advertisement, but a radio listener had no means of rehearing one. What if audiences did not listen closely enough, or grasp the meaning well enough? Rather than compare radio to print, consider it analogous to billboards, advised JWT staffer Colwell, and effective even though passing viewers may catch only a glimpse, an impression, and may not see the entire message. Colwell advised radio copywriters to keep the advertising copy simple and "avoid quick transitions, complex ideas, or concepts which the listener cannot grasp as the words fly by."[105] Keeping copy short and simple was also necessary because of the limitations of audience attention. Young & Rubicam radio department head Robinson underlined this principle when he explained that "the public's memory is conspicuous chiefly for its brevity, its loyalty chiefly conspicuous for its ability to waver."[106] Admen could not rely on audiences to focus or remember; they would have to catch an audience's attention and make the message memorable.

As to the third issue, the use of the human voice as a medium rather than typeface or type size, some admen extolled the advantages of voice over print. Referring to the admen who wrote radio scripts that incorporated both program and advertising copy, adman George W. Smith claimed, "Continuity writers have transformed the *divinity* of the printed word into the still more divine eloquence of the spoken word. They tug at heart strings; they inspire appetites; they change deep-rooted habits. ... In so doing, they sway millions as if by some magic wand."[107] Other admen did not share Smith's confidence in the power of speech to sway millions. BBDO staffer J. T. W. Martin argued that print was intrinsically more credible: "The very fact that advertising copy is printed lends it a sincere appearance. Any size or style of type seems to stamp a statement as truth."[108] Advertising copy that seemed "sincere" in print, Martin argued, had a different effect when spoken on the air: "It is astonishing how exaggerated and ridiculous an extravagant claim for a product sounds over the air."[109] While claiming that the differences between radio and print advertising had been overblown, another adman acknowledged, "It is, of course, easier to commit the sin of blatancy over the air than in print."[110] How could admen avoid the pitfalls of applying print strategies to radio? Hill Blackett, of Blackett-Sample-Hummert, argued, "There are two entirely different techniques" for copywriting. "One is the technique of the spoken word, and the other the technique of the printed word. ... [I]n the early days of radio, the commercials sounded like somebody getting up and reading a piece of advertising."[111] Continuity writers, those writing scripts that incorporated both advertising and program text, must, according to one adman, avoid "unnatural or 'advertisy' dialog" that would undercut the seamless integration of program and advertisement.[112]

The program's announcer translated the printed word into the spoken. Announcers mediated between the program and the advertising: When introducing the program and the players, they usually spoke the text of the advertisement as well, in effect representing the sponsor. After a short musical introduction, a 1930 broadcast of *The Coca-Cola Top Notchers* is introduced thus: "Good evening, ladies and gentlemen of the radio audience. This is Graham MacNamee speaking. We bring you a period of delightful entertainment sponsored by Coca-Cola, the pure drink of natural flavors, served nine million times a day."[113] Victor Ratner, from the Lennen & Mitchell agency, characterized announcers as "the 'type-faces' of radio," and as in print, their proper use was essential: "the right announcer adds a dynamic quality to any copy he is given to deliver. He can step-up advertising 'voltage' as much as a poor announcer can step it down."[114] Some announcers were stars in their own right, announced by another, no-name announcer, as in an episode of *The Chase & Sanborn Hour* in which the first announcer introduced the program title "and your host, Don Ameche!"—who then introduced the stars and the sponsor.[115] In a 1930 staff meeting, JWT staffer Colwell described the different styles of well-known announcers: "Graham MacNamee races along, Alwyn Bach is very slow and dignified, Alois Havrilla is about half way between."[116] Some announcers were prized for their skills at delivering the advertisement and setting up the comedy talent, such as Don Wilson for Jack Benny, Bill Goodwin for George Burns and Gracie Allen, and Bill Baldwin for Edgar Bergen and Charlie McCarthy. The continuity writers needed to take their announcer's style into account. As Colwell explained, "A good continuity man will 'write to his announcer.' Like an actor in a play, an announcer suffers when he is given a part that is out of character. Listeners realize ... when an announcer is saying something that does not sound sincere and spontaneous."[117] Ernest S. Green provided advice to copywriters in a *Printers' Ink Monthly* article titled "What 'Typeface' for Your Radio Commercials?" (see Figure 5.2).[118] The illustration depicts announcers labeled variously "corny" or "smooth" or "punchy" or "factual" and then dressed to reflect that style: The "corny" announcer wears a farmer's hat, the "punchy" announcer wears boxing gloves. To emphasize the importance of announcement style consistency, a list of questions set in different fonts further illustrates the issue: "Am I being *smooth* in a Corny Commercial?" and so on.

WHAT "TYPE FACE"
for Your Radio Commercials?

by ERNEST S. GREEN

Corny   Smooth   PUNCHY

Figure 5.2 "What 'Type Face' for Your Radio Commercials?" (Ernest S. Green, "What 'Typeface' for Your Radio Commercials?" *Printers' Ink Monthly*, May 1938, 18–19.)

Agencies worried about their reliance on announcers to mediate between the advertising and the audience. JWT's Colwell warned his coworkers that one could never be sure if an announcer would "say it in the right way." Consequently, JWT exercised close control over announcers. According to Colwell, "To insure this we have generally a production man at all of our programs to be certain that the announcer gives the words the exact shade of meaning that they should have."[119] Fears that listeners would be alienated by the apparent insincerity or wooden delivery of an announcer prompted another adman to urge agencies to use announcers whose "words must be felt as well as spoken."[120] Credibility and sincerity depended on announcers' emoting rather than reciting. An announcer who was too glib and smooth could undercut an advertisement's effectiveness. For this reason, the JWT Radio Department would also, on occasion, use a radio performer who was not an announcer to present the advertising message: He or she would provide a "fresh voice, a voice which may not be quite so much on its guard and more sincere, frank and open than [that of] the ordinary 'announcer.'"[121] Authenticity and credibility, then, occasionally required the employment of the not-announcer, whose sincerity would be less questionable.

The push to enter radio in the late 1920s came not from within the advertising industry but from without, especially from clients who wanted to sponsor programs and were frustrated with other program producers. Advertising industry resistance to radio arose primarily from its dependence on print publishers, who feared the competition of a new medium, in addition to concerns that the industry's hard-fought path to professional respectability could be undermined by associations with show business and the memories of patent medicine "medicine shows." Advertising agencies, facing competition for clients from other program producers, soon moved into radio with varying levels of enthusiasm and commitment. Well-established agencies founded radio departments to complete the range of services it could offer clients. Upstart agencies specialized in radio to gain the competitive edge over the more conservative agencies. Once in radio, agencies were responsible for overseeing programming and integrating it with advertising strategies. Translating their print strategies into an aural medium proved challenging because radio's ephemeral nature, lack of visuals, and reliance on human voices limited admen's options. Analogizing the human voice as a "typeface," admen began to explore alternative strategies for engaging audiences. By the beginning of the 1930s, the significance of radio to the advertising industry had become clear. As a JWT staffer explained, "Rarely—if ever—can a single printed advertisement result in doubling returns. ... In radio, however, this is a rather common experience, and one which we who are immersed in radio day and night are only beginning to understand."[122]

Notes

1. Stephen Fox, *The Mirror Makers* (New York: William Morrow, 1984), 118.

2. "And All Because They're Smart," *Fortune*, June 1935, 82.

3. E. P. H. James, interview, 27, James Papers, Wisconsin Historical Society, Madison (hereafter James Interview, James Papers).

4. *Printers' Ink*, 27 April 1922, 201.

5. "Radio an Objectionable Advertising Medium," *Printers' Ink*, 8 February 1923, 175–76.

6. Fox, *Mirror Makers*, 153.

7. "Inland Newspapers Demand Pay for Radio Programs," *Printers' Ink*, 2 March 1933, 33.

8. Roland Marchand, *Advertising the American Dream* (Berkeley: University of California Press, 1985), 26–28.

9. Ralph Starr Butler, "Radio Tomorrow," *Printers' Ink Monthly*, July 1936, 73; J. Walter Thompson Staff Meeting Minutes, 5 January 1932, 18, John W. Hartman Center for Sales, Advertising and Marketing History, Duke University, Durham, North Carolina (hereafter JWT Staff Meeting Minutes).

10. "National radio broadcasting with better programs permanently assured by this important action of the Radio Corporation of America in the interest of the listening public." Advertisement reproduced in Erik Barnouw, *The Sponsor: Notes on a Modern Potentate* (New York: Oxford University Press, 1978), 23.

11. "Agencies View Radio Advertising in Survey by Station," *Advertising & Selling*, 30 April 1930, 90.

12. Alexander Russo, *Points on the Dial* (Durham, N.C.: Duke University Press, 2010), 7.

13. S. H. Giellerup, "It's Time We Took the 'Blue Sky' out of the Air," *Advertising & Selling*, 16 October 1929, n.p.

14. From a Batten agency memo, ca. 1924, quoted in Ed Roberts, "Radio and Celebrities," unpublished manuscript, commissioned by BBDO, ca. 1966.

15. John Gordon Jr., "Says Mr. Gordon to Mr. Giellerup," *Advertising & Selling*, 13 November 1929, 32.

16. Lawrence Doherty, "Adman Sample? He's Florida Land Tycoon," part 2, *Advertising Age*, 7 May 1962, 66.

17. Robert Colwell, JWT Staff Meeting Minutes, 8 July 1930.

18. JWT Staff Meeting Minutes, 13 January 1931, 8.

19. George Lewis, "Audit Bureau for Radio Organized by ANA," *Advertising & Selling*, 19 March 1930, 83.

20. "Agencies View Radio Advertising in Survey by Station," *Advertising & Selling*, 90.

21. "Acute Inflammatory Radioitis," J. Walter Thompson *Newsletter*, 15 February 1928, 81, 82, JWT Newsletter Files, John W. Hartman Center for Sales, Advertising and Marketing History, Duke University, Durham, North Carolina (hereafter JWT *Newsletter*).

22. Ibid., 82.

23. Clayton R. Koppes, "The Social Destiny of Radio: Hope and Disillusionment in the 1920s," *South Atlantic Quarterly* 68, no. 3 (1969): 367.

24. Clifford Doerksen argues that this class divide played out in early radio as AT&T/WEAF, seeking to protect commercialism in a "highbrow" context, went so far as to sue the local commercial station WHN, broadcaster of jazz and other "lowbrow" programs, for patent infringement for airing advertising. *American Babel: Rogue Radio Broadcasters of the Jazz Age* (Philadelphia: University of Pennsylvania Press, 2005), ch. 2.

25. Edgar H. Felix, "Broadcasting's Place in the Advertising Spectrum," *Advertising & Selling*, 15 December 1926, 19.

26. Letter from L. A. Jenkins to B. F. Goodrich Company, 26 May 1925, Box 3, Folder 126, NBC Records, Wisconsin Historical Society, Madison (hereafter NBC Records).

27. Letter from L. A. McQueen, Advertising Manager, B. F. Goodrich Company, to L. A. Jenkins, The Kolynos Company, 3 June 1925, Box 3, Folder 126, NBC Records.

28. "Less Radio Advertising Asked," *Advertising & Selling*, 27 November 1929, 73.

29. "Broadcasters and Agencies Condemn Blatant Advertising," *Broadcast Advertising*, May 1930, 20ff.

30. An Advertising Agency Executive, "When Will Radio Quit Selling Its 'Editorial Pages'?" *Advertising & Selling*, 22 July 1931, 17.

31. Martin P. Rice, "Radio Advertising," *Advertising & Selling*, 30 June 1926, 72.

32. "When Will Radio Quit Selling Its 'Editorial Pages'?" 17ff.

33. "Acute Inflammatory Radioitis," 83.

34. "When Will Radio Quit Selling Its 'Editorial Pages'?" 18.

35. Ibid., 18.

36. Gordon Best, "Radio Has Brought a New Responsibility to Advertising Agencies," *Broadcast Advertising*, July 1932, 6.

37. L. Ames Brown, "Radio Broadcasting as an Advertising Medium," in Neville O'Neill, ed., *The Advertising Agency Looks at Radio* (New York: D. Appleton, 1932), 7.

38. Robert Colwell, "The Program as an Advertisement," in O'Neill, ed., *Advertising Agency Looks at Radio*, 26.

39. John T. Flynn, "Radio: Medicine Show," *American Scholar* (Autumn 1938): 430–37; Peter Morrell, *Poisons, Potions and Profits: The Antidote to Radio Advertising* (New York: Knight Publishers, 1937). For more on radio's critics, see Kathy M. Newman, *Radio Active: Advertising and Consumer Activism, 1935–1947* (Berkeley: University of California Press, 2004).

40. George Faulkner, JWT Staff Meeting Minutes, 12 August 1930, 2.

41. Mark Woods, "Reminiscences," 11, Oral History Research Office, Columbia University, New York (hereafter Woods Reminiscences).

42. William Banning, *Commercial Broadcasting Pioneer* (Cambridge, Mass.: Harvard University Press, 1946), 103.

43. Edgar H. Felix, "Organizing Broadcasting and Publicity Bureaus in Advertising Agencies," *Advertising & Selling*, 20 February 1929, 25; Edward L. Bernays, "What Future for Radio Advertising?" *Advertising & Selling*, 8 February 1928, 27.

44. M. Lewis Goodkind, "How Radio Department Can Add to Its Importance as Agency Adjunct," *Printers' Ink*, 23 December 1937, 83. Raymond Rubicam, founder of Young & Rubicam, a successful agency in radio, avoided listening to Y&R programs. Fox, *Mirror Makers*, 157.

45. JWT Staff Meeting Minutes, 2 February 1932, 3.

46. Ibid., 2.

47. JWT Staff Meeting Minutes, 8 July 1930, 3.

48. Roy Durstine, "Function of the Agency in Broadcast Advertising," *Broadcast Advertising*, June 1929, 29.

49. Felix, "Organizing Broadcasting and Publicity Bureaus in Advertising Agencies," 84; Durstine, "Function of the Agency in Broadcast Advertising," 15.

50. Ralph M. Hower, *The History of an Advertising Agency: N. W. Ayer & Son at Work, 1869–1939* (Cambridge, Mass.: Harvard University Press, 1939), 167.

51. "Why Writers Flop," *Variety*, 5 September 1933, 57.

52. Woods Reminiscences, 51–52.

53. Charles F. Gannon, "The Agency's Place in American Broadcasting," *Broadcast Advertising*, August 1931, 15.

54. Robert Simon, JWT Staff Meeting Minutes, 2 February 1932, 2, 3.

55. Chester Bowles, "Agency's Responsibility in Radio," *Printers' Ink Monthly*, July 1936, 82.

56. J. Fred MacDonald, *Don't Touch That Dial!* (Chicago: Nelson-Hall, 1979), 32.

57. Christopher Sterling and John Kittross, *Stay Tuned: A Concise History of American Broadcasting* (Belmont, Calif.: Wadsworth, 1978), 516.

58. Woods Reminiscences, 48.

59. "The News Digest," *Advertising & Selling*, 13 November 1929, 104.

60. Woods Reminiscences, 49.

61. H. A. Batten, "A Confidential Statement of Policy and Practice in Radio Broadcasting," 5 January 1938, 4–5, N. W. Ayer Archives.

62. Ibid., 9–10.

63. *The Literary Digest*, 17 December 1927, n.p. Author's collection.

64. Remarkably, N. W. Ayer kept AT&T as a client until the early 1990s.

65. Ralph M. Hower, *The History of an Advertising Agency: N. W. Ayer & Son at Work, 1869–1949*, rev. ed. (Cambridge, Mass.: Harvard University Press, 1949), 178.

66. James Hanna, interviewed by Howard Davis, 2 May 1988, 33a.1, N. W. Ayer Archives.

67. Hower, *History of an Advertising Agency*, rev. ed., 179.

68. Fred McClafferty, interview with Howard Davis, February and March 1989, 29, N. W. Ayer Archives.

69. JWT Staff Meeting Minutes, 2 February 1932, 8.

70. Charlie Brower, *Me, and Other Advertising Geniuses* (Garden City, N.Y.: Doubleday, 1974), 87.

71. BBDO *Newsletter*, February 1966, 16.

72. *Printers' Ink*, 7 July 1932, 38–39.

73. Bernays, "What Future for Radio Advertising?" 59.

74. Robert Simon, JWT Staff Meeting Minutes, 2 February 1932, 5.

75. Ed Roberts, "Radio and Celebrities," unpublished manuscript commissioned by BBDO, ca. 1966, 4.

76. "Audible Advertising," *Advertising & Selling*, 16 April 1930, 31.

77. Ibid.

78. Quoted in "'Variety' Tells All," *Printers' Ink*, 24 August 1933, 90.

79. JWT Staff Meeting Minutes, 2 February 1932, 12.

80. One claim is that Pepsodent sales increased 100 percent in the first year of its sponsoring *Amos 'n' Andy*. Jeffrey L. Cruikshank and Arthur W. Schultz, *The Man Who Sold America* (Boston: Harvard Business Review Press, 2010), 275.

81. Melvin Patrick Ely, *The Adventures of Amos 'n' Andy: A Social History of an American Phenomenon* (New York: The Free Press, 1991).

82. *Amos 'n' Andy* continuity script, 1 April 1932, Box 13, Folder 1, NBC Records.

83. Quoted in "'Variety' Tells All," 90.

84. And both *The Goldbergs* and *Amos 'n' Andy* would go on to television, albeit with less successful results. For an interesting analysis of these ethnic programs, see Michele Hilmes, *Radio Voices* (Minneapolis: University of Minnesota Press, 1997).

85. William Ensign, JWT Staff Meeting Minutes, 11 July 1928, 3.

86. "The Story of Lennen & Mitchell," *Advertising Agency and Advertising & Selling*, August 1949, 62.

87. Robert Simon, JWT Staff Meeting Minutes, 2 February 1932, 9.

88. Ruth Cornwall, "McCann Practice: What About Radio?" Pamphlet, McCann Company, 1930, 31.

89. Ibid., 44.

90. "'Variety' Tells All," 90.

91. Joan Hafey, "Young & Rubicam and Broadcasting," in *Y&R and Broadcasting: Growing Up Together* (New York: Museum of Broadcasting, n.d.), 21.

92. Robert Simon, JWT Staff Meeting Minutes, 2 February 1932, 10.

93. JWT *Newsletter*, 15 May 1928.

94. William Ensign, "Radio-Raze," JWT *Newsletter*, 5 May 1928, 17; William Ensign, "What Price Radio," JWT *Newsletter*, 18 November 1928, 1; William Ensign, JWT Staff Meeting Minutes, 11 July 1928, 4.

95. William Ensign, JWT Staff Meeting Minutes, 11 July 1928, 5.

96. JWT Staff Meeting Minutes, 14 January 1930, 7.

97. JWT Staff Meeting Minutes, 2 February 1932; Roy Witmer to Mark Woods, 21 July 1933, Box 22, Folder 28, NBC Records.

98. "'Variety' Tells All," 90.

99. Goodkind, "How Radio Department Can Add to Its Importance as Agency Adjunct," 26ff.

100. JWT Staff Meeting Minutes, 2 February 1932, 4.

101. For a different perspective on the struggle over who would run JWT's radio department, see Hilmes, *Radio Voices*, 144–46.

102. JWT Staff Meeting Minutes, 12 August 1930, 2. The censorship issue is addressed in Chapter 4, "Who Owns the Time?" and the need for showmanship is addressed in Chapter 6, "The Ballet and Ballyhoo of Radio Showmanship."

103. J. T. W. Martin, "Copy for the Ear," in O'Neill, ed., *The Advertising Agency Looks at Radio*, 69. Pamela Laird argues that the distrust of the visual within the advertising industry had led to the earlier shift away from chromo-lithography as a major advertising medium. *Advertising Progress* (Baltimore: Johns Hopkins University Press, 1998), 293.

104. JWT Staff Meeting Minutes, 21 December 1932, 2.

105. JWT Staff Meeting Minutes, 8 July 1930, 6; Robert Colwell, "The Program as an Advertisement," in O'Neill, ed., *The Advertising Agency Looks at Radio*, 38.

106. Hubbell Robinson, "What the Radio Audience Wants," in O'Neill, ed., *The Advertising Agency Looks at Radio*, 53.

107. George W. Smith, "Continuity's the Name," *Radio Showmanship*, September 1942, 301.

108. Martin, "Copy for the Ear," 72.

109. Ibid., 73.

110. F. B. Ryan Jr., "Copy on the Air," *Printers' Ink Monthly*, March 1934, 55.

111. Hill Blackett, "Agency Operation," *Printers' Ink*, 12 August 1937, 38.

112. John Archer Carter, "But Do They Really Listen?" *Printers' Ink Monthly*, March 1936, 45.

113. *The Coca-Cola Top Notchers*, broadcast on 19 March 1930.

114. Victor Ratner, "Maybe It's 'Copper and Brass'?" *Advertising & Selling*, 29 March 1934, 40.

115. *Chase & Sanborn Hour*, broadcast on 12 December 1937.

116. Robert Colwell, JWT Staff Meeting Minutes, 8 July 1930, 7.

117. Colwell, "The Program as Advertisement," 39.

118. Ernest S. Green, "What 'Typeface' for Your Radio Commercials?" *Printers' Ink Monthly*, May 1938, 18–19.

119. JWT Staff Meeting Minutes, 8 July 1930, 5.

120. Norman Brokenshire, "Announcer—or Advertising Man?" *Broadcast Advertising*, October 1930, 20.

121. Robert Colwell, JWT Staff Meeting Minutes, 8 July 1930, 8.

122. JWT Staff Meeting Minutes, 11 August 1931, 9.

Bibliography

Archival Collections

John H. Hartman Center for Sales, Advertising and Marketing History, Duke University Library, Durham, North Carolina

    J. Walter Thompson

N. W. Ayer Archives, New York

Oral History Research Office, Columbia University, New York

    Mark Woods

Wisconsin Historical Society, Madison

    E. P. H. James

    NBC Records

Trade Publications

Advertising Age

Advertising Agency and Advertising & Selling

Advertising & Selling

Broadcast Advertising

Printers' Ink

Printers' Ink Monthly

Radio Showmanship

Variety

Books and Articles

Banning, William Peck. *Commercial Broadcasting Pioneer: The WEAF Experiment, 1922–26.* Cambridge, Mass.: Harvard University Press, 1946.

Barnouw, Erik. *The Sponsor: Notes on a Modern Potentate.* New York: Oxford University Press, 1978.

Brower, Charlie. *Me, and Other Advertising Geniuses.* Garden City, N.Y.: Doubleday, 1974.

Cruikshank, Jeffrey L., and Arthur W. Schultz. *The Man Who Sold America: The Amazing but True Story of Albert D. Lasker and the Creation of the Advertising Century.* Boston: Harvard Business Review Press, 2010.

Doerksen, Clifford J. *American Babel: Rogue Radio Broadcasters of the Jazz Age.* Philadelphia: University of Pennsylvania Press, 2005.

Ely, Melvin Patrick. *The Adventures of Amos 'n' Andy: A Social History of an American Phenomenon.* New York: Free Press, 1991.

Flynn, John T. "Radio: Medicine Show." *American Scholar* (Autumn 1938): 430–37.

Fox, Stephen. *The Mirror Makers: A History of American Advertising and Its Creators.* New York: William Morrow, 1984.

Hilmes, Michele. *Radio Voices: American Broadcasting, 1922–1952.* Minneapolis: University of Minnesota Press, 1997.

Hower, Ralph M. *The History of an Advertising Agency: N. W. Ayer & Son at Work, 1869–1939.* Cambridge, Mass.: Harvard University Press, 1939.

Koppes, Clayton R. "The Social Destiny of Radio: Hope and Disillusionment in the 1920s." *South Atlantic Quarterly* 68, no. 3 (1969): 363–76.

Laird, Pamela Walker. *Advertising Progress: American Business and the Rise of Consumer Marketing.* Baltimore: Johns Hopkins University Press, 1998.

MacDonald, J. Fred. *Don't Touch That Dial! Radio Programming in American Life, 1920–1960.* Chicago: Nelson-Hall, 1979.

Marchand, Roland. *Advertising the American Dream: Making Way for Modernity, 1920–1940.* Berkeley: University of California Press, 1985.

Morrell, Peter. *Poisons, Potions and Profits: The Antidote to Radio Advertising.* New York: Knight Publishers, 1937.

Newman, Kathy M. *Radio Active: Advertising and Consumer Activism, 1935–1947.* Berkeley: University of California Press, 2004.

O'Neill, Neville, ed. *The Advertising Agency Looks at Radio.* New York: D. Appleton & Co., 1932.

Russo, Alexander. *Points on the Dial: Golden Age Radio beyond the Networks.* Durham, N.C.: Duke University Press, 2010.

Sterling, Christopher, and John Kittross. *Stay Tuned: A Concise History of American Broadcasting.* Belmont, Calif.: Wadsworth, 1978.

Y&R and Broadcasting: Growing Up Together. New York: Museum of Broadcasting, n.d.

QUESTION TO CONSIDER

- In what way did radio become popular in the 1920s?

1920s xenophobia in America.

Another Thing to Think About.
—From *The Indianapolis News.*

CHAPTER 6

The Xenophobic 1920s

By Bill O. Hing

Editor's Introduction

Attoney-General A. Mitchell Palmer is best known for the "Palmer Raids" of 1919–1921, better known as the "Red Scare." One reason for this was the Bolshevik Revolution in Russia as well as radicalism at home. Palmer considered the radicals (many of whom were foreigners) as influenced by the Bolsheviks. Many in the government felt that the Bolsheviks were out to overthrow the government. As a result, xenophobia gripped the nation in the 1920s. In the following chapter, Hing looks at the xenophobic 1920s.

The Xenophobic 1920s

By Bill O. Hing

M anifested in the Red Scare of 1919–20, the reactionary, isolationist polit- ical climate that followed World War I led to even greater exclusionist demands. To many Americans, the ghost of Bolshevism seemed to haunt the land in the specter of immigrant radicals, especially after the 1919 wave of industrial unrest in immigrant-dominated workforces of the coal, steel, meatpacking, and transportation industries. In 1919, an anarchist placed a bomb on the doorstep of Attorney General A. Mitchell Palmer, and while the blast's only victim was the would-be terrorist, it sparked Palmer and his young assistant, J. Edgar Hoover, to launch a crusade to deport all alien "Reds." [...] In reaction to the isolationist political climate, Congress passed a variety of laws placing numerical restrictions on immigration.

The reactionary, exclusionist sentiment of the time was combined with the ethnic. The 1917 literacy law [...] was inadequate for restrictionists, who remained concerned about the continuing entry of southern and eastern Europeans. Southern and eastern European immigrants numbered 4.5 million in 1910; by 1920 the figure surged to 5.67 million. The 100 percent American campaign was alarmed that one-fifth of the California population was Italian American by then.

Shortly after the 1917 act, the Anarchist Act of 1918 expanded the provisions for exclusion and deportation of subversive aliens and authorized their expulsion without time limitations. Until that time, the law had dealt only with the quality of the aliens who sought to enter from Europe through the literacy requirement. The number of Chinese, Japanese, and most other Asians was under control by then. No attempt had been made to limit the number of eastern and southern European entrants. At the conclusion of World War I, immigration again began to increase. Widespread fear of inundation by a flood of immigrants from the war-devastated countries of Europe developed. The isolationist mood of the period and a severe postwar depression augmented the already strong sentiment for further restrictions.[1]

In addition to the menace of leftist political influence emanating from parts of Europe, public and congressional arguments in support of more restrictive legislation stressed recurring themes: the racial superiority of Anglo-Saxons, the fact that immigrants would cause the lowering of wages, the unassimilability of foreigners, and the usual threats to the nation's social unity and order posed by immigration. Popular biological theories of the period alleging the superiority of certain races were influential. The theories of Dr. Harry N. Laughlin, a eugenics consultant to the House Judiciary Committee on Immigration and Naturalization in the 1920s, were influential:

> We in this country have been so imbued with the idea of democracy, or the equality of all men, that we have left out of consideration the matter of blood or natural born hereditary mental and moral differences. No man who breeds pedigreed plants and animals can afford to neglect this thing. ...
>
> The National Origins provisions of the immigration control law of 1924 marked the actual turning point from immigration control based on the asylum idea ... definitely in favor of the biological basis.[2]

The immigration laws of the 1920s were the culmination of strong political and social arguments that eastern and southern Europeans were not the right stock from which true Americans were bred.

Understanding the Sacco and Vanzetti Case in the Context of America in the 1920s

The confluence of negative social and political images of certain unwanted immigrants in the 1920s is epitomized by the Sacco and Vanzetti case. Negative sentiment toward Italian immigrants was exacerbated by the arrest of two immigrants, Nicola Sacco and Bartolomeo Vanzetti, for armed robbery and murder. Sacco and Vanzetti were poor, atheists, and draft dodgers. They were exactly the kind of people Americans felt might be guilty of anything. In addition, they were anarchists who believed, as many anarchists did, that violence could remedy the injustices of society.[3]

At 3:00 P.M. on April 15, 1920, a paymaster and his guard were carrying a factory payroll of $15,776 through the main street of South Braintree, Massachusetts, a small industrial town south of Boston. Two men standing by a fence suddenly pulled out guns and fired on them. The gunmen snatched up the cash boxes dropped by the mortally wounded pair and jumped into a waiting automobile. The bandit gang, numbering four or five in all, sped away, eluding their pursuers. At first this brutal murder and robbery, not uncommon in post-World War I America, aroused only local interest.

Three weeks later, on the evening of May 5, 1920, Sacco and Vanzetti fell into a police trap that had been set for a suspect in the Braintree crime. Both men were carrying guns at the time of their arrest and their behavior aroused suspicion. As a result they were held and eventually indicted for the Braintree crimes. Vanzetti was also charged with an earlier holdup attempt that had taken place on December 24, 1919, in the nearby town of Bridgewater. This marked the beginning of one of twentieth-century America's most notorious political trials.

Contrary to the usual practice of Massachusetts's courts, Vanzetti was tried first in the summer of 1920 on the lesser of the two charges, the failed Bridgewater robbery. Despite a strong alibi supported by many witnesses, Vanzetti was found guilty. Most of Vanzetti's witnesses were Italians who spoke English poorly, and their trial testimony, given largely in translation, failed to convince the jury. Vanzetti's case had also been seriously damaged when he, for fear of revealing his radical activities, did not take the stand in his own defense.

For a first criminal offense in which no one was harmed, Vanzetti received a prison sentence that was much harsher than usual—ten to fifteen years. This signaled to the two men and their supporters a hostile bias on the part of the authorities that was political in nature and pointed to the need for a new defense strategy in the Braintree trial. The arrest of Sacco and Vanzetti coincided with the intensive, politically repressive Red Scare era of 1919 to 1920. The police trap they had fallen into had been set for a comrade of theirs, suspected primarily because he was a foreign-born radical.

While neither Sacco nor Vanzetti had any previous criminal record, they were long recognized by the authorities and by their communities as anarchist militants who had been extensively involved in labor strikes, political agitation, and antiwar propaganda. They were also known to be dedicated supporters of Luigi Galleani's Italian-language journal *Cronaca Sovversiva,* the most influential anarchist journal in America, feared by the authorities for its militancy and its acceptance of revolutionary violence.

Cronaca, because of its uncompromising antiwar stance, had been forced to halt publication immediately upon the entry of the U.S. government into World War I in 1917. Several of its editors were arrested and at war's end deported to Italy in 1919. The repression of the journal involved a bitter social struggle between the U.S. government and the journal's supporters. It was a former editor of *Cronaca* who was suspected of blowing himself up during a bombing attempt at Attorney General Palmer's home in Washington, D.C., on June 2, 1919; that act led Congress to vote funds for antiradical investigations and launched the career of J. Edgar Hoover as the director of the General Intelligence Division in the Department of Justice. The Sacco-Vanzetti case would become one of Hoover's first major responsibilities.

In 1920, as the Italian anarchist movement was trying to regroup, Andrea Salsedo, a comrade of Sacco and Vanzetti, was detained and, while in custody of the Department of Justice, hurled to his death. On the night of Sacco's and Vanzetti's arrests, authorities found in Sacco's pocket a draft of a handbill for an anarchist meeting that featured Vanzetti as the main speaker. In this treacherous atmosphere, when initial questioning by the police focused on their radical activities and not on the specifics of the Braintree crime, the two men lied about their political views.

The Trial and Its Aftermath

These falsehoods created a "consciousness of guilt" in the minds of the authorities, but the implications of that phrase soon became a central issue in the Sacco-Vanzetti case. Did the lies of the two men signify criminal involvement in the Braintree murder and robbery, as the authorities claimed, or an understandable attempt to conceal their radicalism and protect their friends during a time of national hysteria concerning foreign-born radicals, as their supporters were to claim? On the advice of the anarchist militant and editor Carlo Tresca, a new legal counsel was brought in—Fred H. Moore, a well-known socialist lawyer from the West. He had collaborated in many labor and IWW trials and was especially noted for his important role in the celebrated Ettor-Giovannitti case, which came out of a 1912 textile strike in Lawrence, Massachusetts.

Moore completely changed the nature of the legal strategy. He decided it was no longer possible to defend Sacco and Vanzetti solely against the criminal charges of murder and robbery. Instead, he would have them frankly acknowledge their anarchism in court, try to establish that their arrest and prosecution stemmed from their radical activities, and dispute the prosecution's insistence that only hard, nonpolitical evidence had implicated the two men in common crimes. Moore would try to expose the prosecution's hidden motive: its desire to aid the federal and military authorities in suppressing the Italian anarchist movement to which Sacco and Vanzetti belonged.

Moore's defense of the two men soon became so openly and energetically political that its scope quickly transcended its local roots. He organized public meetings, solicited the support of labor unions, contacted international organizations, initiated new investigations, and distributed tens of thousands of defense pamphlets throughout the United States and the world. Much to the chagrin of some anarchist comrades, Moore would even enlist the aid of the Italian government in the defense of Sacco and Vanzetti, who were still, nominally at least, Italian citizens. Moore's aggressive strategy transformed a little known case into an international cause célèbre.

On July 14, 1921, after a hard-fought, six-week trial, during which the themes of patriotism and radicalism were often sharply debated by the prosecution and the defense, the jury found Sacco and Vanzetti guilty of robbery and murder. However, the verdict marked only the beginning of a lengthy legal struggle to save the two men. It extended until 1927, during which time the defense made many separate motions, appeals, and petitions to both state and federal courts in an attempt to gain a new trial.

The petitions and motions contained evidence of perjury by prosecution witnesses, indications of illegal activities by the police and the federal authorities, a confession to the Braintree crimes by convicted bank robber Celestino Madeiros, and powerful evidence that identified the actual gang involved in the Braintree affair as the notorious Morelli Gang. All of the requests were rejected by Judge Webster Thayer, the same judge who earlier had so severely sentenced Vanzetti. Judge Thayer even ruled on a motion accusing him of judicial prejudice. His conduct—or misconduct—during the trials and the appeals was another of the controversial issues surrounding the case, but it too would prove insufficient to bring about a new trial.

From the beginning, Moore's strategy of politicizing the trial in tradition-bound Massachusetts had been controversial and confrontational. His manner of utilizing the mass media was quite modern and effective in terms of publicizing the case, but it required enormous sums of money, which he spent too freely in the eyes of many of the anarchist comrades of Sacco and Vanzetti, who had to raise most of it painstakingly from workingpeople, twenty-five and fifty cents at a time. Moore's efforts were called into question even by the defendants, when he, contrary to anarchist ideals, offered a large reward to find the real criminals. As a result, in 1924 a respected Boston lawyer, William Thompson, replaced Moore and assumed control of the legal defense. Thompson, a Brahmin who wanted to defend the reputation of Massachusetts law as well as the two men, had no particular sympathy for the ideas of the two men, but he later came to admire them deeply as individuals.

Thompson's defense focus no longer emphasized the political, but these aspects of the case, once they had been set in motion, could not be stopped and continued to gain momentum. Throughout America, liberals and well-meaning people of every sort, troubled and outraged by the injustice of the legal process, joined the more politically radical anarchists, Socialists, and Communists in protesting the verdict against Sacco and Vanzetti. Harvard law professor Felix Frankfurter, the future

Supreme Court justice, who did more than any individual to rally "respectable" opinion behind the two men, saw the case as a test of the rule of law itself. His own research revealed that members of the "Joe Morelli gang" and "Celestino Madeiros" were the culprits at South Braintree, not Sacco and Vanzetti. Standing against the defenders of Sacco and Vanzetti were conservatives and patriots who wanted to defend the honor of American justice and to uphold law and order. The defendants' detractors came to see these protests as an attack upon the "American way of life" on behalf of two common criminals.

On April 9, 1927, after all recourse in the Massachusetts courts had failed, Sacco and Vanzetti were sentenced to death. By then the dignity and the words of the two men had turned them into powerful symbols of social justice for many throughout the world. Public agitation on their behalf by radicals, workers, immigrants, and Italians had become international in scope, and many demonstrations in the world's great cities—Paris, London, Mexico City, and Buenos Aires—protested the unfairness of their trial. Prominent individuals like Albert Einstein, Anatole France, Dorothy Parker, Thomas Mann, John Dos Passos, and Edna St. Vincent Millay spoke in favor of the defendants. Letters of protest flooded American consulates and embassies in Europe and South America. Judge Webster Thayer's house was placed under protection. The *Communist International* urged all Communists, Socialists, anarchists, and trade unionists to organize efforts to rescue Sacco and Vanzetti.

This great public pressure, combined with influential behind-the-scenes interventions, finally persuaded the governor of Massachusetts, Alvan T. Fuller, to consider the question of executive clemency for the two men. It was at this penultimate moment that Fuller asked Harvard President Lawrence Lowell to head a special commission—one of the century's notorious "blue-ribbon panels" designed to legitimate state authority—to review the Sacco and Vanzetti case. The Lowell Commission began with an assumption of guilt and, while it criticized certain aspects of Judge Thayer's conduct, the panel upheld the verdict and sentence. An appeal to President Calvin Coolidge was refused. Sacco and Vanzetti were electrocuted on August 21, 1927.[4]

After their execution, the fight to clear Sacco's and Vanzetti's names continued for the next fifty years. In 1977, then-Massachusetts Governor Michael Dukakis issued a proclamation declaring August 23 a memorial day for Sacco and Vanzetti, as well as all the Italian immigrants who had been denied a fair trial. This proclamation, which was based on the review of the case by Dukakis's legal counsel, recognized for the first time that the prosecutors and Judge Webster Thayer had committed a variety of abuses during the trial. It sought to vindicate the names of Sacco and Vanzetti and their families, and called for vigilance "against our susceptibility to prejudice, our intolerance of unorthodox ideas and our failure to defend the rights of persons who are looked upon as strangers in our midst."

Massachusetts's attempts to clear Sacco and Vanzetti—and its own reputation—continued as recently as 1997. On the seventieth anniversary of their execution, Thomas Menino, the first Italian American mayor of Boston, formally accepted and dedicated a memorial to Sacco and Vanzetti that had been previously rejected three times. The bronze sculpture, made in 1927 by Gutzon Borglum, who is best known for carving the presidential faces in Mt. Rushmore, shows Sacco and Vanzetti facing tilted scales of justices. Borglum carved it when President Calvin Coolidge refused to grant them a stay of execution. Merino said that accepting the memorial was Boston's acknowledgment that Sacco and Vanzetti did not receive a fair trial.[5]

The 1927 outcome of the Sacco and Vanzetti case effectively killed the anarchist movement in the Italian American community. Italian anarchists created a sort of "alternative society" within American capitalism. They formed in their communities small enclaves, close networks of family and friends. Their strong ethical imperative was part of their culture as much as the belief in the necessity of violence in political activity. It informed not only the urge to political action as a means to obtain freedom and justice, but their social norms and personal code of behavior as well. Their networks were bound by deeply felt solidarity, by a sense of belonging to a community with a mission, and by a commitment to the betterment of humanity. The vivid vignettes of militant anarchists support, albeit with romantic overtones, such a contention.[6]

The revolutionary anarchists believed that social revolution was not just a remote possibility. They may have been mistaken, but their view was far from irrational. Before 1914 the world—at least the world of Europe and the cultures derived from it—was still full of hope.[7]

When the United States entered the war in 1917, a great wave of repression was mobilized against all radical movements in the country. The war meant the triumph of American finance-capitalism and the American state, and it brought down the curtain on the radical movements of the time.[8]

By the time that Sacco and Vanzetti were arrested, the work of repression had been done. The Italian-immigrant anarchist movement did not disappear but it gradually ceased to be a significant force, and with the cut off of immigration its years were numbered.[9]

Italian immigrants did, of course, come from a country where traditions of antiauthoritarianism—antistate, anticlerical, antipadrone—were strong and the same kind of battles as in the United States were in fact fought out in Italy during the same era. More than immigrants from some other countries, Italian immigrants may have brought with them a certain intolerance toward authoritarian systems. But only a few came with radical ideas; they sought a better life and found a world that was not very different from the old. If in Italy they had been despised as peasants, here they were despised as Italians. Their life-situations and job-situations in the United States, and the political and economic developments here, were the reasons why many Italian immigrants, like immigrants from other cultures, were responsive to radical ideas, including anarchism. The Italian immigrants heard these anarchist ideas mainly from intellectuals who escaped persecution at home by going off to the New World, where they helped create new circles of anarchism. Unintentionally, the Italian government contributed to the dissemination of anarchism around the world: the anarchist ideas of the exiles found resonance in the lives immigrants were living.[10]

National Origins Quotas

On the immigration policy front, the result of the continued assault on southern and eastern European immigrants was the Quota Law of 1921, enacted as a temporary measure. This legislation introduced for the first time numerical limitations on immigration. With certain exceptions, the law allocated quotas to each nationality totaling 3 percent of the foreign-born persons of that nationality residing in the United States in 1910, for an annual total of approximately 350,000. Since most of those living in the United States in 1910 were northern or western European, the quota for southern and eastern Europeans was smaller (about 45,000 less). The latter groups filled their quotas easily, but northern and western European countries did not fill their quotas under this law.[11] This law was scheduled to expire in 1922, but was extended to June 30, 1924.

In the meantime, a permanent policy of numerical restrictions was under consideration and was enacted in 1924. One problem with the 1910 model for the 1921 law was that that was the end of the decade that had witnessed a large influx of southern and eastern Europeans. So a 1910 population model would include a higher proportion of southern and eastern Europeans than earlier years. Thus, the landmark Immigration Act of 1924, opposed by only six senators, took an even greater malicious aim at southern and eastern Europeans, whom the Protestant majority in the United States viewed with dogmatic disapproval.

The 1924 legislation adopted a national origins formula that eventually based the quota for each nationality on the number of foreign-born persons of that national origin in the United States in 1890—prior to the major wave of southern and eastern Europeans. The law provided that immigrants of any particular country be reduced from 3 percent under the 1921 law to 2 percent of the group's population under the new law. And instead of 1910 as the population model year for determining how many could enter, the 2 percent was based on a particular nationality's population in 1890, when even fewer immigrants from southern and eastern Europe lived in the United States. The message could not have been clearer: the racial and ethnic makeup of the country in 1890 should be perpetuated, prior to the influx of southern and eastern Europeans (and, for that matter, Asians). The quota formula was hailed as the "most far reaching change that occurred in America during the course of this quarter century," enabling a halt to "the tendency toward a change in the fundamental composition of the American stock." The *fundamental American stock* was western European, and the quota laws were designed to keep it that way.

This formula resulted in a sharp curtailment of immigrants from southern and eastern Europe, and struck most deeply at Jews, Italians, Slavs, and Greeks, who had immigrated in great numbers after, and who would be most disfavored by such a quota system. Quota immigrants were limited to approximately 165,000 per year, with the proportion and number even smaller for southern and eastern Europeans than before. However, natives of the Western Hemisphere countries could enter without numerical restriction. Other nonquota groups included wives and children of U.S. citizens and returning lawful residents. Those who entered in violation of visa and quota requirements were deportable without time limitation. Another provision, aimed at Asians, barred all aliens ineligible to citizenship, thus completely barring Japanese (as well as all other Asians), some of whom had continued to enter under the 1907 Gentlemen's Agreement. [...]

The 1924 law provided that in 1929 a new quota would take effect. The national origins formula used the ethnic background of the entire U.S. population, rather than the first-generation immigration population, as its base for calculating national quotas. Because the U.S. population was still predominantly Anglo-Saxon, the national origins quota restricted the newer immigrant groups more severely than the foreign-born formula of the previous quota laws. The national origins quota allotted 85 percent of the total 150,000 to countries from northern and western Europe, while southern and eastern countries received only 15 percent of the total.

The national origins formula was complicated by economic times. Soon after it took effect, the U.S. economy collapsed. The Great Depression limited immigration; only about half a million immigrants arrived during the 1930s. [...] In 1932, at the height of the Great Depression, emigration far exceeded immigration, as 35,576 entered while over 100,000 departed. The potential for immigration increased during those years, however, with the growth of highways and increased airplane traffic. By 1938, there were 186 ports of entry into the country. On June 14, 1940, the INS was transferred from the Department of Labor to the Department of Justice.[12]

The impact of the national origins quota system on the southern and eastern European population in the United States is evident from census information on the foreign-born population of the country. They numbered about 1.67 million in 1900. After the big immigrant wave of the first decade of the twentieth century, the figure almost tripled to 4.5 million in 1910. The population surged again in the next decade to 5.67 million in 1920. However, after the quota systems of 1921 and 1924 took effect, the number of immigrants from those regions of Europe declined. (See charts in the Introduction.) The population increased to only 5.92 million by 1930. The figures for immigrants from specific countries are also telling. The population of Italian immigrants increased only 11.18 percent between 1920 and 1930, after experiencing a 176 percent jump in the first decade of the century. The number of Polish immigrants in the United States increased only 11.4 percent during the 1920s, and the number of Hungarians in the country actually declined from 397,283 to 274,450.

Conclusion

The national origins quota laws of the 1920s resulted from the continued sense of ethnic and racial superiority of Anglo or western European stock for the foundation of who could become a true American. The 1917 literacy law alone was insufficient to stem the flow of Jews, Catholics, and Italians seeking to immigrate. By reverting to the 1890 population as the model from which to gauge the "right" proportion of immigrants to enter, southern and eastern Europeans were blatantly targeted, since their U.S. populations were relatively small in that census. The 1920s also witnessed increasing hysteria aimed at Socialists and anarchists, many of whom were believed to be developing in southern and eastern Europe. Sacco and Vanzetti and their supporters came to epitomize all that was potentially wrong with Italian immigrants: they were poor, not particularly educated, non-English-speaking, Catholic, and filled with radical anarchist ideals on behalf of the working class.

The Immigration Acts of 1917 and 1924 thus became the twin elements of immigration policy, one proclaiming qualitative restrictions and the other numerical limitations. These provisions remained pillars of immigration policy for decades.

Notes

1. Charles Gordon and Harry Rosenfield, *Immigration Law and Procedure* 1–11 to 1–12 (New York: Matthew Bender, 1981).

2. Arnold H. Leibowitz, *Immigration Law and Refugee Policy* 1–10 to 1–11 (New York: Matthew Bender, 1983).

3. Interview with Arthur Schlesinger, Jr. accessed at <http://www.courttv.com/greatesttrials/sacco.vanzetti/schlesinger.html on October 18, 2001>.

4. "The Sacco-Vanzetti Project 2002: 75 Years Since the Execution" accessed at <http://www.saccovanzettiproject.org/pages/hstrcl.html> on October 8, 2001.

5. Drawn from *The Case of Sacco and Vanzetti,* an article running in March 1927, in The Atlantic by Feliz Frankfurter. Accessed at <wysiwyg://104/http://www.theatlantic.com/unbound/flashbks/oj/frankff.html> on September 22, 2001.

   For more information on this topic see also *Men, Mobs and the Law: Defense Campaigns and United States Radical History* by Rebecca Nell Hill, Ph.D. diss., University of Minnesota, 2000.

6. Another example of the influence the two men played in social culture was the Official Bulletin of the Sacco-Vanzetti Defense Committee of Boston, Massachusetts. The committee was concerned with efforts to obtain a new trial for Sacco and Vanzetti after their conviction for the murder of F. A. Pamenter and A. Bardelli in Massachusetts.

7. David Wieck, *What Need Be Said,* Sacco Vanzetii Project 2002: 75 Years Since The Execution, at <http://www.saccovanzettiproject.org/pages/context/wiecke.html>.

8. Id.

9. Id.

10. Id.

11. There was a nonquota exception of which some southern and eastern Europeans took advantage. The law permitted a person to be admitted to the United States as an immigrant if the individual had resided in the Western Hemisphere for one year (later changed to five years). So by temporarily living in a Western Hemisphere country, the quota could be avoided.

12. David Weissbrodt, *Immigration Law and Procedure* 13 (St. Paul, Minn.: West Group, 1998).

QUESTION TO CONSIDER

- Why were the American people leery of foreigners in the 1920s?

PART IV

Hard Times

The Depression Years

A small baby wearing spectacles in the early days of industrial baby food.

CHAPTER 7

Industrial Food, Industrial Baby Food

The 1890s to the 1930s

By Amy Bentley

Editor's Introduction

Who would deny that babies are some of the most important people in this world? They are, after all, symbols of the future as well as our nostalgic past. Prior to the twentieth century, babies were fed with breast milk. However, by the early twentieth century, mothers began supplementing breast milk with evaporated condensed milk. Some brands of condensed milk, like Borden, even had directions printed on the back of the can explaining how to mix the product with water in order to create baby formula. In the 1920s, scientists discovered that fruit and vegetables contained vitamins and minerals. With this discovery, it seemed that the market was ready for industrialized canned baby food—enter Gerber. The following excerpt looks at Gerber's rise as an industrial baby food producer during the Depression of the 1930s.

Excerpt From: "Industrial Food, Industrial Baby Food"

The 1890s to the 1930s

By Amy Bentley

Enter Commercial Baby Food: Origins and Icons

Thus by the 1920s, with the discovery and promotion of vitamins and changing attitudes toward fruits and vegetables, the market was ripe for the introduction of industrialized canned food for babies, especially produce. The new baby food products met with great success and solid growth, even during the 1930s Depression.[1] Despite competitors' early development of their own mass-produced strained baby foods, Gerber (then officially named Gerber's, the "s" being dropped later) dominated the baby food market from the beginning.[2]

The conditions were such that mass-produced baby food struck a chord with consumers, mothers, and health professionals alike, and commercially canned baby food provided mass quantities of prepared strained fruits and vegetables to a public ready to accept them. Canned goods were becoming more affordable and familiar to more Americans; advertising was hitting its stride; fruits and vegetables were more commonly recommended for infants; and doctors and health professionals were becoming more and more involved in (and controlling of) infant health and everyday care. Both full-time mothers and the considerable number of working mothers—employed as domestics, factory workers, seamstresses, teachers, secretaries, clerks, or telephone operators—no doubt embraced and benefited from already-prepared solid infant food. Moreover, commercially produced baby food was not the only new phenomenon at the time that significantly altered child rearing. Commercial diaper services, increased wiring of homes for electricity, washing machines, refrigerators, and other technological innovations altered women's work in general and childcare in particular.[3]

Although Gerber dominated the commercial baby food market early on, it was not the first company to commercially manufacture solid baby food. Evidence suggests that Harold Clapp of Rochester, New York, developed Clapp's Baby Foods a few years earlier. In 1921 Clapp, on the advice of doctors, developed a type of "baby soup," a combination of beef broth, vegetables, and cereal, when his wife was too ill to feed and care for their infant son. Apparently their son did so well on this mixture that Clapp made large batches and began selling to individuals and through local drugstores. At its height, Clapp's Baby Food advertised and distributed nationally its hundred-item product line. Clapp's was eventually sold to the American Home Products Company, which in turn sold the brand to Duffy-Mott in the early 1950s.[4]

Gerber baby food entered the market a few years after Clapp's. Begun by father and son Frank and Daniel Gerber in Fremont, Michigan, the company was founded in 1901 as the Fremont Canning Company, a general cannery built to service local fruit producers. According to a 1983 biographical dictionary of business leaders, in 1926 the younger Gerber "began urging his father to begin the production of strained baby foods at the cannery."[5] The dictionary entry mentions that, given the new practice of feeding infants solids before the age of one year, "if [the Gerbers] were to begin manufacturing baby foods, they would be bucking long-held traditions of baby care, and had no idea of what their potential market might be."[6] The elder Gerber commissioned tests of both the potential market and the possible products themselves. "Experimental batches were tested on Daniel's daughter, Sally, and other babies, with great success."[7] While pharmacies sold a small number of canned foods for infants for about 35 cents a can, the Gerbers' new business plan included selling their product in general grocery stores for 15 cents a can.[8]

As part of the canned goods industry, which in general experienced solid growth during the Depression years, baby food in general and Gerber in particular did extremely well.[9] First producing pureed vegetables and fruits—the process was termed "strained" or "sieved" at the time—Gerber soon added a line of cereals and within a few years introduced chopped produce and dinner combinations for older toddlers. In 1930, the company produced 842,000 cans of baby food; by 1931 the number had risen to 1,311,500 cans; one year later, in 1932, Gerber manufactured 2,259,818 cans of baby food.[10] Despite competitors' quick development of their own mass-produced strained baby foods, Gerber dominated U.S. market share over such competitors as Clapp's, Heinz, Beech-Nut, Stokeley, and Libby.[11] The new baby food products were so successful that by 1941 the Fremont Canning Company changed its name to Gerber's Baby Foods (and in the 1960s became the Gerber Products Company), and two years later it abandoned its line of regular vegetables to make baby foods exclusively.

Americans in the early twentieth century were still becoming acquainted with mass advertising, which was designed to create new needs where none had existed before, such as for mouthwash or deodorant, or to promote products, such as baby food, that responded to and enabled a more fast-paced life brought on by technological innovation.[12] With the mass production and advertising of goods, memorable packaging and branding became an essential part of the product, "an integral part of the commodity itself," as one business executive noted in 1913.[13]

Thus as soon as manufacturers began mass producing baby food in the late 1920s they began to advertise their products in print media. Baby food manufacturers, like other manufacturers of new products, found it necessary not only to educate and persuade the public to feel comfortable enough to buy and use their products, but to acclimate and familiarize people with the manner in which baby food was packaged and presented—the metal cans (glass jars came later) and the labeling. Mass producing any industrial product, especially during the Depression-era 1930s, when consumer purchasing slowed to a minimum, meant establishing and expanding a steady market of buyers by acquainting the public with products through advertising campaigns. At the same time that Gerber launched its baby food, for example, it undertook an ambitious advertising campaign in several women's magazines as well as professional medical and nutrition journals. Gerber knew its task was not only to promote its novel product but to convince parents to adopt a new philosophy of infant food and feeding practices. These early baby food advertising campaigns document the emergence of the idea of introducing solids at an earlier age.

The Gerber Origins Story and the Mainstreaming of Commercial Baby Food

While the 1983 biographical sketch describing the origins of Gerber baby food makes no mention of Daniel Gerber's wife, she plays a large role in the narrative promoted by the Gerber firm itself. According to this corporate narrative, the Gerber Products Company grew not out of a corporate-driven search to develop a new product and generate a consuming public, but out of the genuine need and inventiveness of a mother trying to prepare mashed peas for her seven-month-old child. Those canned fruits and vegetables for infants previously brought to market were expensive, manufactured in limited quantities, and available only at drugstores. Now that fruits and vegetables were a recommended part of a six- to twelve-month-old's diet, women had to cook and strain fruits and vegetables for their toddlers, an often onerous process. Thus, in the summer of 1927, Dorothy Gerber, wife of Fremont Canning Company owner Dan Gerber, "following the advice of a pediatrician," was trying to strain peas for her infant daughter. Finding the job tedious and time-consuming, she asked her husband to try his hand at it. According to the company history, "After watching him make several attempts, she pointed out that the work could be easily done at the Fremont Canning Company, where the Gerber family produced a line of canned fruits and vegetables. Daniel Gerber, covered in strained peas, thought his wife had a good point."[14] From this, we are told, came the idea to market strained vegetables and fruits along with the company's regular line of canned produce. By late 1928, strained peas, prunes, carrots, spinach, and beef vegetable soup were ready for the national market.[15]

Though this story has taken slightly different forms over the decades, the facts are plausible.[16] Because women at the time performed most of the child-rearing work, it makes sense that one mother, frustrated at the time it took and messes it created to prepare the now-vital fruits and vegetables for infants, would seek time- and labor-saving methods. That Dorothy Gerber's husband owned a produce-processing plant makes it more plausible. The story creates a compelling, personalized portrait of the beginnings of Gerber—a homey, "authentic" happening far removed from the cacophony of noise and detritus of the industrial canning factory. The story of a woman's ingenuity transforming child rearing in the United States enhances the purity and trustworthiness of the product, and also mutes the profit motive of the company.

By playing on parents', especially mothers', emotions, presenting medical doctors as the ultimate baby experts, and positing the uncontested assumption that commercially prepared foods are superior to, or at least far more efficient than, those cooked at home, the new commercial baby food advertising in the 1930s successfully imbued its products with qualities of exceptional purity and wholesomeness, convenience and modernity, and scientific efficiency. As evidence, a survey of 1930s' issues of the *Journal of the American Dietetic Association* and *Ladies Home Journal,* while by no means an exhaustive study of Gerber promotion pitches, reveals that Gerber quickly undertook an ambitious national campaign to convert health professionals and consumers to its baby foods. In its earliest years of advertising Gerber focused on helping consumers and dietitians become comfortable with the idea of using canned goods in general and Gerber products in particular, and persuading women that it was in their best interest, and in their babies' interest, to use commercially produced food, especially Gerber baby food.

Convincing the Dietitians

From the late 1920s well into the 1930s Gerber placed full-page advertisements in each monthly issue of the *Journal of the American Dietetic Association,* the official publication of the American Dietetic Association (ADA).[17] The ADA, founded in 1917, was the professional organization for the overwhelmingly female field of dietetics and nutrition. The field was growing rapidly at this time: between 1925 and 1938 the ADA's membership expanded from 660 to 3,800. The ADA in the 1920s and 1930s became influential in coordinating and promoting dietary policy and guidelines for optimal health and nutrition.[18] By advertising in the organization's journal, Gerber was clearly aiming to promote baby food as scientifically prepared and thus free of contaminants, a vitamin-filled, healthy, and wholesome food for infants. "Care in every detail makes the Gerber products better for Baby," began one 1932 advertisement.[19] Two 1934 advertisements, each complete with photos of workers dressed in white, operating sparkling clean machinery, began, respectively, "Oxygen is excluded in the Gerber straining process [to conserve vitamins]," and "Careful sorting—rigid inspection, another reason why Gerber's are better for Baby."[20] In the same issues, the American Canning Company ran advertisements designed to resemble scholarly articles on the safety and healthfulness of canned foods. "The Canning Procedure," "Vitamins in Canned Foods: Vitamin A," and "Canned Foods for Infant and Early Child Feeding"[21] were three such ads, each providing scientific information on the benefits of canned foods. Such ads, along with the Gerber ads, were attempting to combat suspicion toward canned foods.

Since fully automated canning factories had been in operation for only a relatively short while, Americans still held lingering suspicions about the quality of canned goods. Though it had been two decades since Congress had passed the Pure Food and Drug Act, some remembered well the days of adulterated and spoiled foods concealed by opaque packaging.[22] While many middle-class women in the United States used commercially canned goods with some regularity by this time, dietitians in particular still questioned whether canned produce was as nutritious and safe as fresh, especially if the products were designed specifically for infants. In what would become standard practice, some 1930s ADA journal issues included research, funded by Gerber, touting the safety, health, and full vitamin content of canned baby foods. Flora Manning, a home economist at Michigan State College, published two such articles in the 1930s, "Canned Strained Vegetables as Sources of Vitamin A" and "Further Studies of the Content of Vitamins A and B in Canned Strained Vegetables."[23] Manning found a minimal difference between the vitamin content of (Gerber) canned, strained vegetables and fresh, noncanned vegetables (a slightly lower vitamin content in the former), but whether intentionally or not, the articles minimized this difference through opaque, indirect language.

Another set of Gerber ADA journal advertisements situated dietitians as the intermediaries between women and their children's doctors. Revealing their faith in the power of persuasion through advertising, ads targeting dietitians and nurses began with such openings as "Gerber advertises … so that mothers will cooperate with you."[24] Other taglines included "Yes, Doctor, we do talk to your patients … and we tell them facts which help you and help us" and "Thanks, Doctor, this helps me carry out your instructions."[25] The copy construed the reader as a female dietitian conversing with a (male) medical doctor about how to persuade women to feed their children Gerber baby food. The ads and articles function to advance the idea that commercial baby food, Gerber's in particular, is just as nutritious as fresh as home-prepared foods, and even more appropriate because it is so scientifically prepared.

Convincing the Mothers

Like the advertising campaigns for many new mass-produced products in the early twentieth century, Gerber's first campaign in 1929 focused on selling its products directly to women, since many grocers did not carry Gerber baby foods.[26] The ads were placed in such leading women's magazines as *Ladies Home Journal*, subscribed to by over a million women.[27] In what was common practice at the time, the advertisement urged women to send in one dollar for a set of Gerber items and asked them to provide the name of their grocer, whom Gerber would then persuade to carry its products. Doctors, however, could request the products free of charge. Emphasizing its products as scientifically prepared and thus trustworthy, Gerber informed women that they "provid[ed] in a scientific, wholesome manner … the important vegetable supplement to baby's milk diet." Advertisements also focused on the products' ability to impart freedom and mobility, notably modern concepts, to both women and their infants: "The new Gerber Products make Mother and Baby alike independent of the kitchen's restrictions. Baby can really travel now."[28]

Later advertising focused on this theme of freedom for Mother and Baby. Not only did Gerber provide freedom from kitchen drudgery, but ads informed that preparing baby foods by hand was essentially a disservice to the woman herself, her baby, and her husband. "For Baby's Sake, Stay Out of the Kitchen!" read the headline of one 1933 advertisement. "It isn't fair to baby—really—to spend long hours in the kitchen. … For baby's sake and for your own—learn what doctors tell young mothers just like you."[29] Moreover, the ads argued that women could not provide the same quality no matter how hard they tried: "You can't, with ordinary home equipment, prepare vegetables as safe, as rich in natural food values, as reliably uniform as ready-to-serve Gerber products!"[30] The opening of another Gerber ad read, "Square Meals for Baby ... and better for him than vegetables you could prepare yourself with ten times the work!" "Don't serve Gerber's for your sake," the ad went on, "*serve them for Baby's sake! ...* They're the finest vegetables Baby can eat—and Baby deserves the best!"[31]

Perhaps most strikingly, the advertisements focused on a woman's relationship with her husband. An early Gerber ad in the *Ladies Home Journal* opened with a photo of a concerned-looking man's face. Surrounding the male face was the text, "To puzzled fathers of rather young children. If you've had to exchange a charming wife for a tired mother who spends endless hours in the kitchen dutifully scraping, stewing and straining vegetables for your child—you'll be glad to read this story." It continued with a version of the Gerber creation story different from the late twentieth-century one mentioned earlier, one that focused on a male persona entirely. "Five years ago, Mr. Dan Gerber faced the same situation, and knowing a great deal about vegetables he set out to solve this problem."[32] Although an accompanying photo depicted a woman identified once more as "Mrs. Dan Gerber" feeding a baby, there was no mention whatsoever of her involvement in the creation. The narrative implies that Dan Gerber's frustration and dissatisfaction (at "having to exchange" his once-charming wife for a now tired and haggard-looking spouse) led to Gerber baby food's invention. Although the advertisement carried a masculine persona, it was clearly designed for women's consumption, appearing as almost a warning to mothers of small children. Gerber advertising as a whole aimed not only to increase women's confidence in the wholesomeness of the product but also implicitly to reduce their confidence in their ability to care for their infants—and also that hardworking provider—without the help of these experts and these products.

In addition, both sets of advertising indirectly or directly advocated the earlier introduction of these foods. Many ads referred to the use of solids at three months or earlier. Under the above-mentioned photo of "Mrs. Dan Gerber" and her daughter Paula, for example, the caption notes, "Paula began to eat Gerber Strained Cereal at 3 months, and had her first Gerber's Strained Vegetables at 3 1/2 months."[33] Gerber's competitors did the same. A 1937 ad for Clapp's baby food included photos of three-month-old baby "John Curlett" being fed his Clapp's Baby Cereal. "At 4 months," the copy informed women, "he'll be introduced to all of Clapp's Strained Vegetables." The final photo showed John at eleven months of age, "flourish[ing]" because of his Clapp's diet.[34] Figure 3, a 1938 Libby's baby food ad picturing a baby barely able to hold up its head, was perhaps one of the most blatant. The caption reads: "Hurry, Mother—it's Libby time! Tiny babies love the vegetables that Libby prepares so carefully."[35]

Not only did specific ad copy and photographs encourage the notion that infants under four months need solid food, but the icon of the Gerber Baby itself legitimated the idea. Nongovernmental organizations that monitor compliance with the International Code of Marketing of Breast-Milk Substitutes argue that the Gerber Baby, whose sketch has graced every Gerber product and advertisement since 1931, appears much younger than six months of age. They argue that the appearance of the Gerber Baby itself gives the implicit impression that babies this young should be eating solid foods, despite World Health Organization guidelines that deem six months the appropriate age for infants to begin receiving solids.[36]

The Gerber Baby

The iconic Gerber Baby proved to be a powerful and effective tool in many ways, including as an indivisible part of the commodity, allowing the company to bypass such traditional middlemen as grocers and appeal directly to women as dietitians or as mothers. Few Americans today are unfamiliar with the winsome, compelling Gerber Baby, who has graced the labeling and advertising of the Gerber Products Company since the early 1930s. The Gerber name has long been synonymous with baby food, and the icon of the Gerber Baby traditionally has symbolized quality and trustworthiness; indeed, a late twentieth-century survey found Gerber to have the highest consumer loyalty of any commercial brand in the United States.[37] In 1928 the Fremont Canning Company solicited illustrations of a baby face for the advertising campaign to introduce its newly developed baby food. Dorothy Hope Smith, an artist who specialized in drawing children, submitted a simple, unfinished, charcoal drawing, indicating she could finish the sketch if it were accepted. Again, according to the company narrative, Gerber executives were so taken with the simple line drawing of an infant's head that they acquired it as it was. The illustration proved so popular that Gerber adopted it as its official trademark in 1931 and offered consumers copies for 10 cents. Recognizing a good marketing opportunity, Gerber offered free copies to doctors and nurses, as illustrated in figure 7.1.[38] Americans mused over the identity of the sketch's model, and at one point it was widely believed that Humphrey Bogart had posed for the sketch.[39]

The Gerber Baby turned out to be a pitch-perfect icon for this new product. Consumers had been primed to respond favorably to the sketch by a couple of decades' worth of advertising of a variety of products, including food, clothing, furniture, and health elixirs, featuring children and infants cast with wondrous

"Hurry, Mother—it's Libby time!"

Tiny babies love the vegetables that Libby prepares so carefully for them. First they're strained—then *specially homogenized* to make them extra-easy to digest. Usually fed as early as 3 months. Ask your doctor when to begin your baby on Libby's Baby Foods. *Free Booklet—"Your Baby's First Vegetables and Fruits." Write today, Libby, McNeill & Libby, Dept. LJ128, Chicago.*

COPR. 1938, LIBBY, McNEILL & LIBBY

Figure 7.1 "Hurry, Mother—it's Libby time!" December 1938 ad in the *Ladies Home Journal*. Advertising for baby food frequently included text referring to "tiny babies," as well as photos and illustrations of babies only a few weeks old, giving the impression that even newborns could be fed solid baby food.

and innocent expressions.[40] The Gerber Baby's large eyes and dilated pupils, round symmetrical head, button nose, and tiny bow-like mouth typifies the "cuteness" and perceived vulnerability that evolutionary biologists surmise increases the likelihood of parents' protecting their young.[41]

Further, the Gerber Baby cultivated a powerful connection with female consumers in a unique respect. Unlike most of the advertising of the period, which featured infants in the presence of adults, mostly their mothers, the Gerber Baby is alone, its large round eyes looking straight out into those of the viewer. This mode of typification Daniel Thomas Cook has termed "matriocularity," that is, "seeing with or through mothers' eyes" an image of an infant that "seek[s] to evoke the emotional response of what companies wish mothers to see and to feel as a consequence of possessing or contemplating their products."[42] Cook further explains that "this mode of depiction ... represent[s] her viewpoint and perhaps her desires or aspirations for what they presume she hopes to see," a happy, contented infant or child.[43] Thus in the early years of commercial baby food production, the Gerber Baby sketch, along with a good percentage of baby food advertising, which featured the matriocular gaze of babies seeking to connect with the mother-consumer, proved visually distinctive and commercially compelling.

As mentioned in the introduction, the appealing sketch of the Gerber Baby and the abundance of advertising in the 1930s by the major commercial baby food makers contributed to the emerging phenomenon of the "mother-consumer."[44] Mothers were to provide both love and material comfort to their infants, and the early twentieth-century era of rapid industrialization and increased availability of goods made it difficult for women to separate the nurturing and capitalism-facilitated

May we send you a GERBER BABY?

In a recent Gerber advertisement the suggestion that pictures of the Gerber Baby were available was mentioned as a matter of relative unimportance.

We were both pleased and surprised at the number of requests that resulted from this suggestion. In a similar manner, we have been gratified during the past year at the number of physicians and nurses who have expressed interest in pictures of the Gerber Baby at our various medical convention exhibits.

It is because of these things that we are taking this present opportunity of indicating more definitely that it would, of course, be a matter of pride and pleasure to us to have the opportunity of sending pictures of the Gerber Baby to anyone in professional work who might be interested.

The black and white lithographed reproductions of the original Dorothy Hope Smith drawing measure 10″ x 11″, and are free from any objectionable advertising matter. If we may do so, we would be glad to forward one of these on receipt of the coupon below.

GERBER PRODUCTS DIVISION
FREMONT CANNING CO.   FREMONT, MICH.

STRAINED VEGETABLES

for baby—
for the older
children — for dia-
betic, colitic, and
other special
diets

GERBER PRODUCTS DIVISION
Fremont Canning Company
Dept. A-27, Fremont, Michigan

Without obligation on my part, I would like you to forward one of the lithographed reproductions of the Dorothy Hope Smith Gerber Baby to the name and address below.

Name_____

Address_____

Figure 7.2 Early (1931) ad for Gerber baby food in the *Journal of the American Medical Association*. Gerber started to commercially produce baby food in late 1928, and shortly there-after it began to advertise. In 1931 the company began using the sketch of the Gerber Baby, an image that has subsequently appeared on all company advertising. A beloved American cultural icon, by the late 1990s the Gerber Baby was the most identifiable brand icon in the United States. (Hartman Center for Advertising & Marketing History, Rubenstein Rare Book & Manuscript Library, Duke University)

aspects of parenting. Baby food advertising not only shaped a woman's understanding of her role as mother-consumer but also provided an efficient commodified structure through which to perform that role.

Introducing Solids at Earlier Ages

During approximately the same time period as commercial baby food was being developed, the average age at which infants were first fed solid foods, including fruits and vegetables, was decreasing. In the late 1920s, just as commercial baby food manufacturers began national advertising and distribution of canned baby foods, prevailing wisdom advocated introducing strained fruits and vegetables around seven months. By the next decade, however, pediatricians recommended introducing fruits and vegetables between four and six months of age.[45]

But this change did not occur without much discussion, debate, and research. During the 1920s and 1930s the new professionalization of the medical establishment, which included the development of the specialty practice of pediatrics, continued a serious and at times impassioned conversation about the introduction of solid foods. In 1920, for example, one pediatri-cian, clearly an advocate of late introduction of solids, called the early feeding of solids ("early" being six months at this point) the new "liberal diet" and registered his opinion that the "traditional timetable" was still the best for babies.[46] Yet by the mid-1920s several doctors were noting in medical journals that, with the relatively recent discovery of "vitamins," it was necessary to change an infant's feeding timetable.[47]

The discovery of vitamins' importance to human growth and health as well as the awareness of the foods that contained them created a paradigm shift of sorts for the medical community. The existence of scientific evidence for the value of vitamin-laden fruits and vegetables framed the discussion of newer notions of infant feeding. As researchers began to understand the importance of vitamin C, for example, they began to experiment with the assortment and timing of introducing foods rich in vitamin C to young children. Studies found that tomato or carrot juice were appropriate substitutes for the more-expensive orange juice as a source of vitamin C for babies.[48] Another study tested the use of the once-suspect banana as a good source of carbohydrates for infants.[49] As researchers conducted studies to measure food values, others experimented with the age of introducing solids to infants.

In the early 1930s the number of studies on introducing solids to infants increased significantly, and the use and efficacy of commercially prepared canned baby food was integral to this research and the debate. In 1932 one doctor took the dramatic step of introducing solids to infants as young as six weeks of age. In his study "The Nutritive Value of Strained Vegetables in Infant Feeding," George W. Caldwell, MD, noting on the first page that "the vegetables used in this investigation were furnished through the courtesy of the Gerber Products Company, Fremont, Michigan," concluded that infants fed vegetables are healthier, with no adverse side effects. Moreover, Caldwell asserted, commercially manufactured products were better than those prepared at home.[50] Others reached the same conclusion. The chief drawback, according to these physicians, was the manner in which vegetables were cooked at home, which led to diminished nutrients: "The infants ... showed definite ability to digest strained solids, even in the early months of infancy (second and third months). This easy digestibility may be due to the recent great improvements in the manufacture of strained fruits and vegetables."[51] Some medical researchers preferred commercial baby food because its large-batch preparation allowed for nutritional uniformity, an asset to their research studies.[52] The American Medical Association's Council on Foods, a governing body of doctors, in 1937 issued a report on infant feeding of fruits and vegetables. Though the council indicated that home-prepared foods could be used, and "if properly prepared, are not inferior in nutritive value to the commercial product," it noted that the machinery at the processing plants enabled a more finely sieved product that allowed optimal digestion and minimal stomach upset, though "methods of preparing commercial canned sieved foods vary somewhat in different factories."[53] The report recommended feeding infants strained fruits and vegetables at between four and six months of age.[54]

There was perhaps good reason to be troubled by the methods of cooking vegetables at home. Given the long-held cultural distrust of fruits and vegetables, tradition dictated a long boiling time to remove impurities and harmful substances. Recipe books and early infant care advice manuals recommended long cooking times for vegetables. Afraid of stomach upset and diarrhea—which without proper treatment could be lethal, especially for the elderly, infants, and young children— cooks were advised to break down the fiber in produce as much as possible through rigorous cooking. Further, among the more privileged classes fibrous foods were seen as intrinsically too course for delicate ladies' stomachs.[55] So whereas some groups, such as recent Italian immigrants, continued a culinary tradition of lightly cooking vegetables, other Americans did not. Southerners, long noted for their extensive gardens and consumption of fruits and vegetables, commonly cooked their vegetables for a long time in water, a practice that tended to leach out vitamins. Some consumption habits included the practice of drinking the vegetable water, or "potlikker," as it was called in the South.[56] In most regions of the United States, however, it was not a common practice, though housekeeping manuals often advised readers to drink the water in which the vegetables were cooked.

Given the emerging industrial markets for commercial baby food as well as other food products, combined with scientific evidence of the efficacy of fruits and vegetables, it makes sense that baby food manufacturers would assertively advertise their products. Moreover, advertising that advocated the early introduction of their foods was a way to create and expand the market share of this new product that fit right into a society increasingly shaped by technology, convenience, and modernity. Further, the rapid growth of the baby food industry offers evidence that consumers—primarily mothers—were eager to try and stay with the products.

It is not difficult to see how, once the idea of "baby food" in general became a common part of American infant feeding practices, experts could assume that when it came to fruits and vegetables, the more the better and (lacking substantial scientific research indicating otherwise) the earlier and "more scientifically produced" (industrially manufactured) the better. By the mid-twentieth century, as the next chapter details, the prevailing wisdom, which gained credence in the 1930s, was that while the early introduction of solids might not necessarily help infants, neither would it harm them.

Further, although there is not necessarily a causal connection between the decline of breastfeeding and the earlier introduction of solid baby food, it is highly plausible that the widespread acceptance of artificial formulas acclimated mothers and doctors alike to infants' ingestion of non–breast milk substances. Thus it may have felt more comfortable, and seemed more customary, to introduce solid baby food into an infant's diet at earlier and earlier ages. As this early introduction of solids became standard advice and practice, commercially produced baby food functioned not only as a supplement to, but also as a substitute for, breast milk.

Notes

1. "Food Industries Buy," 14, 16; *History of the Fremont Canning Company and Gerber Products Company, 1901–1984.*

2. Nisbet, *Contribution to Human Nutrition,* 15.

3. Cohen, *More Work for Mother.*

4. Greg Lawson, "Clapp's Baby Food Plant."

5. "Gerber, (Daniel) Frank Sr.," 443.

6. Ibid., 444.

7. Ibid.

8. Ibid.

9. "Food Industries Buy," 14, 16.

10. *History of the Fremont Canning Company.* Publication found in the Gerber Corporate Archives, which are closed to the public. (This specific information was supplied by Ms. Sherri Harris, Gerber archivist.)

11. Judson Knight, "Gerber Products Company."

12. Strasser, *Satisfaction Guaranteed,* 89,95.

13. Gerald B. Wadsworth, "Principles and Practice of Advertising," *A&S* (January 1913): 55, as quoted in Strasser, *Satisfaction Guaranteed,* 32.

14. "Gerber Company History," Gerber website, accessed May 1999.

15. "Gerber Company History," Gerber website, accessed May 1999. A similar version is recounted in Ellen Shapiro, "The Consultant Trap," 31–32.

16. Advertising in the 1930s, the late twentieth century, and the early twenty-first century all have slightly different versions of the creation story. The Gerber website circa 2012 tells this story: "Following the advice of their pediatrician in the summer of 1927, Daniel and Dorothy Gerber started straining solid foods in their kitchen for their 7-month-old daughter Sally. Eventually, Daniel and Dorothy decided to strain fruits and vegetables at their canning business, based in Fremont, Michigan. Workers in the plant requested samples for their own babies, and the legacy of GERBER® baby foods began." See "Meet the Famous Gerber Baby," Gerber website, accessed March 19, 2014, www.gerber.com/AllStages/About/Heritage.aspx.

17. In 2011 the organization changed its name to the Academy of Nutrition and Dietetics, and the name of the journal became the *Journal of the Academy of Nutrition and Dietetics.*

18. Lynn K. Nyhart, "Home Economists in the Hospital, 1900–1930," 128.

19. *Journal of the American Dietetic Association* 8 (July 1932): 199.

20. *Journal of the American Dietetic Association* 10 (July 1934): 183; *Journal of the American Dietetic Association* 10 (May 1934): 79.

21. *Journal of the American Dietetic Association* 11 (January 1936): 493; *Journal of the American Dietetic Association* 12 (September 1936): 271; *Journal of the American Dietetic Association* 15 (April 1939): 305.

22. Strasser, *Satisfaction Guaranteed*, 33–35.

23. Flora Manning, "Canned Strained Vegetables as Sources of Vitamin A"; Flora Manning, "Further Studies of the Content of Vitamins A and B in Canned Strained Vegetables."

24. *Journal of the American Dietetic Association* 11 (September 1935): 293.

25. Ellipses in the original. *Journal of the American Dietetic Association* 15 (June–July 1939): 513; *Journal of the American Dietetic Association* 16 (January 1940): 85.

26. Strasser, *Satisfaction Guaranteed*, 11, 126.

27. Ibid., 91.

28. *Ladies Home Journal* 46 (July 1929).

29. Ellipses in the original.

30. *Ladies Home Journal* 50 (August 1933): 77.

31. Italics and ellipses in the original. *Ladies Home Journal* 50 (October 1933): 127.

32. *Ladies Home Journal* 50 (July 1933): 51.

33. This is in contrast to the 1990s and 2011 company narratives that mention that the infant as a "seven month old." Elsewhere I have seen the baby's name given as "Sally." See Shapiro, "The Consultant Trap."

34. *Ladies Home Journal* 54 (September 1937): 60.

35. *Ladies Home Journal* 55 (December 1938): 99.

36. World Health Organization, *International Code of Marketing of Breast-Milk Substitutes*; World Health Organization, *Cracking the Code: Monitoring the International Code of Marketing of Breast-Milk Substitutes*. See also June 13, 1997, correspondence from David Clark, Legal Officer, UNICEF, in author's possession.

37. Mercedes M. Cardona, "WPP Brand Study Ranks Gerber 1st in U.S. Market," 3.

38. At the start of the twenty-first century, the Gerber Baby continues to appear on all company packaging and advertising, including in its recently redesigned labels and new line of organic foods. Judann Pollack, "Gerber Starts New Ads as Agency Review Narrows," 6.

39. Knight, "Gerber Products Company," 664.

40. Gary Cross, *The Cute and the Cool: Wondrous Innocence and Modern American Children's Culture.*

41. See Stephen Jay Gould's 1979 essay "A Biological Homage to Mickey Mouse."

42. Daniel Thomas Cook, "Through Mother's Eyes: Ideology, the 'Child,' and Multiple Mothers in U.S. Mothering Magazines."

43. Ibid.

44. Ibid.

45. Meyer, *Infant Foods and Feeding Practice,* 143; Walter W. Sackett, *Bringing Up Babies: A Family Doctor's Practical Approach to Child Care,* chapter 6. See also Cone, "Infant Feeding," 17; Adams, "Use of Vegetables"; Nisbet, *Contribution to Human Nutrition,* 11, 19.

46. John Lovett Morse, "The Feeding of Normal Infants During the Second Year."

47. Thomas D. Jones, "Feeding the Normal Infant the First Year."

48. Eva Mae Davis and Hannah A. Stillman, "Fruit and Vegetable Juices Used in Infant Feeding: A Comparison of Their Growth Promoting Qualities."

49. Jessie Boyd Scriver and S. G. Ross, "The Use of Banana As a Food for Healthy Infants and Young Children."

50. George W. Caldwell, "The Nutritive Value of Strained Vegetables in Infant Feeding."

51. Manuel M. Glazier, "Advantages of Strained Solids in the Early Months of Infancy," quote on 888.

52. F. W. Schlutz, Minerva Morse, and Helen Oldham, "The Influence of Fruit and Vegetable Feeding upon the Iron Metabolism of the Infant."

53. Council on Foods, "Strained Fruits and Vegetables in the Feeding of Infants," 1259.

54. Ibid., 1261.

55. Joan Jacobs Brumberg, *Fasting Girls: The History of Anorexia Nervosa,* chapter 7.

56. Zell Miller, "Pot Liquor or Potlikker?"

Bibliography

Adams, Suzanne F. "Use of Vegetables in Infant Feeding Through the Ages." *Journal of the American Dietetic Association* 35 (July 1959): 692–703.

Brumberg, Joan Jacobs. *Fasting Girls: The Emergence of Anorexia Nervosa as a Modern Disease.* Cambridge, MA: Harvard University Press, 1988.

Caldwell, George W. "The Nutritive Value of Strained Vegetables in Infant Feeding." *The Journal of Pediatrics* 1, no. 6 (December 1932): 749–753.

Cardona, Mercedes M. "WPP Brand Study Ranks Gerber 1st in U.S. Market." *Advertising Age,* October 5, 1998.

Cohen, Ruth Schwartz. *More Work for Mother: The Ironies of Household Technology from the Open Hearth to the Microwave.* New York: Basic Books, 1985.

Cone, Thomas E., Jr. "Infant Feeding: A Historical Perspective." In *Nutrition and Feeding of Infant and Toddlers,* edited by Rosanne B. Howard and Harland S. Winter, 1–7. Boston: Little, Brown, and Company, 1984.

Cook, Daniel Thomas. "Through Mother's Eyes: Ideology, the 'Child,' and Multiple Mothers in U.S. Mothering Magazines." *Advertising and Society Review* 12, no. 2 (2011).

Council on Foods. "Strained Fruits and Vegetables in the Feeding of Infants." *JAMA: The Journal of the American Medical Association* 108, no. 15 (April 10, 1937): 1259–1261.

Cross, Gary S. *The Cute and the Cool: Wondrous Innocence and Modern American Children's Culture.* Oxford: Oxford University Press, 2004.

Davis, Eva Mae, and Hannah A. Stillman. "Fruit and Vegetable Juices Used in Infant Feeding: A Comparison of Their Growth Promoting Qualities." *The American Journal of Diseases of Children* 32 (1926): 524–529.

"Food Industries Buy." *Business Week,* December 15, 1934.

"Gerber, (Daniel) Frank Sr." In *Biographical Dictionary of American Business Leaders, A-G,* edited by John N. Ingham, 443–445. Westport, CT: Greenwood Press, 1983.

Glazier, Manuel M. "Advantages of Strained Solids in the Early Months of Infancy." *The Journal of Pediatrics* 8, no. 3 (1933): 883–890.

Gould, Stephen Jay. "A Biological Homage to Mickey Mouse." *Ecotone* 4, nos. 1–2 (Winter 2008): 333–340. Accessed September 6, 2012. http://muse.jhu.edu/journals/ecotone/v004/4.1-2.gould.pdf.

History of the Fremont Canning Company and Gerber Products Company, 1901–1984. Fremont, MI: Gerber Products, 1986.

Jones, Thomas D. "Feeding the Normal Infant the First Year." *Virginia Medical Monthly* 53 (September 1926): 372–378.

Knight, Judson. "Gerber Products Company." In *Encyclopedia of Major Marketing Campaigns,* edited by Thomas Riggs, 664–667. Farmington, MI: Gale Group, 2000.

Lawson, Greg. "Clapp's Baby Food Plant." *Senior Life Newspapers,* August 29, 2012. Accessed July 3, 2013. http://seniorlifenewspapers.com/news/2012/aug/29/clapps-baby-food-plant/.

Manning, Flora. "Canned Strained Vegetables as Sources of Vitamin A." *Journal of the American Dietetic Association* 9, no. 4 (November 1933): 295–305.

———. "Further Studies of the Content of Vitamins A and B in Canned Strained Vegetables." *Journal of the American Dietetic Association* 12 (September 1936): 231–236.

Meyer, Herman Frederic. *Infant Foods and Feeding Practice: A Rapid Reference Text of Practical Infant Feeding for Physicians and Nutritionists.* Springfield, IL: Thomas, 1960.

Miller, Zell. "Pot Liquor or Potlikker?" *New York Times,* February 23, 1982. Accessed March 13, 2014. www.nytimes.com/1982/02/23/us/pot-liquor-or-potlikker.html.

Morse, John Lovett. "The Feeding of Normal Infants during the Second Year." *JAMA: The Journal of the American Medical Association* 74, no. 9 (February 28, 1920): 577–580.

Nisbet, Stephen S. *Contribution to Human Nutrition: Gerber Products since 1928.* New York: Newcomen Society in North America, 1954.

Nyhart, Lynn K. "Home Economists in the Hospital, 1900–1930." In *Rethinking Home Economics: Women and the History of a Profession,* edited by Sarah Stage and Virginia B. Vincent, 125–144. Ithaca, NY: Cornell University Press, 1997.

Pollack, Judann. "Gerber Starts New Ads as Agency Review Narrows." *Advertising Age,* December 16, 1996.

Sackett, Walter W., Jr. *Bringing Up Babies: A Family Doctor's Practical Approach to Child Care.* New York: Harper and Row, 1962.

Schlutz, F. W., Minerva Morse, and Helen Oldham. "The Influence of Fruit and Vegetable Feeding upon the Iron Metabolism of the Infant." *Journal of Pediatrics* 3, no. 1 (July 1933): 225–241.

Scriver, Jessie Boyd, and S. G. Ross. "The Use of Banana as a Food for Healthy Infants and Young Children." *The Canadian Medical Association Journal* 20 (1929): 162–166.

Shapiro, Ellen. "The Consultant Trap." *Inc.,* December 1995. Accessed March 13, 2014. www.inc.com/magazine/19951201/2507.html.

Strasser, Susan. *Satisfaction Guaranteed: The Making of the American Mass Market.* New York: Pantheon Books, 1989.

World Health Organization. *Cracking the Code: Monitoring the International Code of Marketing of Breast-Milk Substitutes.* London: World Health Organization, 1977.

World Health Organization. *International Code of Marketing of Breast-Milk Substitutes.* Geneva: World Health Organization, 1981. Accessed March 29, 2014. www.who.int/nutrition/publications/code_english.pdf.

QUESTION TO CONSIDER

- Explain the process whereby Gerber became one of the main manufacturers of baby food.

The golf course Camp Gordon in Augusta, Georgia.

CHAPTER 8

Golf in the 1930s

By Richard Moss

Editor's Introduction

During the Great Depression of the 1930s, golf suffered at all levels, but it survived. Many of the 1930s tournaments (known as the "Grapefruit Circuit") were played in California and Florida. Due to the Depression, many country clubs found themselves overspending; thus, they ended up filing for bankruptcy and closing their doors to their customers. Yet, people continued to be attracted to golf during the Depression. Why? Find out by reading Richard Moss's explanation.

Golf in the 1930s

By Richard Moss

I have a friend who claims to know the iron rule of golf history. Its short form goes like this: golf, in all of its manifestations, thrives when the stock market goes up and shrinks when the market goes down. Simple as that.

Certainly there is some truth to this view. Golf is dependent on discretionary dollars, and when the market is up, people have more of these dollars. They play more, buy more equipment, build more expensive courses, travel to see more tournaments, and join more country clubs. During the bull market of the 1920s, affluent Americans poured a fortune into golf. At the time, going into debt seemed like a good idea; everything was going up, so why not expand the country club, buy new clubs (steel shafts!), or travel south for a winter golf vacation? Everything, one assumed, would cost more next year. Luxury crept into every aspect of the game: more cashmere, more leather, more fancy country clubs, more expensive travel to Europe, South America, and the American South and West. Golf was no different than many other aspects of American life; wretched excess and debt crept in, unnoticed, and became the norm.

As the Depression settled in, Americans looked back and saw the foolishness of the previous decade's extravagance. For the golf community, the early thirties was a time of reflection and self-criticism. The collapsing stock market did not merely shrink golf; it made golfers and country clubs reconsider what they had done since the war. Out of this reconsideration, a conflict emerged between two traditions that structured the game. One tradition called for a simple, inexpensive game, while the other tradition called for luxury and complexity (it should be noted, however, that both of these visions of golf called for the exclusion of "undesirable elements"). This conflict between "cheap-simple" and "expensive-complex" is one of the defining elements of the golf community to this day. Also, if we focus solely on the economy of the 1930s and its impact on golf, we will surely overlook the fact that many elements of the game stabilized and became more deeply rooted during the decade. All the basic structural elements of the golf community survived the thirties, and by the early fifties it had emerged from two decades of economic strife and war ready to get big again.

There can be little doubt, however, that the golf community got smaller in the 1930s. The massive growth in courses and players that occurred in the twenties

Richard Moss, "Golf in the 1930s," *Kingdom of Golf in America*, pp. 130-152. Copyright © 2013 by University of Nebraska Press. Reprinted with permission.

slammed to a halt. Despite these setbacks, it is crucial to note that, ultimately, golf never actually went into reverse. The most important golf organizations suffered but survived. A 1936 *Business Week* survey found that membership at social, professional, yacht, and country clubs was down 14 percent between 1929 and 1936. The United States Golf Association struggled throughout the decade. Approximately 1,100 clubs belonged to the organization in 1930, but this number had dropped to 763 in 1936. *Business Week* estimated that the total number of country-club members had shrunk by one million between 1925 and 1936. On the other hand, daily-fee and municipal courses actually increased. Municipal courses tripled their numbers between 1925 and 1936 (184 to 576). Daily-fee courses grew to slightly more than a thousand in 1935.

Certainly, there was a relationship between all of these numbers. It was especially common for a private club to go under and emerge as a municipal or private daily-fee enterprise. Geoffrey Cornish and Ron Whitten, in their very useful history *The Golf Course*, estimate that between 1932 and 1952, six hundred courses closed permanently (ultimately becoming lots or parks), and approximately one thousand new courses opened. Some of these new courses were important in the evolution of golf. Too often the emphasis is on the lost courses of the thirties, rather than on those gained.

In the public realm, one project clearly stands out: the four-course complex installed in Bethpage State Park, located near Farmingdale on Long Island. In 1934 the Bethpage Park Authority acquired almost 1,400 acres that had once been a private estate. The parcel contained a private golf course designed by Devereux Emmet, and plans were drawn to renovate the existing course and construct three additional courses. A. W. Tillinghast was hired as a consultant and designer. The federal government, through the Civilian Works Administration, provided the funds for the labor and material. The most notable of the courses, the Black, opened in 1936 and has hosted many important events, including the 2002 and 2009 U.S. Opens. When completed in the thirties, Bethpage was undoubtedly the largest public golf facility in the world.

Also noteworthy was the construction of the George Wright Municipal Course in the Hyde Park section of Boston. The course was named after the Cincinnati Reds and Boston Red Sox baseball player whose sporting goods store in Boston had become a fixture. Wright was a promoter of public golf; he had laid out the city's first course at Franklin Park in 1890.

The George Wright Course was built on the failed plans for a private course. A group had acquired the Henry Grew estate and was going to establish a club with a course designed by Donald Ross, but these plans were abandoned in 1929.

They were revived in 1931 when the city, by eminent domain, took over the site. The land turned out to be an enormous problem: it was mostly rock and swamp. In a newspaper story, Donald Ross remarked that to build a course on the site, you would need one of two things: "a million dollars or an earthquake."

There was a third possibility: the federal government could decide to fund projects that provided work for the unemployed and produced something worthwhile. By 1938, when the course opened, the project had cost more than a million dollars. At times there were over one thousand workers laboring on the project, which included the construction of a $200,000 clubhouse of indeterminate style designed by Walter Greymont, a Works Progress Administration architect. It had some Norman and Tudor elements; the whole pile reminded one of an English manor house. Over seventy-two thousand cubic yards of soil were spread, thirty tons of dynamite was used to dislodge the rock ledge, and more than eight thousand feet of drainage pipe were used to dry up the wet areas. The best student of Ross's work, Bradley Klein, believes that Ross never had to do more work to make a course "fit the land."

The course opened with great fanfare. Boston's mayor Maurice Tobin hit the first shot wide right and out-of-bounds. This was quickly deemed a "practice shot"; his second attempt was straight and long. Newspaper accounts describe the mayor as surrounded by 250 of the 350 "members" who had paid thirty-five dollars in annual dues. The daily fee was two dollars. Klein suggests that George Wright Municipal was "nominally public, but the clientele was disproportionately upscale." The clubhouse became a favorite site for parties, proms, and weddings. For a public course, the city made great efforts to keep people out, and it was one of the first in the nation to be surrounded by a security perimeter of rock walls and fences.

Both Bethpage and George Wright Municipal suggest that growth in municipal courses during the thirties was not a complete turn toward simple, inexpensive courses for the masses. There were members who had considerable sway over what happened at the course. This led to efforts to keep "rougher" elements out. The model was substantially based on the private clubs and courses built earlier in the century. Bethpage Black was clearly modeled after Pine Valley. A 1934 *Golf Illustrated* article on Bethpage suggests that the courses at Bethpage will allow players "to enjoy a round under conditions parallel to a first-rate private club." The article also notes that "polo matches will be conducted every Sunday afternoon."

The long-term future of the municipal courses built in the thirties was not often good. A steady commitment to facilities built with federal help and deflated Depression-era dollars was frequently not forthcoming. In addition, upscale golfers who took to municipal courses in the thirties often returned to private clubs when the economy improved after the war. Golf and golf courses were hard to defend during downturns. The history of George Wright Municipal serves as an example. By the middle of the 1970s, Boston's city golf courses had deteriorated considerably. In 1976 the Franklin Park Course was closed, and George Wright was on life support. City officials struck notes that were familiar in city after city. Staffer Barry Brooks, from the mayor's office, explained that closing (and not funding) golf courses was a matter of priorities. He claimed: "You must maintain vital services. A recreational program serving so few, and mostly adults, does not compare in need with some of the city's other programs." In 1975 Boston's city courses recorded a deficit of $146,637. These courses had 315 full-time members and 13,155 paid single rounds. These numbers were the product of a decline in the conditions at the city's courses. Indeed, Franklin Park had been in an "almost unplayable condition" for years, the *Boston Globe* claimed. The paper also noted that Franklin Park was close to a "deteriorating area." There had been robberies and muggings on the back nine. The course had given up putting pins and flags in the cups; they were stolen as quickly as they were replaced. In 1975 the Franklin Park clubhouse burned to the ground.

The George Wright Course was in a better condition than Franklin Park. The *Globe* reported, however, that vandalism was much worse, because there was more to damage. There was more play at George Wright, but the operating deficit was much larger than at Franklin Park. The culprit was a decline in daily-fee players, coupled with the low daily charge of only three dollars on weekends. There were accusations that members were routinely given special privileges by those running the course, referred to as the "inner club." One city official charged that the course was run "like a private club." Members dominated weekend-morning tee times and actively discouraged walk-ons. The *Globe* also claimed that many city workers paid no fee at all. This was especially true of policemen and firemen.

George Wright lives on in good shape. There is considerable irony to this situation: a course and a clubhouse built as a social and economic experiment, built by men paid by the federal government, was saved by the intervention of a private, voluntary association. In 1983 the Massachusetts Golf Association leased the course from the city. The mga turned to Bill Flynn, a professional who had won the New England Professional Golfers' Association (pga) Championship and had considerable experience running golf courses. His plan was simple: "We want to turn this [George Wright] into a public country club with a good course and a good restaurant." Faced with a tax-cutting ballot initiative (Proposition 2½), the city had no choice; they could either close the course or lease it to the mga. In 2004 the city regained control of the course, and it is widely considered one of the best public courses in New England.

Public municipal courses, since the thirties, have often gone the way of George Wright. Bethpage slowly deteriorated until a huge infusion of cash from the usga saved it and made it into the poster child for public courses. Other cities have done better, but clearly cities in general have often proven to be poor stewards of good golf courses. Taxpayers generally do not like to subsidize golf. Courses often fail as the section of the city in which they reside slides downhill. Finally, private daily-fee courses and the companies that operated them complained that tax-supported courses constituted unfair competition. In the end, the golf community has often found public ownership of courses to be problematic and unreliable.

Among the private courses that the golf community produced and maintained in the thirties, there are two that serve as pertinent examples. Both took root outside the Northeast homeland of golf (one in California, and one in Georgia). Both were connected back to Scotland, since both were—for the most part—designed by the transplanted Scot, Alistair MacKenzie. The two courses—Pasatiempo, in California, and Augusta National, in Georgia—were three thousand miles apart, but deeply connected in a number of other ways. They both illustrated some of the fundamental realities that confronted golf during the Depression.

Pasatiempo was the production of Marion Hollins, certainly one of the most important women in golf history. Hollins grew up on Long Island in an atmosphere shaped by affluence. Her father, Harry B. Hollins, was wealthy enough to provide Marion with whatever she wished on the family's Long Island estate, Meadow Farm. At first it was horses, then Marion took up golf at the Westbrook Golf Club (1894), where her father had been one of the founders. Marion traveled extensively in Europe and Great Britain, where she saw all the famous courses and picked up the habits of the English upper class.

After 1913, when her father went bankrupt, Marion was on her own. She continued to play golf and became one of America's best players. She won the usga Women's Amateur in 1921 and routinely did well in most of the better women's events. Perhaps more importantly, she was drawn to the creation of clubs and courses. She was the prime mover in the creation of the Women's National Golf and Country Club on Long Island near Glen Head. Hollins was a genius at raising money for such projects. The Women's National was financed by women, most of them recruited by Hollins, and only women could become members. Hollins was adept at getting to the wives of the ultra rich. Money came in from ladies with notable last names: Mellon, Pratt, Whitney, and Frick. The club, which opened in 1923, survived for eighteen years, and is today part of the Glen Head Country Club.

By the midtwenties, Hollins had fallen in love with California. She had met Samuel F. B. Morse III while on vacation in the West, and he offered Marion a position that would place her in the middle of Morse's attempt to develop the Monterey Peninsula as the golf capital of the West. In this position, she did many things, but most notably, she was the key figure in the founding of Cypress Point Golf Club. This club and its course have, over the years, become iconic.

Hollins was not satisfied to be just an agent of someone else's success. In 1928 she purchased a piece of land near Santa Cruz, and after raising money in the East, she built Pasatiempo Country Club and Estates. It opened on September 8, 1929, just before the crash. The club had everything: an expensive course designed by MacKenzie, a polo field, a steeplechase course, a swimming pool, a huge clubhouse, and housing lots for sale along the fairways. Hollins thought, with good reason, that she could ignore the deepening Depression. Just as she was opening Pasatiempo, Hollins entered into an oil venture with Franklyn R. Kenney. Marion, once again, was able to raise money from back East, and the first hole they punched into Kettleman Hills produced a gusher. In May 1930, Hollins sold out for $2.5 million.

Even this fortune did not insulate Hollins and Pasatiempo from the challenge of the Depression. In the thirties, the club had been a center of elite social life in California. Movie stars like Mary Pickford and Brian Aherne were frequent visitors, where they mingled with the Vanderbilts and the Crockers. By 1937, however, Hollins was hopelessly in debt. The cost of water to keep her course alive was a major factor. Never had the phrase "sucked dry" been more appropriate. That same year, she was seriously injured in an automobile accident. In 1940 she sold her interest in Pasatiempo and returned to work for Del Monte Properties. She had lost all of her oil money, plus $650,000 in an attempt to save her club. In 1937 her childhood club, the Westbrook Golf Club, where she had learned to play golf and love the life, folded for financial reasons.

After Hollins gave up on Pasatiempo, it went through a long period of strife and litigation. It emerged as a hybrid; there were private owners, but the public played the course for a daily fee. Today, it ranks as one of the nation's very best courses open to the public.

At about the same time that Hollins was beginning to pour her oil money into Pasatiempo, two men in Georgia were planning a club that would become more than iconic (if that is possible) in the golf community. Augusta National Golf Club was the product of Bob Jones and Clifford Roberts. Not only did they create a club and a course, they created a tournament to promote the club. This tournament, of course, has become one of the four most important golf events in the world, and the only one played on the same course each year.

Jones had often expressed a desire to build a championship course in the South. After the Grand Slam and his retirement, Jones returned to Atlanta and his legal career. He also produced a series of instructional films that may have netted him more than a quarter of a million dollars. He signed a lucrative deal with Spalding, and by 1932 golfers were the target of a glossy ad urging them to buy a set of clubs that included a replica of Jones's famous putter, Calamity Jane. As a celebrity, he found certain aspects of his life difficult. He discovered that a weekday round with friends at East Lake could easily turn into something like an exhibition with sizable gallery. Jones wanted a place to play that would protect his privacy.

In 1926 Jones had met Roberts and the two had become friends. Roberts knew that Bob wanted to build a course as a private preserve. In 1930 it was Roberts who suggested that such a club could be built in Augusta, Georgia.

Clifford Roberts was to become a very important person in the history of American golf. Born Charles DeClifford Roberts Jr., in 1894, on a farm near Morning Sun, Iowa, he was not from a background that one would associate with the world of exclusive golf clubs. David Owen, whose *Making of the Masters* is the most well-researched and careful picture of Roberts, the club, and the Masters, has painted Roberts's early life as grim and strange. Basing his conclusions on the diary of Roberts's mother, Rebecca, Owen suggests that "the underlying themes are of dislocation and despair." His father was something more than restless. He would purchase a business and quickly trade it for a store or some other kind of business. The family moved often, and their financial status and security would wax and wane dramatically. Clifford's father was often absent pursuing some deal in another state, and his mother was often ill with one of a number of ailments. She was clearly depressed. In 1909, at age sixteen, through a careless act with a match, Clifford burned down the family home. In 1913 his mother gave up the fight; she went out early one morning and shot herself in the chest with a shotgun.

By 1915 Clifford was on his own, selling men's clothing wholesale in a huge territory that included most of the Midwest. Roberts, at this point in his life, reflected the values we associate with the young men in the Horatio Alger stories. His goal was to rise in the world, and like many Alger heroes, the rise began with a move to New York City. He purchased new clothes, he studied the lives of men who had become wealthy, and he learned whatever he could about colleges and universities that had produced the Eastern elite. School for Clifford Roberts had stopped with the eighth grade.

After one failed attempt to establish himself in New York, Roberts tried again in 1918. This time he put down some roots. He was drafted into the army, where he trained at Camp Hancock in Augusta, Georgia; Roberts spent much of the decade after the war struggling to make it as an investment adviser and broker. It is important to note that Roberts never became wealthy in the twenties. When he met Jones, Roberts was, at best, a minor figure in the New York financial world.

Why exactly did Bob Jones and Clifford Roberts become partners of a sort in the making of Augusta National? I have never read a satisfactory answer to this question. Certainly, Roberts proved to have a knack for assisting heroes; he proved this with both Bob Jones and Dwight Eisenhower. In any event, for almost fifty years, Clifford Roberts contributed in countless ways to the construction and evolution of golf's most iconic and controversial club and course. He was the most important influence in shaping the Masters Tournament.

The first step in the building of Bob Jones's course was to determine a place to set the club. Augusta, Georgia, made a lot of sense for a number of reasons. It was convenient to Atlanta and familiar to both Jones and Roberts. There was already a resort hotel and the Augusta Country Club in place. Perhaps most crucial was the existence of a virtually perfect piece of land. Jones and Roberts saw a 365-acre parcel that, since 1858, had been the Fruitland Nurseries, owned by Prosper Berckmans. By 1918 the nursery had gone under, and in the twenties it had been the site of a failed attempt to construct a golf course and hotel. In January 1931, they took an option to buy the property.

This set in motion the creation of the business side of the endeavor. Roberts assembled a group of underwriters, which included Bob Jones and his father. A real estate company was created—the Fruitland Manor Corporation—which purchased the land for fifteen thousand dollars in cash and the assumption of sixty thousand dollars in debt.

The plan for the club was modeled after the megaclubs of the 1920s. There would be 1,800 members, two golf courses (a championship course and one for the "ladies"), tennis and squash courts, and a new, expensive clubhouse. When this plan was drawn, Roberts and Jones no doubt thought the economic downturn was temporary and that raising money for a club connected to Bob Jones would be easy. The incorporated club would lease the land for the courses and, over time, eventually buy it. The real estate company would retain a sizable chunk to sell as house lots. Almost none of this came to pass. As the economic darkness spread, Roberts slowly and steadily pared back the original plan.

Roberts began his membership drive in the spring of 1931. Armed with massive mailing lists and an aggressive pitch that emphasized the uniqueness of the club and the connection to Jones, Roberts had high hopes. A year into the drive, the club had attracted thirty-six members. The search for a membership whose fees would fund operations never really worked until after World War II. The club was able to limp along only because the costs were born by a small group of underwriters who loaned the club money that was never repaid.

The irony is that economic reality forced Augusta to greatly simplify the original plan and, in the long run, this is what made the club successful. The plan for a grand multipurpose country club was abandoned, and the focus was put on building the course. There would be no tennis courts, no house lots, no new grand clubhouse, and no women. Instead, there would be just the one course, and they would remodel and enlarge the existing manor house into one of the most familiar buildings in golf.

The course grew directly out of the desire of Bob Jones to duplicate in Georgia the golf design he had seen in California and Scotland. In 1929 Jones lost in the first round of the U.S. Amateur played at Pebble Beach. After the loss, he and others, including Francis Ouimet, played a round at Cypress Point. The next day, he was a part of an opening-day exhibition match at Pasatiempo in Santa Cruz. This was his introduction to the work of Alister MacKenzie. Jones already knew Marion Hollins. Cypress Point and Pasatiempo convinced Jones that when he built a course he wanted MacKenzie as its architect.

MacKenzie first visited Augusta and appraised the site in July 1931. Construction had, at that point, not been approved. This did not come until February 1932. Once started, the course was built with astonishing speed. MacKenzie returned to oversee the final contouring of the greens. Workers were mowing the course early in June. By one account, the course was completed in seventy-six days. The total cost: approximately $115,000. The club paid the workers who labored on the course, but MacKenzie was not so lucky. When he died in January 1934, the club still owed him most of his fee and related expenses.

The resulting course was clearly the product of Jones and MacKenzie, but there was also input from Marion Hollins. At MacKenzie's request, she visited the course just before construction and passed her observations on to MacKenzie. Since the club famously became a male bastion, it is ironic that a woman played some part in the design.

Some have assumed that the invention of what was to become the Masters helped the club get on its feet in the 1930s. Gene Sarazen's legendary double eagle on fifteen, in 1935, made great newspaper copy but it did little to help the tournament or the club. Actually, the tournament, by one measure, shrank during the thirties. In 1934 seventy-two players accepted an invitation to play, but that number had sunk to fifty-six in 1939. Pros found it difficult to add the Masters to their schedule when they had to get back to their northern club jobs. Many simply gave up playing the so-called winter tour altogether.

The most interesting aspect of Augusta's early history is that it did by necessity what many in golf thought the whole sport needed to do. Augusta National survived because it simplified its original plans. Instead of building a multicourse, multi-purpose family country club with lots for sale, the club, led by Roberts, focused on the single golf course, and on being "just golf."

As Augusta was taking its first steps in this direction, several commentators were calling for all of golf to embrace a return to simplicity. In the end, the demand for simplicity turned out to be not so simple. As the Depression set in, there was a tendency to examine the excesses of the twenties. Golf clubs were deemed to be one such excess. A *New York Times* survey of Westchester clubs found that the average budget was $101,000, but that the cost of course maintenance was only $38,000. The *Times* suggested that many golf clubs had evolved to serve as high-class social gathering spots, with "liveried flunkeys everywhere and a general air of expensiveness." Another *Times* survey found that at a number of clubs, the high cost of golf was often caused by expensive nongolf amenities like pools, club houses, and tennis courts.

In 1933, in the *American Mercury*, Kenneth P. Kempton portrayed the situation in a mildly fictionalized essay. He laid out the history of an imaginary club founded in 1899. The early history of the club was simplicity itself. The "fathers" of the club built a simple course on a few acres of pasture. Golf took root and the membership grew. Women began to play along with the men. Kempton believes Americans tend to take everything to excess. Every aspect of "White Brook," the imaginary club, grew and became more expensive. Kempton notes that in the old days, members played in "rough and comfortable clothes," but by the end of the twenties, players needed "plus fours," matching sweaters and hose, chamois gloves, leather windbreakers, rubber cape coats, and every new device to improve your swing. Manufacturers saw the simple game of 1900 as a place to sell things to an affluent clientele.

At White Brook, the members grew disenchanted with the early clubhouse. They decided to buy more land for the clubhouse, and they began to sell lots on the edge of the club property to pay for it. Soon they were adding onto the clubhouse. By the end of the 1920s, White Brook, once a simple male golf club, had women members, a skating rink, house lots for sale, a toboggan run, tennis courts, and a new caddie house. Many of the additions had one goal: to expand the use of the club by the whole family.

The costs were enormous, but Kempton claims that in the twenties, the members were "as happy as larks." But then, late in 1929, the curtain began to gently fall on the happy 1920s. Resignations from the club increased, membership drives failed, and the club began to offer bargain memberships. By the end of 1932, White Brook was in profound financial trouble.

The essay ends with Kempton's account, again fictionalized, of the 1933 annual meeting. Barely 10 percent of the membership attends. Those in attendance hear some sound advice from an old gentleman who joined the club in 1900. He claims that golf is not a rich man's game, but that it had become one at White Brook. His program calls for a return to the simple days of 1900. Shut the clubhouse and fire all but ten of the caddies, who will only work for players over seventy. Members should do much of the course maintenance themselves. The members can no longer have a country estate, but they can have a Spartan, austere golf club. Kempton vaguely suggests that the mindless expansion of his club had something to do with the arrival of women. The old club of 1900 was a simple male place; the club of 1927 was a family affair, aristocratic and feminized.

In a 1934 *Golf Illustrated* essay, the New York newspaperman George Trevor was not so subtle. He begins with a question: "How do you like your golf? Simple, home-spun, unadorned, with emphasis on the game and its good fellowship, or dolled up in sybarite luxury, embellished with such extravagant and exotic side-shows such as swimming pools, billiard rooms, banquet halls, a solarium, Turkish baths, formal drawing rooms, dance pavilions, and all the other flamboyant accessories which have distorted the original purpose of a golf club."

Trevor favors simplicity. For him, simple golf clubs were done in by "the opulent boom era." This process had a lot to do with women. Trevor sees the old austere clubs as "emasculated" after the war. They lost their "virile qualities" and were "sickled over with feminine fripperies." For women have been "chiefly responsible for the sumptuous excrescences which have transformed golf clubs from plain, unvarnished hang-outs for the devotees of Scotland's game into palatial country clubs." In the new, transformed clubs, men are afraid to "sit in the Louis XV chairs"; they crave a "a soft yet substantial Morris chair." Perhaps most important, a man wishes to be able to "swear like a boatswain if he chooses." The presence of women inhibited this desire. The Depression will tend to create more male-oriented places and peel back the excesses of the roaring twenties. Trevor believes that "the pendulum is swinging back to the bread and butter of recreation after an orgy of pink-iced angel cake."

Thus it was clear that the thirties did more than merely shrink the golf community. As American culture took stock of itself, there was a sense that, during the twenties, things had gotten out of control. There had been too much money, and too much of that money had been spent foolishly. In golf this theme had played itself out in a number of forms. Equipment and clothes had become too expensive—too much cashmere and leather. The most crucial issue was the venue upon which the game was played. From the beginning, there had been two tendencies when it came to courses. One was the simple golf club where the clubhouse was merely functional, and the emphasis was on the course and the game. The second was reflected in the evolution of the American country club. These clubs were significant business enterprises, where land sales and future appreciation of club property was too often uppermost in a member's mind. At the American country club, the game was linked with the social aspirations of affluent American families. The golf course became just one of a number of amenities. The country clubs of the twenties became a way for affluent Americans to have, collectively, a country estate and to take on aristocratic pretensions.

During the 1930s the basic rules under which the game was played were fundamentally stabilized and simplified. Two decisions by the USGA, concerning the ball and the number of clubs allowed, created a stable platform that, to a great extent, has lasted to the present. Late in the 1920s, the USGA grew concerned about the great distances the best players could drive the ball. From 1921 to 1931, the dimensions of the official ball were set at 1.62 inches in diameter and 1.62 ounces in weight. In 1930 the USGA tried an experiment with a lighter ball, and the results were not good. Ordinary players disliked the ball because they believed it reduced the distance on full shots. While the better players seemed to lose no distance at all, people began to call it the "balloon ball." In November 1931, the USGA announced that starting on January 1, 1932, the official ball should not be less than 1.68 inches in diameter and weigh no more than 1.62 ounces. This left ball makers with considerable latitude to make a ball either larger or lighter than the official standard. As any contemporary player knows, this hardly ended the debate about the ball, perhaps the most important piece of a golfer's equipment.

In January 1937 the USGA made another even more basic ruling. Starting a year hence, on January 1, 1938, players would have to make do with a maximum of fourteen clubs. Up to this point, players were allowed any number of clubs; the only limitation was the ability of the player or caddie to lug the clubs around the course. Some very good players, Chick Evans, for example, played and won major events with seven or eight clubs. The ruling came as players and club manufacturers began to experiment with an ever-increasing number of clubs. The USGA thought that "shot making" skill was being taken out of the game by the growing number of clubs. Some players carried as many as thirty clubs. The limit on clubs applied, of course, only to championships; the weekend golfer was still free to employ as many clubs as he or she could get the caddy to carry.

Over time, however, the fourteen-club limit has become virtually universal. Players at all levels accept it as a basic condition of play. I have seen few players, in any context, carry more than fourteen clubs. Fourteen has become, like nine, eighteen, and seventy-two, one of golf's basic numbers. This does not mean that within the fourteen-club limit anything like a standard set was created by the USGA edict. Certainly, a player would find in the 1930s pro shop something like a standard set. It would include four woods, eight irons, and a putter. Over the years, the number of woods has decreased; the two-wood, or brassie, has virtually disappeared. The iron set has come to include as many as four specialized wedges for short shots. This proliferation of wedges also began in the thirties, when Gene Sarazen invented the sand wedge. In doing so, Sarazen took some of the terror out of bunker play and clearly made the game easier. Today one of the little joys of golf is manipulating your frame of mind by subtracting a club (a one-iron, a two-iron) and adding a new, useful implement (a five-wood, a utility club, a lob wedge), all within the fourteen-club limit.

High-level competition during the early thirties entered what might be politely referred to as a lull. The number of lesser events contracted, and in the major events, no compelling figures appeared. Attendance went down as hard-pressed spectators found cheaper alternatives, or simply gave up being fans until the economy improved. Golf missed Bob Jones, and it missed Hagen, who faded rapidly after 1930.

There were some high points. Gene Sarazen had a spectacular year in 1932. He won the British Open at Prince's, a course next to Royal St. George's in Sandwich. This victory came with one of the great caddy stories in golf history. In 1928 Sarazen had purchased from Hagen, for two hundred dollars, the right to employ Old Daniels, a legendary caddy at Royal St. George's. Sarazen played superior golf, except on one hole: the fourteenth at Royal St. George's. In the second round, Sarazen hit his drive far left, avoiding the out-of-bounds to the right. Old Dan suggested an iron to get the ball back in play. Sarazen took a wood instead, and barely advanced the ball. He was lucky to take a seven. He lost the tournament to Hagen by two shots.

When Sarazen arrived at Prince's in 1932, he was advised not to employ Daniels. Near seventy, the once great caddy was nearly blind. During the practice rounds Sarazen did not get on well with his new caddy. As the first round approached, the American was mired in a siege of poor form that he blamed on his caddy. He fired the replacement and returned Old Dan to his rightful place. The old caddy acted like a magic spell on his employer; Sarazen's play improved. Sarazen won by five shots. Old Dan died a few months later.

Sarazen returned to the United States and began to tune up for the U.S. Open, to be played at Fresh Meadow Country Club. Since Sarazen had once been the pro at the club, he was quickly installed as one of the favorites. He played cautiously in the first two rounds and it did not work; he was trailing badly. In the middle of the third round, he changed his approach and began to aim for the pins and go for broke. A third-round 70 got him back in the tournament. His 66 in the last round gave him the title. He would come close again, but Sarazen would never win another national title.

In both the wins in 1932, Gene carried his new creation, the sand wedge, in his bag. It was a simple invention; he had merely added a heavy flange to the bottom edge of a standard nine-iron. Sarazen said that the new club took away his fear of bunkers and made it easier to shoot at pins. Golfers everywhere noted Gene's success in 1932 and began demanding sand wedges for themselves. The manufacturers were happy to oblige.

A final word about Sarazen: he first attracted notice with his Open win in 1922. From that point until his death, in 1999, Sarazen was a significant and positive figure in the golf community. A man with little formal education, Sarazen came literally to personify class, civility, and personal charm. Golf has had no better ambassador. Coming from a humble Italian background, Sarazen, together with Hagen, proved that a golf professional could be more than a humble employee of a golf club. Sarazen represented the game that made him famous with class and humility for over *seventy* years.

Sarazen's fellow pros in the 1930s were, for the most part, fine fellows, but they lacked the qualities of Hagen, Sarazen, and Jones. In describing the pros of the thirties, Herbert Warren Wind (who saw them all) wrote, in *The Story of American Golf*, "There was no denying the skill of the young men who had become leaders in professional golf, but when it came to color and the ignition of personal ardor, the new stars couldn't hold a candle to the old boys." Of Ralph Guldahl, who won two U.S. Opens in a row, Wind thought he "was sensationally dull to watch, but steady as rock." There were "comers" sure enough, but they would blossom later. The age of Jones and Hagen would be followed, after more than a decade-long lull, by the age of Nelson, Hogan, and Snead. Herb Wind did make several interesting and important points about the infant PGA Tour in the thirties. He presented the earnings, in dollars, of the top twelve money winners for the calendar year 1936:

Horton Smith	7,884
Ralph Guldahl	7,682
Henry Picard	7,681
Harry Cooper	7,443
Ray Mangrum	5,995
Jimmy Thomson	5,927
Jimmy Hines	5,599
Gene Sarazen	5,480
Byron Nelson	5,429
Johnny Revolta	4,317
Tony Manero	3,929
Ky Laffoon	3,592

Wind then offered an objective, eye-witness-based account of how they played and what factors were shaping the game at the very top. First of all, he noted that no player made enough money to distinguish himself. Wind also noted that, almost without exception, the best pros of the midthirties were long hitters. They benefited from new high-compression golf balls and improved steel shafts. The generally lower scores were also the product, until 1937, of the fact that while pros often carried as many as thirty clubs, the sand wedge was clearly the most important. Wind also contended that golf courses were made easier in the thirties: roughs were shorter, fairways improved, and dangerous bunkers removed.

Wind points out correctly that the money list was the product of fewer tournaments, but he also argues that they were "well-paid for their services." In the full context of the time, he is certainly right. Most of the twelve men on the 1936 money list also had club jobs that paid them a salary. They also made money from endorsements and the publication of instructional articles and books. We can put the yearly take of the touring pro into context if we remember that the men who built the Augusta National Golf Course received a dollar a day for their labors.

Wind notes that the fortunes of the touring pro were enhanced after 1936 by the arrival of Fred Corcoran. Born in Boston, Corcoran had been connected to golf most of his life. He caddied at the Belmont Country Club and became the caddie master. He worked for the Massachusetts Golf Association, where he learned to manage tournaments. In 1936 he was hired by Pinehurst to run the press relations at the PGA Championship being held at the resort. This led to a job with the PGA as its tournament director.

Corcoran was very good at his job. He possessed both the ability to work hard and something that might be called marketing genius. Taking advantage of improved economic conditions and the arrival on the scene of new, compelling figures like Nelson and Snead, Corcoran grew the PGA Tour dramatically. In 1936 the tour consisted of twenty-two events; a decade later there were approximately forty-six money events. Total money available in these events had increased six fold. When World War II ended, the American public was actually more aware of the PGA Tour than it had been in 1932.

It's easy to skip over the 1930s as a hard time for the golf community. It was a decade in which many Americans turned against the rich and, to some extent, all businessmen. For some, it was the reckless business class that had caused the Depression and who fought Roosevelt's attempts to help the little guy. And golf was, for many, still the rich man's game, the businessman's game.

Beneath this black-and-white view of things, however, there was another reality. It involved the relationship between work and leisure. The Depression seemed to call for a return to the solid values of the Protestant work ethic. For others, the Depression called for a different attitude, one that put an emphasis on the acceptance of leisure and a reformed attitude toward work.

Many commentators noted that the Depression had not been caused by laziness or a lack of work. In fact, the problem was overproduction. Work in the half-century after 1880 had been transformed by technological and social advances. Humankind had become more productive than anyone prior to the Civil War could have ever dreamed. At Pinehurst, where Leonard and Richard Tufts watched American attitudes toward leisure like hawks surveying a rabbit patch, their newspaper, *The Outlook*, consistently took a radical attitude toward leisure and work. Speaking through the editor, Arthur S. Newcomb, the Tufts articulated attitudes that would have shocked their Protestant ancestors. The paper argued that mankind did not need to work so hard. Science and technology had overcome the problem of production. For centuries the issue had been whether humankind could produce enough. Now the issue was overproduction. Why else were we plowing under cotton and pouring milk down the sewer? Newcomb concluded that the time had come "for men and women to give more hours and thought to leisure and diversion." Of course, when this came about, places like Pinehurst would "take on a new and added importance and responsibilities."

In an *Atlantic Monthly* article, in April 1933, the advertising executive Ernest E. Calkin took a less self-interested view: "It is obvious that the necessary work of the world can now be done in comparatively few working hours." Calkin noted that his first job in 1885 took up sixty-five hours of his week. Since then, the coming of the Saturday half-holiday and the move to the eight-hour day and Daylight Saving Time had dramatically cut into that sixty-five-hour week. But now the rise of leisure had become "a problem." What would men and women do with this time? Calkin believed that Americans, unfortunately, had not turned to authentic play, but instead "[their] playing [was], for the most part, by proxy." In his article, Calkin advocates a childlike sense of play in the citizen who is healthy and active. He praises walking, reading, community work, study, learning, and gardening. Americans, he fears, are becoming addicted to activities that are passive and "destitute of the spirit of play." The movies, radio, and sport spectacles are really not play; they are "distractions" and "amusements." He concludes with a prediction: the future of American civilization will in some sense depend on how we solve the problem of leisure. Will we play ourselves, or will we merely watch and become addicted to "vicarious amusements"? Will we have "paid entertainers" to solve the problem of leisure for all of us?

This debate about leisure had profound relevance for golf. When good economic times returned, would Americans play golf, or would they watch golf? Would they turn increasingly to vicarious experiences, or would they seek to play themselves? There were many developments in the future that would influence this decision, most notably the advent of television. But before we could get to the age of television, all Americans would have to endure another experience as daunting as the Depression—a half-decade of war.

QUESTION TO CONSIDER

- Why were people attracted to golf during the Depression of the 1930s?

PART V

World War II Morale

1941–1945

A 1942 photo of Glenn Miller.

CHAPTER 9

Swing Goes to War

Glenn Miller and the Popular Music of World War II

By Lewis A. Erenberg

Editor's Introduction

The one man who would most inspire the World War II generation with his music was Glenn Miller. Joining the military in 1942, Miller was assigned to lead the 62-man Army Air Force Band. Hearing his songs—"Moonlight Serenade," "In the Mood," or "Sing, Sing, Sing," just to mention a few—boosted troop morale during the war. By mid-1944, Miller toured dozens of bases throughout the United Kingdom. His unfortunate disappearance on December 15, 1944, while flying a single-engine plane in bad weather with two other men over the English Channel to Paris, France, was a tragic loss to the troops and the music world. The following essay looks at the impact Glenn Miller's music had on popular music during World War II.

Swing Goes to War

Glenn Miller and the Popular Music of World War II

By Lewis A. Erenberg

I n September 1942, thirty-eight-year-old Glenn Miller disbanded his successful swing orchestra to enlist in the army. "I, like every patriotic American," he declared, "have an obligation to fulfill. That obligation is to lend as much support as I can to winning the war." Having lived and worked as "a free man," he would use his music to defend "the freedom and the democratic way of life we have that enabled me to make strides in the right direction." In doing so, Miller embodied the wartime ideal of sacrifice for a nation that allowed individuals to succeed and prosper. Besides lifting morale and recruiting GIs, he created a model of patriotic duty and a web of connections between military obligation and an American way of life known by millions of young people.[1]

His sacrifice was real: in giving up the nation's most lucrative band Miller lost millions. The orchestra had broadcast three nights a week on the prestigious Chesterfield Hour, set theater, hotel, and ballroom attendance records, and produced a string of hit records. His Army Air Force (AAF) Orchestra, however, soon surpassed its civilian predecessor. Under Captain (then Major) Miller's command, the AAF Orchestra s forty-two-man marching band, nineteen-person dance unit, radio outfit, string ensemble, and small jazz combo engaged in bond drives, made Victory Discs for the troops, and entertained them at home and abroad. Miller's disappearance in a small plane over the English Channel on 15 December 1944—his ultimate sacrifice—made him a national icon. His story highlights the powerful role that swing played in World War II and helps explain what American soldiers were fighting for.[2]

In going to war, Miller infused the depression's popular music with national purpose. As swing became enmeshed in the conflict, it signified that the defense of popular values nurtured during the depression and imbued with particular conceptions of American life—rather than an ideological or militaristic crusade—would be the basis of the war effort. Indeed, the music played by popular bands was the conflict's music, although the Office of War Information and Tin Pan Alley wanted to produce patriotic songs like those of World War I. Except for "Coming in on a Wing and a Prayer" and "Praise the Lord and Pass the Ammunition," few tunes met the test of popularity. With unity relatively easy to attain because of the unprovoked attack and a clearly defined enemy, it was possible to ideologize the war as a defense of a superior American culture embedded in everyday life. As Miller saw it, GIs wanted "as narrow a chasm as possible between martial and civilian life." Radio, films, records, and big bands made popular music "a great new factor in the American way of life." To the young, listening and dancing to popular bands was "almost as important a part of its daily habits as eating and sleeping," as vital "as food and ammunition." Part of dating, personal freedom, and consumption as well as a measure of ethnic cosmopolitanism, in the minds of young people big band music was firmly associated with the benefits of American life. Hence Miller's proposal to streamline military music and lift morale with swing met with conditional government acceptance.[3]

Big band swing heralded the triumph of modem urban culture during the 1930s as jazz-inflected dance music appealed to a mass audience composed of black and white middle- and working-class college and high-school students. As first played by King of Swing Benny Goodman, the music made the rhythm and soloing of black jazz palatable for whites. Arrangers provided for jazz solos and individual players improvised, but with the power of the group behind them. Audiences did hot jitterbug steps that freed their bodies, and flew through the air transcending earthly reality. Or they listened intently as each soloist acted as an agent of his own fate while the band took them to new levels of ecstatic release from the demands of organized society and of families worried about the depression. In relations between the sexes, swing offered sensuous movements, and the band singers expressed an ironic rather than a sentimental approach to love. As utopian alternatives to the world around them, the bands of Count Basie, Benny Goodman, Artie Shaw, and Charlie Barnet held out a more inclusive vision of American culture. Created largely by urban blacks and the children of immigrants, the bands were exciting examples of big city music and ethnic pluralism. And despite a segregated music business, Goodman pioneered the integration of black musicians in white bands ten years before organized baseball hired African Americans.[4]

Miller's achievement lay in taking the safest parts of this youth culture to the war. His military career lay atop his civilian accomplishments, which had codified swing, polished its jazz elements, and used it to paint an idealized picture of American life. In his person and his art, Miller blended swing with more traditional conceptions of national life and made it acceptable to a vast audience. Unlike most other swing band leaders, Alton Glenn Miller had roots in the "typically American" farms and small towns of the West and Midwest. Bom in Clarinda, Iowa, in 1904, he grew up in Fort Morgan, Colorado, where his itinerant handyman father and prohibitionist mother, head of a WCTU chapter, instilled in him values of self-control, persistence, and success. Miller's heroes were Horatio Alger and Theodore Roosevelt, and he hungered for musical and commercial success. He took up the trombone as a youngster, and after two years at the University of Colorado he left to turn professional. Discovering jazz in the 1920s, he played with the best white musicians in the Ben Pollack Orchestra. When his career took him east in 1928, he became an enthusiastic New Yorker. There he played in top bands, freelanced in radio and recording studios, and enjoyed big city life. A midwesterner who achieved his musical identity in New York, Miller fused disparate traditions to create a type of swing that had national appeal.[5]

Miller made swing all-American by merging the two popular music strains of the 1930s—adventurous swing and romantic, more melodic sweet music—into a powerful amalgam. Once he decided he would never outswing Goodman, Shaw, or Count Basie or best Tommy Dorsey on the trombone, Miller went on to his strength—arranging and organizing the talents of others into a more unified, romantic sound. The result was a synthesis: "sweet swing," a clean-cut version of jive suitable for expansion into the nation's heartland via jukeboxes and radio. Tex Beneke, the band's singer-saxophonist, noted that Miller was successful because the public "liked sweet ballads, reminiscent melodies, sentimental words. He found that it liked new pleasant sounds which did not clash." Miller succeeded by taking the standard swing motif—setting brass against reeds over a four-four rhythm section—and using clarinetist Willie Schwartz to play lead melody over the other reeds. These woodwinds smoothed out the sound, giving a "silvery," romantic context to the swing beat. Uniting adventure and security, the Miller style took the edge off the hard-charging Goodman approach and made it comfortable for less experienced dancers.[6]

In his desire to draw large audiences, Miller codified the major elements of big band performance with taste and ingenuity. When all elements worked, the band was a flexible, exciting, and beautiful soloist. "I haven't a great jazz band, and I don't want one," Miller told *Down Beat*. "Our band stresses harmony." Years of legitimate study "finally is enabling me to write arrangements employing unusual, rich harmonies, many never before used in dance bands." At the same time, he organized his band according to a "formula" or, in Gunther Schuller s words, a "sound world." He used his formidable leadership ability and arranging skill to create a totally streamlined sound built on everyone's fitting into an arranged concept. He frowned on long solos, and even hot choruses had to be the same in arrangements imposed from above. He demanded ensemble perfection rather than "one hot soloist jumping up after another to take hot choruses." One critic noted that "the band solos more than any one individual in it." As a result, though, the band suffered from a stiff rhythm section. As trombonist Jimmy Priddy put it, "If you're not going to be a little sloppy, you're bound to be stiff. And that band was stiff!"[7]

Creating a uniform sound required patriarchal authority and discipline. An extremely image-conscious corporate executive, Miller demanded perfect deportment and perfect notes. Musicians had to have everything "just right," recalled trumpeter Billy May, uniform, neckties, socks, handkerchiefs, "or else you'd be fined." This fit the music too. "He would hit on a formula and then he would try to fit everything into it. There was no room for inventiveness. Even the hot choruses were supposed to be the same. [Arranger] Jerry Gray was perfect for the band. He followed the patterns exactly." His insistence on band uniformity and his "sharply disciplined routines bugged many of the musicians." According to singer Chuck Goldstein, Miller "was always the General. Everybody knows what a disciplinarian he was."[8]

Although his commanding style angered some musicians, many players and fans appreciated his authority and patriarchal air, which later enhanced his stature as an air force officer. His aura of fatherly reassurance and authority was heightened by modesty and stoicism that helped him overcome the many problems that plagued traveling bands. He was a confident model of masculinity, capable of meeting any uncertainty. Tall, "bespectacled and scholarly looking," he "was a commanding guy, youthful but mature," according to his press agent, Howard Richmond. As he noted, Miller "looked like security, like all the things Id never found in a band leader." True, "Mickey Mouse band leaders looked like security. I'm talking about jazz leaders. To me they always looked like they didn't know where they were going to sleep the next night." Seventeen-year-old singer Marion Hutton concurred. As her legal guardian, "he was like a father. … He represented a source of strength. … He fulfilled the image of what a father ought to be." As a leader and organizer he brought these same traits to jazz, making it clean-cut and respectable, less a challenge to society than one of its commodities.[9]

Similarly, Miller's hits combined big city swing with the currents of a more stable and conservative Midwest. Music critic Irving Kolodin noted that Miller had "a kind of inland sentiment that differed considerably from the 'big town' aura that pulses in Ellington or Goodman." For example, his best-known swing numbers like "In the Mood," "Tuxedo Junction," "String of Pearls," and "Pennsylvania 6–5000" reveled in big city excitement and sophistication. At the same time, the band was known for music about distinctively American regions and symbols: "Dreamsville, Ohio," the folksy "Little Brown Jug," "[I got a gal in] Kalamazoo," and "Boulder Buff." In 1941 "Chattanooga Choo-Choo" became the first song to sell a million records by combining a thrusting train imagery and a "carry me home" theme. In fact, "Chattanooga" was the first popular song hit since 1935 to yearn for the old hometown. "Don't Sit under the Apple Tree" also conjured up a small-town couple hugging in the backyard. In Miller's music, the romantic context and the small-town imagery made freedom less open-ended and more the product of typical American places and settings, found somewhere in a harmonious past. During the war, audiences could defend those real places, not just some abstract ideal.[10]

Figure 9.1 Captain Glenn Miller shortly after his enlistment. Courtesy of the Glenn Miller Archives, University of Colorado, Boulder.

Besides merging swing and sweet, city and town, Miller consciously sought to build an all-American team that fused the ethnic big city and the Protestant heartland. A New Yorker with a midwestern face, glasses, and a folksy tinge to his voice, he recruited clean-cut all-American musicians and singers like Tex Beneke and Marion Hutton. Initially Miller introduced Hutton as Sissy Jones, which he felt connoted "apple pie, ice cream and hot dogs better than Marion Hutton did," and dressed her to emphasize her American look. Yet Miller's concept of an orchestra was still a pluralistic vision of an all-American team. The Modemaires, his singing group, included a Jew, a Catholic, a Presbyterian, and a Christian Scientist. This sense of a mixed group applied to the musicians too, whom he stereotyped. "Italian trumpeters," he said, "seldom play good jazz," but they made "great lead men." He also would quote Ben Pollack's remark that "you can't have a good band without at least one Jew in it." Hence the Miller all-American team, like his "sweet swing," included big city ethnics, but in an idealized middle-class depiction of the nation.[11]

Black musicians, however, played no role in this homogenized assemblage. The band used the energy of black jazz but, unlike the harder-swinging Goodman, Shaw, Barnet, or even Jimmy Dorsey, employed no black players. Eddie Durham wrote arrangements for "In the Mood," but Miller never allowed black musicians onstage. His racial conservatism probably derived from his desire to attract the largest possible white audience and his lack of sympathy for rough improvisers and gritty musical expression. Including blacks would have disrupted the band's carefully tended image and total streamlined sound and denied the orchestra bookings at top hotels and ballrooms that were segregated. His personal predilections fit well with army policy, which maintained strict segregation in service bands. In the expanded all-American team, blacks stayed on the bench while a polished black music played a prominent role.

As Miller hoped, the music appealed widely to white teens. Jitterbug dancers loved his medium tempo, which, unlike Goodman's frantic style, allowed them to do lindy hop steps with ease. As a result, jitterbugging spread rapidly in the 1940s. As a reviewer described it, "The frenzy and the ecstasy he created in the auditorium" seemed to be "a case of eveiy emotion for itself and it stirs other emotions as well as other individuals to be up and doing—and shouting." For middle-class youth the music was a romantic backdrop for dating and for establishing independence from one's family. But swing's appeal transcended class lines. As one working-class Polish American noted, his parents did the polka, but "Miller was the music of [his] generation." For him and his ethnic friends swing was the door to new personal and American identities.[12]

The war brought this popular music into the conflict on an unprecedented scale as part of the attempt to define national objectives and create national unity around familiar symbols of everyday life. According to Broadway impresario Billy Rose, show business had to "make us love what is good in America and hate what Hitler and the minor thugs around him stand for," including the Nazi suppression of jazz, popular music, and American films created by "inferior" black and Jewish races. In this context, swing symbolized a war to defend an American way of life under attack.[13]

As central figures in the youth culture of swing, Miller and other big band musicians helped make the music of the home front a vital part of the war. Many enlisted or were drafted, and they were permitted to lead or perform in military musical units. Moreover, the government and the army cooperated with the music industry to bring popular music to the troops. Victory Discs, for example, brought together musicians, singers, music publishers, record companies, the American Federation of Musicians (AFM), and radio executives under armed forces leadership to record and distribute popular music overseas. Despite an AFM strike against the recording industry, union musicians were permitted to record for the sole benefit of the troops. "Wherever there are American soldiers with juke box and jazz tastes," declared music critic Barry Ulanov, "there are V Discs to entertain them." The newly created Armed Forces Radio helped spread the word, just as the enemy attempted to compete for the allegiance of the troops with the swing-laced radio propaganda of Tokyo Rose and Axis Sally.[14]

Of all the popular bandleaders, Miller played an especially important role as he created a military version of his sweet swing, all-American band for battle against the Nazis. Under the leadership of a reassuring father figure who had sacrificed profit for duty, the military band smoothly melded civilian values and military goals in a common cause. Miller's swing was capable of turning the rigidly old-fashioned army marching band into a modernized emblem of cosmopolitan American society. "The interest of our boys lies definitely in modern, popular music, as played by an orchestra such as ours," he declared, rather than in their fathers' music, "much of which is still being played by army bands just as it was in World War days." In a letter to Brigadier General Charles D. Young, Miller offered to "do something concrete in the way of setting up a plan that would enable our music to reach our servicemen here and abroad with some degree of regularity." An army band under his leadership might put "more spring into the feet of our marching men and a little more joy into their hearts."[15]

Yet his most ambitious plans clashed with those of the army. Relying on his arranging and organizing skills, Miller initially proposed to transform the entire army band structure with a fourteen-man arranging staff "to provide music for the Army Air Forces Technical Training Command." When army brass vetoed this plan, Miller instead built a modernized super marching band for the Army Air Force Training Corps. Unveiled at the Yale Bowl during a giant bond rally in July 1943, the forty-man band electrified the cadets. Instead of the usual twelve marching snare and bass drums, the band's rhythm derived from two percussionists using complex swing drum kits and two string bass players, who rode in two jeeps that rolled beside the marching orchestra. When they blared Sousa's "Stars and Stripes Forever"—"in jive tempo," charged *Time*—"sober listeners began to wonder what U.S. brass-band music was coming to. Obviously, there was an Afro-Saxon in the woodpile." Other jazz influences surfaced in the swinging marches created out of blues and swing numbers like "St. Louis Blues," "Blues in the Night," and "Jersey Bounce." Music critic George Simon recalled this fusion of jazz and military music as "the loosest, most swinging marching band we'd ever heard," filled with syncopation. "The horns played with zest and freedom, occasionally bending some notes and anticipating others, the way true jazz musicians do so well."[16] Military brass were aghast at the idea of transforming the military band—and by implication the army itself—into a loose, jazzy organization. As United States Army Bandmaster Franko Goldman put it, "Personally I think it's a disgrace! There isn't any excuse for it. But no one can improve on a Sousa march. … My God!" Given official opposition, Miller turned his attention overseas, where his AAF Orchestra raised troop morale with its brand of sweet swing from 1944 to 1946. Although official military march units resisted swing, Miller succeeded in injecting it into the war effort. Few military bands could omit swing entirely, since modem troops demanded the personally freer and more vital music played by cosmopolitan former civilian musicians. As long as they did not threaten military discipline, swing bands were permitted by the army to perform a variety of roles.[17]

At home and abroad, Miller's swing band helped personalize the war for his radio listeners. As early as 1940 his civilian band had broadcast from army camps and dedicated songs to particular units, a practice the AAF Orchestra continued in England. On a Chesterfield program of 1940, for example, Miller dedicated "Five O'clock Whistle" to "the boys" in the "New Fighting 69th," from "around New York way," but now at Fort McClellan, Alabama. "They were among the first to leave in service for our country." Other broadcasts featured a "top tune of the week" for soldiers at various bases. Interspersed were references to other aspects of home: Ebbets Field, baseball, and other bandleaders.[18]

His Armed Forces Network broadcasts also included propaganda playlets that dramatized the Four Freedoms, the official goals of the war, and equated American music with free expression and American culture. Just as the AAF Orchestra served as the ethnic platoon writ large underneath the reassuring baton of a good American leader, its novelty tunes hailed America as a cosmopolitan country. "There Are Yanks" (1944) praised the unity of ethnically diverse Americans in the war effort, linking Yanks from "the banks of the Wabash" to "Okies, crackers," and "every color and creed / And they talk the only language the Master race can read." Miller's weekly broadcasts for the Office of War Information's "German Wehrmacht Hour," beamed from England to the German enemy, also equated a cosmopolitan nation and its music. Using "Ilse," a German announcer, Johnny Desmond's vocals, and German dialogue, the show trumpeted the blessings of music and democracy. After the band played the "Volga Boatmen" on one show, for example, Ilse declared that an American could play any music he liked without "barriers," "whether the music is American, German, Russian, Chinese or Jewish." Miller underlined the point: "America means freedom and there's no expression of freedom quite so sincere as music." The band then did a swing tune by Miller, Ellington, or Goodman.[19]

Figure 9.2 Glenn Miller's AAF Orchestra, somewhere in England, performing in an airplane hangar. Note servicemen sitting atop planes and hanging from the rafters. Courtesy of the Glenn Miller Archives, University of Colorado, Boulder.

The orchestra became the living embodiment of American culture for troops in the European theater. In England the band endured a grueling schedule to bring American music to GIs away from home. They broadcast thirteen times a week over the Armed Forces Network, flew up and down the British Isles for live concerts, performed for special occasions, and recorded Victory Discs. According to one estimate, the band played seventy-one concerts for 247,500 listeners in England, often on makeshift stages in huge airplane hangars. As drummer Ray McKinley noted, the live performances consisted of a seventy/thirty swing to sweet ratio that included the older hits soldiers demanded and a series of army songs like "Tail-end Charlie," "Snafu Jump," and "G.I. Jive," which humorously relieved the pressures of war and reminded GIs that they were defending the nation responsible for such personally liberating music. Audiences wanted familiar music. As Miller put it, "We came here to bring a much-needed touch of home to some lads who have been here a couple of years" and were "starved for real, live American music."[20]

In its ability to recreate familiar and personal ties, Miller's twenty- piece unit became "the most popular band among boys in the service." As a private noted of one concert, "The troops were a cheering mass of swing-hungry GIs. The Joes ate up everything the massive band dished out, most of them in a dream world for an hour or so." But he tired of the repetitious arrangements "that have been played and replayed, all in the same precise, spiritless manner." Miller replied angrily. The musicians might want to experiment, but "we play only the old tunes," because the GIs were away from home and out of touch with current hits, and "know and appreciate only the tunes that were popular before they left the States." Most GIs agreed. One declared that the band pleased millions "who want to hear things that remind them of home, that bring back something of those days when we were all happy and free." The GI wanted "songs he used to know played as he used to hear them played." He looked to music "strictly for its emotional content." Separated from loved ones, facing death, "your pent-up emotions run for just one avenue of escape, an avenue leading to the thing you want most of all, *your home, and all your loved ones and all that they stood, stand and will stand for*" Perhaps this explains why GIs created their own nightclubs and swing bands, and at "mission parties," guys who used to go to Roseland or the Paramount "now knock themselves out to the music of GI bands with the English lassies jumping with 'em."[21]

The look homeward was often nostalgic in the face of death and military regimentation. If freedom was to be achieved, it would be either in the past or in a future after the army. Miller himself gazed backward as his presentiments of death rose and his frustrations with army red tape grew. His radio director recalled, "I don't know of anyone who was as homesick as Glenn." The day before he died he envisioned the postwar world as a suburban ranch home, Tuxedo Junction, a balsa replica of which he carried with him, where he planned to get away, relax, play golf, and devote time to his family. The preoccupation with family togetherness and security, removed from bureaucracy and public purpose, surfaced increasingly in the sweeter, more romantic songs played in person and on "I Sustain the Wings," his radio program. With their lush chords and wafting clarinet lead they established a dreamy remembrance of romantic togetherness and security to be found back home. One of his hit songs put it well: "When I hear that Serenade in Blue / I'm somewhere in another world alone with you / Sharing all the joys we used to know / Many moons ago."[22]

At the center of the homeward gaze was the American woman, who embodied the virtues of American civilization and the personal obligation to defend them. Pinups, according to Robert Westbrook, reminded servicemen of their personal ties to the home front, occasioning emotions of love, lust, and longing. The Miller band acknowledged this in novelty tunes such as "Paper Doll" (1943), a hit for the Mills Brothers, and "Peggy, the Pin-up Girl" (1944). The former speaks of a lonely soldier looking for solace, while the latter chronicles innocent 'Peggy Jones," "with a chassis that made Lassie come home," whose pictures in *Life* and *Look* were carried into battle "all over the world" by American soldiers. The song ends with an explicit statement of obligation: "Pilot to Bombardier, Come on boys, let's drop one here, for Peggy the Pin-up Girl." The band experience itself, moreover, evoked in listeners memories of women and the home front. An RAF pilot remembered the Miller outfit in a smoke-hazed English hangar, crowded "to capacity with uniformed boys and girls swaying gently or jiving' wildly," with the vocalist "singing of love not war." As the band wove its spell, they "were conscious of the music ... the exhilarating rhythm and of course, the girl in our arms ... she was Alice Faye, Betty Grable, Rita Hayworth or whoever our pin up' of that particular week may have been." Perhaps it was sweet-voiced Dinah Shore, on a USO tour with the band, who as a living equivalent of the pinups represented the idealized image of girls left behind.[23]

Women singers and sentimental ballads rose in popularity during the war as they personalized American civilization and the anguish that lay behind the war-enforced separation of the sexes. Women dominated the music audience at home, and they wanted ballads that expressed the pain of waiting for their men to return or the normal life of boys and dating to begin. Under these conditions, love flared intensely, in a race with the relentless march of events. Miller's rendition of Kurt Weill's "Speak Low" conveys passion growing under the pressure of time as the vocalist sings, "Our moment is swift / Like ships adrift, we re swept apart, too soon."

Ostensibly, women waited and thereby symbolized home front faithfulness to the war. The anguish of parting became the subject of "dialogue" songs between soldiers at war and the women back home. Miller's version of "Don't Sit under the Apple Tree" (1942), for example, features a soldier and his girl urging each other to remain true. While he tells her, "Don't go walking down lover's lane with anyone else but me," she demands, "Watch the girls on foreign shores / You'll have to report to me." In Ellington's "Don't Get around Much Anymore," also done by Miller, the singer goes out but finds, "It's so different without you." Often loneliness and frustration led to songs like "No Love, No Nothin' [until my baby comes home]," or "Saturday Night Is the Loneliest Night in the Week." Separation and loneliness also produced pledges of faithfulness by women aimed at soldiers far away, as in "I'll Walk Alone," and "I Don't Want to Walk without You," top hits of 1944. These and many other such songs conveyed the gender disjunctures as girls stayed home and boys went off to war. Both felt the anguish of separation and suspended personal lives.

Sweeter bands and singers able to express the pain of separation and the dream of future togetherness increased in popularity. Harry James s Orchestra, for example, shot to the top in 1942 with a string section, a syrupy trumpet style, and beautiful ballads. One reviewer caught the appeal to an unhappy seventeen-year-old out with a soldier: "Tomorrow he will have gone back to duty and you to the dull, lonely routine of your life without him—waiting, waiting for the day of his return." While James played, "her innermost feelings were taking shape and finding expression, almost as if she had never thought them until that moment." Helen Forrest helped James's rise with increasingly romantic songs of loss and parting. They both had "the same feeling for a song," and her longing for James meshed with the feelings of millions of women. As Forrest put it, her songs "aimed at wives and lovers separated by the war from their men in the service." In a war that set the sexes apart for long periods, women vowed to wait, as in "If That's the Way You Want It Baby," and be the idealization of stability and civilization that men were fighting for. Male singers idealized the "true" woman, as in the Ink Spots' "I'll Get By [as long as I have you]" and the Mills Brothers' "Please wait for me / Till then." In the face of death, both sexes sought peace and security in small pleasures: "I'll Buy That Dream" and when daddy returns, "Shoo, Shoo, Baby" asserts, "we'll live a life of ease."[24]

Under the surface, however, songs of home front devotion and unity contained deep anxieties about sexuality. "Don't Sit under the Apple Tree" and "Everybody Loves My Baby" expressed jealousy and fears about women's sexual activity at home and the lack of home front support for the war. Frank Sinatra brought these concerns to a head as a bobby-soxers' idol who made adolescent girls scream and swoon with sexual fervor. "I looked around at the faces of the girls," noted the narrator of Frederick Wakeman's *Shore Leave*. "It was mass hysteria, all right. Those lads were having a mass affair with Sinatra." In an era of loneliness he gave young girls a vulnerable, dark boy next door as a sex object who expressed their desires. Ballads like "I'll Never Smile Again" and "All or Nothing at All," sung in bel canto style, stretched the emotions to the breaking point and made girls think of clinging forever to their partners. At the same time, as a figure of female desire with a medical exemption from service, Sinatra challenged wartime images of male toughness. He was narrow shouldered and frail, but his appeal to women of all ages was strong. As one girl told *Time*, "My sister saw him twice and she was afraid to go again because she's engaged." Sinatra's songs expressed the hopes of a generation for pure love in a mad world, but his strong sex appeal for women of all ages underscored the fragility of those dreams of home. Moreover, at the USOs and canteens where true women served the cause, they danced with strange men and tested the limits of their faithfulness.[25]

Although sexual tensions remained an undercurrent, it was in the area of race that musical tensions reached their height. Miller's orchestra fed both government purpose and popular desire for unity between home front and war effort, but it was undeniable that for most listeners his home front was white. As part of the goal of including blacks in a unified war effort, the orchestra continued to incorporate elements of black swing, and even particular songs—doses of Ellington, Basie, Fats Waller—into its national musical repertoire. Yet Miller's musical preferences for a clean-cut version of American jive and a sanitized conception of American culture worked with the government policy of military segregation and its desire not to disturb deeply held racial values. As a result, the AAF Orchestra was all-white rather than all-American. Black players remained excluded, relegated to performing in second-class military bands under segregated conditions. By playing black music, however, Miller brought race to the surface of national musical identity.

During the war racial tensions increased in the music world over the meaning of American "home" values. At its simplest, black musicians encountered increasing racial conflict as southern white soldiers and civilians hassled black musicians and entertainers for "race mixing" in the clubs and ballrooms where they played. Black bands, moreover, had problems getting buses, gas, and tires for their tours. Dependent on endless one-night engagements in the South, black bands were forced to abandon their buses and ride segregated trains in which they encountered an endless series of racial humiliations. They no longer reacted quietly. Increasingly, they viewed American society, engaged in a war for democracy, as a hypocritical white supremacist nation. Having ridden the segregated trains and heard tales of black soldiers on leave from fighting for their country who also had had to face discrimination, trumpeter Dizzy Gillespie forcefully expressed his hostility toward white society at his draft hearing and was exempted as psychologically unfit. He refused to accept "racism, poverty, or economic exploitation."[26]

At the same time, the conflicts engendered by a segregated society fighting against a white supremacist enemy heightened the elements in swing that were favorable to racial integration. Black and white radicals and many swing musicians and fans believed that swing carried a vision of democratic community rooted in ethnic and racial pluralism. The war sent conflicting messages to black and white jazz fans about the meaning of American culture. For example, although USO canteens and entertainment units generally were segregated as a matter of government policy, civil rights organizations and white and black progressives in the music and entertainment community established racially integrated Hollywood and Broadway canteens where top bands, among them Benny Goodman's and Count Basie's, entertained free and couples could dance together regardless of race. According to Margaret Halsey, the racially liberal manager of the Stage Door Canteen, the policy was designed "to close the unseemly gap between our democratic protestations and our actual behavior." As a result, she employed black and white hostesses who were instructed to dance with GIs regardless of color. Whereas southern whites often protested, black GIs wrote to her that "we had given them hope for the first time in their lives." Some white servicemen also wrote that "we were the kind of people they were glad to go overseas and fight for."[27]

The discrepancy between defending democracy and the racial realities of American life intensified black attacks on segregation at home. As the *Pittsburgh Conner* put it when Ellington's orchestra was denied hotel accommodations, "It didn't happen in Tokio or Berlin, but right here in the good American city of Moline, Illinois, U.S.A." Music magazines joined the black press in a campaign to recognize Ellington as America's top bandleader and composer and pointed out that he was denied his own radio show and lucrative bookings because of racism. Indeed, the jazz, black, and Left press now protested segregated music venues and audiences as officially un-American.[28]

The black press and African American entertainers did the most to challenge the definition of the home Americans were defending. The *Pittsburgh Courier*, for instance, launched the Double V Campaign for Victory Abroad and Victory at Home and, as part of their efforts, focused on how black entertainers fared at home and abroad in the face of segregation. Black entertainers participated by actively supporting the war effort and openly protesting the segregation and discrimination they encountered. They toured segregated army bases in separate USO troupes, for instance, but objected to performing before segregated audiences. Black bands also appeared in benefits for black soldiers victimized by violence and discrimination. Singer Lena Home played a special role. Because black troops could not have white pinups, she became the unofficial African American pinup queen, who represented what they were fighting for. As part of that mutual obligation, she vociferously refused to perform before segregated army audiences and objected strongly to the army's policy of giving German POWs front-row seats at shows for black soldiers. In many ways, then, black activists, white radicals, and sympathetic black entertainers saw themselves in a fight for a new national identity. It was in this spirit that Duke Ellington launched his Carnegie Hall concerts with "Black, Brown, and Beige," which memorialized black military contributions in the past, and in "New World a Cornin'" held out hope for cultural pluralism and racial democracy as the definition of American freedom in the near future. As the *Amsterdam News* declared, "To accept half a loaf as better than none is silly in the light of what a war is being fought over."[29]

As the realities of war undercut the perfect dreams of racial and gender unity on the home front, the epitome of American culture, the swing band, began to lose its energy. Sweet music enjoyed an upsurge, and the highly organized war effort altered swing. In a total war dominated by large-scale bureaucracy and rigid military hierarchy, swing was no longer an outsider to the establishment. Following Miller's lead, other bands became more organized, arranged, and sentimental, adding string sections to play sweet songs. Miller became an officer, his band a military unit, and his style even more arranged, laid out from on high with less room for invention. The result was a subtle taming of the musical and utopian vision of swing. Ironically, Miller himself resented the struggle he waged with the military brass over the type of band he wanted, and many of his players felt alienated from him as a rigid authority figure who demanded full military discipline. Wary of military distrust of jazz musicians, he wanted his men to conform to military standards. His demand that they shave off mustaches proved the last straw, especially for horn players, who considered this hard on their embouchures. Many other musicians found the military intolerable and turned to more spontaneous traditional jazz as the voice of improvisatory individualism and organic music making. As one observed, "The individuality of a hot musician became a liability when orchestrators, who are the draftsmen of the music business, started to devise arrangements of popular music for bands of twenty or thirty men." In jazz, fans and creators were on the verge of revolt. Hence, although Glenn Miller and his AAF Orchestra conveyed important conceptions about the American way of life, that vision of the home front was a matter of much contention and debate.[30]

Yet Miller's music lived on, rooted in the personal memories of wartime experiences and the collective memory of sacrifice and national unity. Conveying hopes of personal freedom, ethnic assimilation, and security, his band symbolized an American dream of freer lives made possible by American culture. Moreover, his death elevated his personal sacrifice to mythic status. Given the mystery surrounding it, his death became a metaphor for the lost lives and interrupted careers of all GIs. In fact, a year after he disappeared many theaters observed "Glenn Miller Day," the first such tribute accorded a bandleader. Swing remained a symbol of victory too. After his death the orchestra performed a concert for 40,000 allied troops in Nuremberg Stadium on 1 July 1945, marking a victory over Hitler s belief that jazz was a decadent example of a "mongrelized" society and making a statement of the personal and musical freedom accorded by a nation devoted to cultural pluralism. At the National Press Club in Washington, moreover, the country's highest political and military leaders saluted Miller. After the opening bars of "Moonlight Serenade," President Truman and Generals Dwight Eisenhower and Hap Arnold led the assembled dignitaries in a standing ovation for a man who "felt an intense obligation to serve his country" and "made the supreme sacrifice."[31]

Critic George Simon declared that Miller's band was "the greatest gift from home" GIs had "known in all their Army days, a living symbol of what America meant to them, of what they were fighting for." A GI correspondent agreed. Listening to a Miller memorial in an army recreation center in Britain, he "saw men openly crying." The music was "tied up with individual memories, girls, hopes, schools. It's a tangible tie to what we are fighting to get back to." But the message was ambiguous. "We haven't forgotten, nor can we ever. You owe these guys when they get back, not so much money or gadgets, but a shot at the way of life that many of them have been dreaming about." Given a war fought for personal obligation, many soldiers expected a national commitment to their own personal enjoyment of that life in the future. For soldier boys and the girls they left behind, the attempt to capture and define the American way of life would dominate the late 1940s. For many it represented personal dreams and family security removed from public life and bureaucracy; for others it meant opportunities for young ethnic boys and girls to have a place in American life; for many blacks it meant "victory at home" or rejection of that way of life as racially restrictive. These conflicting themes would shape the postwar jazz scene, which became a battle for America's musical soul at the very time the nation embarked on "a sentimental journey home."[32]

Notes

1. Miller quoted in Frank Stacy, "Glenn Miller Day Boosts Bond Sale," *Down Beat*, 15 May 1945, 14.

2. George Simon, *Glenn Miller and His Orchestra* (New York, 1974), covers Miller's career. See also *Current Biography*, 1942, 597–99. On his music, see Gunther Schuller, *The Swing Era* (New York, 1989), 661–77. On political obligation linked to personal ties and consumption, see Robert B. Westbrook, " 'I Want a Girl, Just Like the Girl That Married Harry James': American Women and the Problem of Political Obligation in World War II," *American Quarterly* 42 (1990): 587–614. For the strongest statement of this, see John Morton Blum, V *Was for Victory* (New York, 1976).

3. Glenn Miller, "Travel's Tough but the Jazzmen Hit the Road for Army Camps," *Daily Worker*, 3 July 1942, 7. On the Office of War Information's campaign for "war songs," see John Costello, *Virtue under Fire* (Boston, 1985), 120–21. For Tin Pan Alley, see *Variety*, 5 January 187.

4. James Lincoln Collier, *Benny Goodman and the Swing Era* (New York, 1989), and Benny Goodman with Irving Kolodin, *The Kingdom of Swing* (New York, 1939), cover Goodman's career. Lewis A. Erenberg, "Things to Come: Swing Bands, Bebop,

and the Rise of a Postwar Jazz Scene," in *Recasting America*, ed. Lary May (Chicago, 1989), 221–45, examines the utopian side of swing in greater depth.

5. The phrase "typically American" is in "Glenn Miller," *Current Biography*, 1942, 597.

6. "New King," *Time*, 27 November 1939, 56; Barry Ulanov, "The Jukes Take over Swing," *American Mercury*, October 1940, 172–77, details the jukebox's role in Miller's rise. Tex Beneke, "Swing Was Never Really King," *Metronome*, February 1947, 20–21.

7. For "King of Swing," see "Room at the Top," *Time*, 8 January 1945, 76; Dave Dexter Jr. "I Don't Want a Jazz Band,' " *Down Beat*, 1 February 1940, 8; Irving Kolodin, "A Tonefile of Glenn Miller," *Saturday Review of Literature*, 1953, 63, in Miller file, Institute of Jazz Studies, Rutgers, Newark. *Current Biography*, 1942, 597, and Simon, *Glenn Miller*, 238, 246, for discipline. Priddy is quoted in Simon, 219.

8. Billy May quoted in Simon, *Glenn Miller*, 232; Chuck Goldstein quoted in Simon, 245–46. Tommy Mace, in Mort Good, liner notes to *The Complete Glenn Miller*, 3 (1939–40) (RCA-Bluebird Records, 1976), recalled that musicians considered Miller "a boy-scout leader" and noted Glenn's desire to be called "'Skipper' or 'Captain' or something like that. And that was before the war. Discipline was terrible in that outfit. Rough." See Schuller, *Swing Era*, 671–73, for more on the Miller sound world.

9. For Richmond, see Simon, *Glenn Miller*, 135; for Hutton, Simon, 139.

10. Kolodin, "Tonefile of Glenn Miller," 63. "Choo Chugs to Million Mark," *Metronome*, February 1942, 11. Norman Charles, "Social Values in American Popular Song" (Ph.D. diss., University of Pennsylvania, 1958), 77–78, notes the homeward direction of songs of the 1940s.

11. Simon, *Glenn Miller*, 184.

12. For Cleveland theater, W. Ward Marsh, *Cleveland Plain Dealer*, 10 January 1942, n.p., as quoted in John Flowers, *Moonlight Serenade, a Bio-discography of the Glenn Miller Civilian Band* (New Rochelle, N.Y., 1972), 404. Interviews with Theodore Karamanski, "Big Ray" Murray, Trudy Faso, Lawrence McCaffrey, all in author's possession.

13. Billy Rose, " 'Escapology' Not the Answer, Showmen Must Sell Americanism to Everybody," *Variety*, 7 November 1942, 28.

14. "Pacific Tour for Bob," *Metronome*, October 1944, 9; Barry Ulanov, "The Air Force Jumps!" *Metronome*, May 1944, 15. See also Harry Jaeger, "Buzz Bombs and Boogie Woogie," *Metronome*, May 1945, 11, for bands in England. Frank Mathias, *G.L Jive: An Army Bandsmen in World War II* (Louisville, Ky., 1982), for a swing musician in

the army. Barry Ulanov, "V Discs," *Metronome,* May 1944, 20–21. Bob Klein, who soldiered in New Guinea, told me about Tokyo Rose. For Axis Sally see Robert and Jane Easton, *Love and War* (Norman, Okla., 1991), 243.

15. Miller to Brigadier General Charles D. Young, 12 August 1942, quoted in Simon, *Glenn Miller,* 311–12.

16. Miller to Jerry Gray, quoted in Simon, 324; for the marching band, 311–12; Simons reaction, 337–38, 349–52. *Time,* 6 September 1943, 48–49.

17. Goldman quoted in "Sousa with a Floy Floy," *Time,* 6 September 48–49. See also "Letters," *Time,* 27 September 1943, 4.

18. For broadcasts, see Edward Polic, *The Glenn Miller Army Air Force Band, Sustineo Alas/I Sustain the Wings* (Metuchen, N.J., 1989), 1:3, 714.

19. Polic, *Glenn Miller Army Air Force Band,* 1:51; 2:1027. Examples of the "Wehrmacht Hour" can be heard at the Glenn Miller Archives, University of Colorado, Boulder.

20. For number of performances, Simon, *Glenn Miller,* 369. Miller to Simon, quoted in Simon, 361. On the repertoire, Ray McKinley, "Ooh, What You Said Tex!" *Metronome,* March 1947, 19, 39–41.

21. Pfc. David B. Bittan, "Miller over There," *Metronome,* September 26–27; Miller to Simon, September 1944, quoted in Simon, 384–87; a GI, "Miller a Killer," *Metronome,* November 1944,15. Pvt. William Piatt to *Metronome,* April 1945, 4–5, also extolled Miller's ties to home. Jaeger, "Buzz Bombs and Boogie Woogie," 11, for mission parties. For nightclubs on North African bases, see *Depot Dope,* 29 September 1.

22. Don Haynes, *Diary,* quoted in Simon, 406–7; discussion of Tuxedo Junction, 375–76. For radio repertoire, Polic, *Glenn Miller Army Air Force Band.*

23. RAF pilot quoted in Costello, *Virtue under Fire,* 130–31. Westbrook, "I Want a Girl."

24. Helen Forrest with Bill Libby, *I Had the Craziest Dream* (New York, 1982), 128–37. Richard Lingeman, *Don't You Know There's a War On?* (New York, 1970), 210–21, for World War II songs.

25. David Ewen, *All the Years of American Popular Music* (Englewood Cliffs, N.J., 1977), 430–65, for ballads and singers during the war. Gene Lees, "The Sinatra Effect," in *Singers and the Song* (New York, 1987), 101–15, analyzes Sinatra. Dana Polan, *Power and Paranoia* (New York, 1986), 124–127, explores the sexual tensions around Sinatra. "That Old Sweet Song," *Time,* 5 July 1943, quoted in Polan, 126–27; Frederick Wakeman, *Shore Leave,* quoted in Polan, 125. For more on sexual conflicts, see Elaine T. May, *Homeward Bound* (New York, 1988), and her chapter in this volume.

26. Dizzy Gillespie, *To Be, or Not ... to Bop* (Garden City, N.Y., 1979), 119–20.

27. Margaret Halsey, *Color Blind: A White Woman Looks at the Negro* (New York, 1946), 11–13, 31, 33–34. For USO policy, *Amsterdam News,* 22 May 1943, 14. For more on this, see Bruce Tyler, *From Harlem to Hollywood* (New York, 1992), 137–70.

28. "It Happened to the Duke," *Pittsburgh Courier,* 18 April 1942, 21; " 'Hurricane' Target for Welter of Criticism," *Pittsburgh Courier,* 12 June 1943, 21; and "To Help Woodard," *Pittsburgh Courier,* 17 August 18, offer examples of the black press's growing militance and the role of entertainment. For the music press, see editorials "Why?" *Metronome,* March 1943, 34; "Because," *Metronome,* April 1943, 5; and "Bouquets," *Metronome,* July 1943, 5.

29. For "half a loaf," see "Billie Holiday and the 'St. Louis Incident,' " *Amsterdam News,* 23 December 1944, 9. See also Tyler, *From Harlem to Hollywood,* 171–98.

30. Rogers E. M. Whitaker, "Eddie Condon," *New Yorker,* 28 April 30.

31. On Nuremberg, Simon, *Glenn Miller,* 423; Press Club, 427–31.

32. Simon, "Glenn Miller Lives On," *Metronome,* March 1946, 14–15; Mike Levin, "When Johnny Comes Marching Home," *Down Beat,* 15 June 1945, 1, 4.

QUESTION TO CONSIDER

• Who was Glenn Miller, and why was his music important to American troops overseas during World War II?

Cover page of the *Daredevil* comic book.

CHAPTER 10

War Victory Adventurers

By James J. Kimble

Editor's Introduction

During World War II, comic books were used as propaganda in its war against the enemy. American children were bombarded with some of our most prominent superheroes, such as Captain America, whose character was tailor-made to support America's war effort. Other superheroes were Superman, Batman, and Wonder Woman, just to mention a few. These superheroes embodied the ideal virtues of American soldiers and demonstrated the courage and resolve needed to fight evil during World War II. The following essay looks at the role comic books played in the art of persuasion of American youth.

War Victory Adventures

Figurative Cognition and Domestic Propaganda in World War II Comic Books

James J. Kimble

T he major comic book houses of the Golden Age found World War II to be a golden opportunity. National Periodicals (later known as DC Comics) shot to prominence by featuring heroic Allied partisans such as Superman, Wonder Woman, Batman, and Flash.[1] One of National's primary rivals, Timely Periodicals (later to become Marvel Comics), countered with a formidable cast of superheroes that included Captain America, Human Torch, and Sub-Mariner. Dozens of other publishers joined in the home-front fun during the war, all in support of a vast campaign of comic book propaganda that showcased a horde of superheroes doing everything possible to vanquish the Axis powers (Murray, 2011; Scott, 2007).

It is hard to believe in retrospect, but one of the most ardent book houses to join this colorful propaganda campaign was Family Comics (later to become Harvey Comics). Founded by Alfred Harvey in 1940, the organization is famous nowadays for its nonviolent, child-friendly fare, including characters such as Richie Rich, Wendy the Good Little Witch, Little Dot, and Casper the Friendly Ghost (Jackson & Arnold, 2007). One can hardly picture such characters taking up arms against the Axis powers, as so many comic book figures did in the 1940s. Yet their Family Comics predecessors did become quite involved in the war effort, as when the organization's Captain Freedom, Black Cat, Green Hornet, and Spirit of '76 fought against injustice in general and Nazi spies in particular (Arnold, 2006).

One of Family Comics' wartime series invites detailed scrutiny, since it began in an unprecedented cooperative agreement with the U.S. Treasury (1942). Dubbed *War Victory Comics*, issue number one in the series emerged in the summer of 1942. The entire booklet was an exercise not only in convincing young readers to purchase war stamps and war bonds, but in showing them ingenious ways to finagle those purchases. Given its direct sponsorship by the government, this issue amounted to an official propaganda message, and an imaginative one at that (Kimble & Goodnow, 2009). But although the Treasury was so pleased with the issue's results that it ordered a second printing, the booklet was destined to become a historical footnote. By early 1943 the government was already turning away from the direct sponsorship of comics and comic books, leaving the cartoon war to be fought by the publishers themselves—and leaving subsequent issues of *War Victory Comics* in limbo (Barkin, 1984).

Family Comics evidently saw potential in the fledgling series, even if it was only because the organization hated to lose the large reading audience attracted by the initial publication. Thus, issue #2—now transformed into *War Victory Adventures* (1943a)—appeared in August 1943, with #3 (1943b) appearing at the end of that year. Both issues featured dramatic and lurid perspectives on the war, with story lines about battlefronts, resourceful civilians at home, treacherous fifth columnists, Nazi U-boats, dauntless undercover operatives, and brave allies at war. To be sure, one cannot consider the continued series to be official government propaganda, since the Treasury was no longer involved in its production. Despite its now-unofficial status, however, the series retained a clear propaganda mission, as it offered young readers a distinctly U.S.-centric view of the war even as it depicted the inevitability of an Allied victory on every front.

War Victory Adventures' multifaceted propaganda story lines concerning the war are particularly intriguing from the perspective of cognitive linguistics. Brian Diemert contends that historical narratives tend to transform "individuals, people, classes, and nations into 'characters,' sometimes caricatures, in a piece of historical theatre." In wartime, he continues, such mythical characters "function within the morphology of the discourse as actors (the belligerents), helpers (the allies), and blocking figures (the axis)" (2005, pp. 24–25). George Lakoff offers a similar perspective, suggesting that war narratives construct antagonistic character roles through the process of "metaphorical definition" (2001, p. 23). In this view, a culture's wartime stories inevitably urge members of the culture to experience "one kind of thing in terms of another" (Lakoff & Johnson, 1980, p. 5) by portraying nation-states in the conflict as metaphorically possessing the traits of a hero, an enemy, a victim, or an ally.

This figurative process allows participants and observers to understand the impossible complexities of modern warfare in simpler terms. No one can fully grasp the countless details, motivations, events, and consequences of international conflict, let alone those involved in a world war. To explain or describe a conflict, then, propagandists and media sources rely on a dramatic shorthand in which countries become embodied actors who personally square off on the battlefield and whose personalities and traits represent the best or the worst in humanity. Of course, nations do not have personalities, and they do not literally stab, strike, or parry with other nations on a field of battle. Yet figurative language allows humans to understand war cognitively this personified way, even though the fact that this understanding is inexact remains obscured. At the same time, the figurative encoding of warfare provides a vital tool for propagandists, who can use it to characterize the actions and intentions of nations at war in strategic ways.

Comic books were a potent vehicle for constituting these sorts of figurative characterizations during World War II. One reason for this potency is that the booklets were widely read on the home front, and not just by children (Waugh, 1947). Another reason was that comic books generally lacked the stigma of official propaganda, enabling them to approach readers who might otherwise have been wary of the booklets' depictions (Murray, 2011). A final reason is that the intimate interaction between the visual and the verbal in such artifacts—what Scott McCloud refers to as the mingling of "*partners* in a dance" (1994, p. 156)—allowed readers "quick entry into another space, one that ... [was] private, fantasy-driven, and lodged within a psycho-emotional and subliminal state" (Legrady, 2000, p. 79).[2] In such a state, readers were wholly open to the metaphoric characterizations and narrative story lines that emanated from the comic book industry's numerous wartime publications.

My objective in this chapter is to draw upon the insights of cognitive linguistics and the developing tradition of comic books scholarship in order to explore the rhetorical means by which the *War Victory Adventures* series, in particular, consti-tuted the varied characters in its imagined war. I contend that the series serves as an excellent case study of the intertwining of metaphoric and narrative cognition in order to posit distinctive national character roles in the unfolding drama of World War II. In doing so the comic books tacitly crafted an epic struggle between good and evil, one that gave readers no choice but to sympathize with the Allied war effort. The following sections of the chapter support this perspective by exploring how the series depicted: 1) the United States and its people as transformed, if plucky, heroes; 2) the Axis powers as contemptible, if dangerous, villains; and 3) allies and occupied nations as praiseworthy supporting players in the drama. In a concluding section, the chapter returns to the symbiotic nature of narratives and metaphors in wartime propaganda, suggesting that comic books were the perfect venue for using such figurative devices to establish and reinforce for millions of home-front civilians a mythic understanding of the war and its eventual outcome.

The Accidental Heroes: Where Courage Met Pluck

The United States did not enter World War II with the same sense of invincibility that it would possess nearly four years later on V-J Day. On the eve of Pearl Harbor, much of the country was still in recovery from the greatest economic depression in national history. While President Franklin D. Roosevelt had won a third term promising that no U.S. boys would be sent to fight in a foreign war, the public itself was bitterly divided between determined interventionists and passionate isolationists. And although the defense program had ramped up significantly throughout 1940 and early 1941, the military was hardly prepared for a global war. Indeed, as Christina Jarvis (2004) points out, even media depictions of the American male body—which would typically become virile and muscular during the conflict—remained visibly weakened and occasionally emaciated in the prewar years.

On one level, then, *War Victory Adventures* represented a radical shift in national self-perception. Its story lines featured numerous roles for Americans, ranging from military servicemen to factory workers to diplomats. There was room for nearly every citizen, regardless of role or gender, to play a heroic part.[3] Each individual contribution in some way added to the construction of the larger, nationwide role of a reluctant-but-heroic United States, a metaphoric figure who personified bravery and resourcefulness in the face of undeniable evil. By portraying various Americans in action on the battlefronts and the home front, in other words, the series constituted a compelling and persuasive portrait of the United States itself as a personified participant in the war's dramatic action.

The key to the series' depiction of its U.S. characters revolved around the notion of *transformation*. In accordance with the comic books' fantastical logic, humble youngsters could become formidable forces on the battlefield, while lovable goofs and ordinary civilians could bravely blunder their way into capturing enemy spies. The crisis of wartime was responsible for precipitating such transformations, effectively turning benign American virtues into extraordinary feats and deadly fighting skills. The resulting characters were one part classic everyman (or every-woman) and one part heroic overachiever—figures well suited to inspiring both the imagination and the behavior of young readers.

The series began this transformative work in the very first story of issue #2. Chickie Ricks is, at first glance, a most unlikely hero—let alone a U.S. Marine aviator (Epp, 1943b). The shy 17-year-old volunteer first appears at home, shaving in the bathroom mirror. His younger brother watches adoringly, even as his mother wonders why Chickie is shaving, since he lacks "enough fuzz to cover a peach!" (Epp, 1943b, p. 2). Downstairs, a group of friends, including a lovestruck Betsy, wait to give Chickie a rousing send-off to boot camp. The protagonist's introverted, hesitant nature is evident in his interactions with Betsy, as well as in his final farewell to friends and family as his train pulls away: "G—g'bye—gosh—!" (Epp, 1943b, p. 4).

Predictably, Chickie's first act upon arrival at boot camp is to wander off, then absentmindedly bump into a fierce drill instructor, Shanghai Joe. Yet a few minutes later, it becomes clear that while the raw recruit might be a bumbling kid, he is also a fierce patriot. After he stumbles into Cloe, the young daughter of the camp's commanding officer, they hear the distant sound of "Taps." Immediately, they stand up for the lowering of the flag. Chickie, hat in hand, says "G—gosh—it sure is the purtiest flag in the world! I—it makes ya proud (gulp) to be an American!" Impressed with his heartfelt sentiments, Cloe intones "Hmm!—you'll do! ... Yes sir, we'll make a real leatherneck out of ya!" (Epp, 1943b, p. 5).

Thereafter follows an intense basic training sequence, with Chickie and his fellow trainees running, climbing, and jumping "from dawn to dark—go!—go!" (Epp, 1943b, p. 5). Soon, Chickie has a noticeable swagger, though he remains shy in front of women. His new toughness appears to give him courage and strength in difficult situations. At one point, for instance, his commanding officer is kidnapped by two Nazi spies. Chickie vaults through a skylight and attacks them, interrupting their torture session. "I saw this in a comic book onct [sic]," he exclaims as he leaps, "maybe it'll work!" (Epp, 1943b, p. 8). In a follow-up story line, Chickie has become a Naval Air Corps cadet, and he dauntlessly leads a squadron of lost pilots through heavy fog to a safe landing (Epp, 1943a). Although he has retained his aw-shucks manner and fierce patriotism, it seems, he has gradually transformed into a confident soldier, one who will make a difference on the front lines for the United States.

A slightly different transformation is evident in the adventures of Deanna Dartmouth, a wealthy American heiress ("Rendezvous with Revenge," 1943). When readers meet Deanna, she is coolly sitting in a Marseille café, watching the locals flee from the invading German army. An American reporter, Paul Delton, attempts to rescue her. However, he soon finds that she is in no danger, because she is engaged to Count Boroux, a noted Nazi sympathizer. The reporter *is* in danger from the invading force, however. He is quickly arrested and dragged to an interview with the Gestapo—but not before he accuses Deanna of being a Nazi sympathizer herself.

Later, the action shifts to the count's swanky celebration party, to which Adolf Hitler himself has been invited. Paul has escaped the Gestapo and watches through a window as both the count and Deanna toast Hitler by exclaiming, "To the new order!" ("Rendezvous with Revenge," 1943, p. 17). Yet when Deanna subsequently invites herself to the Führer's bedroom, she suddenly pulls a pistol from her purse and shoots him. As she and Paul escape the party, she explains her gradual change of heart. She had initially "been thrilled at the thought of being a countess. But when I saw what was happening to the people of Europe, well[,] I got wise to myself" ("Rendezvous with Revenge," 1943, p. 20). She had transformed, in other words, from a would-be sympathizer into a de facto American agent. After coming to her senses, she concludes, "I realized who the enemy was and I went after him!" ("Rendezvous with Revenge," 1943, p. 20).

U.S. characters, to include soldiers and civilians of all sorts, underwent such transformations nearly everywhere in the series. Whether a specific story line involved better fighters, more patriotic citizens, or even super-efficient medics, the underlying message was clear: it was possible and perhaps inevitable that the wartime emergency would turn even the most unlikely citizen into a formidable force in the struggle against evil. Christopher Murray suggests that superhero comic books of this era presented home-front readers with icons "of empowerment through transformation" when they depicted the change "from an ordinary person to a superpowered being" (2011, p. 8). But the transformations among Americans in *War Victory Adventures* quite often did not involve superheroes; rather, the central lesson appeared to be that *anybody* could transform into a productive participant on behalf of the war effort.[4] Considered in the aggregate, this massive series of transformations could only invoke images of a very different United States on the world stage than the impoverished persona of the Depression years. Indeed, in the fantastical war of the popular imagination, this transformed United States was itself a courageous and resourceful figure—doubtless useful characteristics in a deadly fight against the personified archenemies of the Axis.

Awkward Evil: Germany and Japan as Contemptible Enemies

The vast majority of citizens on the U.S. home front never saw an Axis soldier or spy in the flesh. Accordingly, their conception of the enemy's appearance and nature had to be constructed. It should be no surprise to find, then, that propaganda accounts of the Axis enemy were a recurring theme throughout much of the war. Newsreels and Hollywood features portrayed enemy advances and atrocities even as they profiled Axis leaders in an unflattering light (Doherty, 1993, p. 132). Newspaper and magazine articles condemned the enemy as brutal and malignant (e.g., Dulles, 1942). And countless posters featured hulking silhouettes and leering storm troopers menacing vulnerable women and children (e.g., Grohe, 1942/1976; Koehler & Ancona, 1942/1980). If the home front needed suitable villains in order to justify its wartime urgency, ample propaganda was clearly available to provide them.

War Victory Adventures, for its part, presented readers with numerous depictions of the Axis enemy. While the series ignored Italy altogether (a choice not inconsistent with a great deal of the home front's propaganda imagery), it had plenty of room to offer unflattering portraits of the Japanese and German opponents. These portrayals took the form of individual glimpses at the appearance and character of various enemy leaders, soldiers, sympathizers, and spies. Each portrayal, in turn, helped foster the comic books' fantastical composites of those two enemy nations and their nefarious role in the war's dramatic story line.

The series' depictions of the enemy were organized as a relentless campaign of *derision*. The comic book format itself, of course, inexorably encouraged a stereotyped, cartoonish approach to its enmification. The outcome was a series of colorful caricatures and over-the-top portraits of awkward evil, all with an underlying tone of contempt. The resulting enemies were often menacing, to be sure. Yet the comic book writers and artists made certain that the depictions of these enemies never came across as infallible or omnipotent. Indeed, for the series' young readers, it must have been a comfort to feel that the Axis powers had flaws that were both comical and practical.

Family Comics wasted no time in featuring the derisive enemy in *War Victory Adventures*. Both comic book covers presented action-packed scenes in which the enemy's shortcomings were quite apparent. Issue #2, for example, depicted a battle involving an assault by U.S. Marines on entrenched Japanese troops (*War Victory Adventures*, 1943a, cover; see Figure 10.1). Here the Anglo Yanks face off against a thoroughly dehumanized enemy, one with greenish-yellow skin, simian features, claws, and (in one case) batlike ears. The enemy in the image is thus undeniably bestial, even evil. It is also remarkably inferior to the Americans. The Marines in the image visibly surpass the Japanese figures in prowess, equipment, and numbers (witness the reinforcements arriving by ship below). Perhaps more importantly, the Americans show no fear in combat, while the two central Japanese figures display anguish and even cowardice. The small explosive soaring toward the charging Marine does introduce some uncertainty into the picture. Still, there can be no doubt that the American forces in this scene will prevail against their very dangerous but ultimately flawed and unworthy opponent.

The cover of issue #3, meanwhile, amounted to a Family Comics character study of the Germany enemy (*War Victory Adventures*, 1943b; see Figure 10.2). In this drawing, Captain Cross bursts through a wall in order to rescue a captured four-star general. Facing the superhero are two brutish German soldiers, while a third frantically calls for help. Interestingly, the layout and feel of the tableau are strikingly similar to the cover of issue #2. Of course, there are some differences:

...the Yanks charge over the top with their guns barking and.....

READ THE STORY BEHIND THE COVER

Figure 10.1 Family Comics portrays the Japanese enemy (War Victory Adventures.1943a, detail from cover).

the American attacker is alone, the wounded general is a fresh element, and the three Germans are not inhuman.[5] Much as in the other scene, however, these enemy figures are somewhat inept as fighters, and they are decidedly on the defensive. Indeed, the general's smug expression foreshadows the outcome of the scene: Captain Cross will knock these hapless, thuglike Nazis out cold, prevailing despite being outnumbered three-to-one. As before, an American victory against an incompetent foe seems all but guaranteed.

To be sure, the story lines in the series did occasionally remind readers not to take such Axis enemies too lightly. In "Masquerade for Prey" (Cazeneuve, 1943a), for instance, the crew of a Nazi ship consistently uses subterfuge to sink Allied vessels and to avoid capture. In "Attack of the Lone Avenger!" (1943), the protagonist declares that Japanese soldiers are "a bunch of die-hards, if I ever met any" (p. 35). "The Death Mask Mystery" (1943) features Nazi spies who are ruthless—they even go so far as to kill a U.S. naval attaché for military secrets. Finally, in the science fiction-themed "Terror Rides the Waves" (Cazeneuve, 1943b), a fleet of U-boat personnel takes over an underwater city through intimidation and violence—a clear

Figure 10.2 Captain Cross attacks the German enemy (War Victory Adventures., 1943b, detail from cover).

reference to the real-world takeover of numerous cities in occupied Europe. The Axis powers, the comic books frequently stressed, were thus crafty and malevolent; defeating them in the war would prove to be a tremendous challenge.

Interestingly, the series occasionally emphasized the nefarious nature of the enemy by featuring *reverse* transformations. Whereas U.S. protagonists typically underwent a positive transformation, as discussed above, others in the booklet's story lines occasionally transformed from seemingly positive characters into evil ones, thereby warning readers of the enemy's perfidy. In "Grimm, Ghost Spotter," for example, a beautiful German countess turns out to be a zombie intent on killing the protagonist (Weaver, 1943). Elsewhere, in "Peril on the Pampas" (1943), an Argentinian rancher seems, at first, to be a victim of Axis saboteurs who are poisoning cattle meant for Allied soldiers. By the story's end, however, he is unmasked as the local Axis spymaster, and he pays the price for his subterfuge. Through these sorts of startling turnabouts, the comic books were able to emphasize in another way that readers should not take the enemy lightly, despite the obvious weaknesses.

Still, *War Victory Adventures* consistently returned to its derisive style of enmification. German spies and fighting men alike universally utter mangled and even humorous English, as when a U-boat captain congratulates a crew member for sneaking up on an American fighter: "Goot vork, Emil—now bring dot swine below!!" ("Uncle Cal Combats Axis," 1943, p. 46). In comparison, Japanese soldiers in the series lack even rudimentary English skills, as the story lines limit them to impenetrable kanji symbols. This awkward note extends to the enemy's behavior, too. Axis partisans, it becomes clear, not only lack social graces but are also prone to Charlie Chaplin–like pratfalls. The Gestapo agents who haul away Paul Delton in "Rendezvous with Revenge" (1943), for example, can barely get out of each other's way as the reporter escapes. Himmler himself witnesses the farce, screaming, "Vot's der matter with you idiots?" while the struggling Nazi goons desperately yell "Shtop! Shtop!" down the hallway ("Rendezvous with Revenge," 1943, p. 15). Even more telling was the series' use of traditional tropes of comic book violence against the enemy. Almost invariably, American soldiers and even civilians in the story lines were able to knock down, knock out, or kill Axis characters at will.[6] To add insult to injury, *War Victory Adventures'* artists often lingered with evident relish on the falling or unconscious enemy figures. Such imagery reinforced the apparent strengths of Allied characters while it simultaneously underlined the vulnerability and awkward nature of the Axis enemy for readers.

Despite their obviously evil nature and ruthless ways, then, the cartoon enemies in the Family Comics series ultimately emerged as contemptible and fallible. Cord Scott contends that World War II comic books tended to portray the Axis villains as "cunning, psychopathic, and malicious" (2007, p. 334). *War Victory Adventures* made those points, of course, but the series seemed to be even more concerned with emphasizing a thoroughly derisive tone that belittled and ridiculed the Axis powers even as it allowed that defeating them would be quite a challenge. For those on the home front who envisioned the enemy nations as personified states in a metaphoric struggle, such visceral propaganda messages could only reinforce the belief that the Axis opponents were bound to lose if the heroic U.S. and its allies rose to the occasion.

Rounding out the Cast: Victims and Allies at War

At first glance, a standard war narrative might seem to have only two relevant roles: us versus them. In narrative terms, these roles become the protagonist and the antagonist, or just the hero and the villain. Scholars who write in the area of cognitive linguistics (e.g., Diemert, 2005; Lakoff, 2001), however, suggest that two additional roles are typically part of the drama. The *victims* are those players whom the villain has assaulted, or figuratively raped.[7] The heroic nation sees itself as coming to the rescue of (or avenging) that victim. In the course of doing so, the protagonist often enlists helpers, or *allies*. These personified states might well diverge from the hero in a variety of ways. Yet a shared interest in redressing the victims' plight at the expense of the villain pushes heroes and allies together, forcing them to seek common ground.

By the time *War Victory Adventures* #2 (1943a) was published, these roles were well established in home-front propaganda narratives. Nations that had succumbed to Japanese incursions or to the German blitzkrieg featured prominently in such appeals, as in Ben Shahn's well-known 1942 poster informing viewers, "We French workers warn you … defeat means slavery, starvation, death" (reprinted in Pohl, 1993, p. 71). Other messages touted U.S. allies, particularly the United Kingdom and the Soviet Union (the other two members of the so-called Big Three). As before, these sorts of messages gave civilians an opportunity to conceptualize both victims and allies as personified states who were playing memorable roles in the drama of the war—if only in support of the leading players in that drama.

The common theme uniting the comic book series' portrayal of victims and allies was an emphasis on *veneration*. The stirring message for readers was that these nations were praiseworthy for their stalwart nature in the face of overwhelming adversity. Victims in the stories came across as particularly valiant, given their status; the series even seemed to downplay the rescue trope that one might expect in such tales. It was abundantly clear, at least in the view of Family Comics, that both victims and allies in the narrative were resisting the Axis powers in every way possible. Consequently, the series took the time and space to feature inspirational portraits of those characters as a way of praising their vital role in the drama.

The primary victim featured in issue #2 was Norway. German forces had invaded in 1940, afterward controlling daily life in Norway with an occupying force of some 300,000 troops. Despite the occupation, however, the Norwegian government continued to operate in exile, while numerous soldiers and civilians who were able to escape the Nazis served the Allied cause. In the "Masquerade for Prey" story line (Cazeneuve, 1943a)—apparently based on real-life events—first officer David Knudsen and a crew of "grimly determined" (p. 21) Norwegian sailors demonstrated that although their homeland was playing the part of a victim in the war's narrative, its partisans retained a fighting spirit as well as good humor in very trying circumstances. In the story the Norwegians' ship is initially bombed by a German plane in the middle of the Atlantic Ocean. "Well, it could be worse!" ("Masquerade for Prey," 1943a, p. 22) exclaims one sailor, as the crew gamely fights the resulting fire. Not much later, however, a German ship disguising its allegiance by using an Allied flag shells them (as the Nazi captain gloats, "Ja! Ve fooled der dumkopfs completely!" ["Masquerade for Prey," 1943a, p. 24]). Their ship sinking, the Norwegians are forced to use lifeboats to rescue drowning crew members. At length, the surviving sailors find themselves prisoner in the attacking ship's hold. Their good spirits in captivity serve them well, however, as they eventually are able to outsmart their German captors. When the Nazi ship tries to fool a passing Allied convoy by deceitfully flying a Norwegian flag, the real Norwegians wave a white shirt from their porthole to alert the Allies to the masquerade. As Knudsen and his compatriots safely watch the Nazi ship sink a while later, one offers this sardonic comment: "Now ain't that just too bad!" ("Masquerade for Prey," 1943a, p. 26). The sarcastic pity in this statement makes for a fitting final word from a brave and praiseworthy victim who never gave up the fight against his oppressors.

Later in the year, issue #3 (*War Victory Adventures*, 1943b) also provided a detailed glimpse at the venerable characteristics of a narrative victim—but this time the tale took the form of a science-fiction allegory. In "Terror Rides the Waves" (Cazeneuve, 1943b), an underwater city—thriving inside a glass dome—serves capably as a symbol of the many real-world European cities that were still suffering under German occupation. As the story opens, a damaged Nazi U-boat has sunk to the bottom of the ocean. The situation looks hopeless, but the crew is unexpectedly rescued by several people in strange diving suits, who escort them to a submerged, Atlantis-like civilization. Of course, the Germans do not waste time by being grateful for the rescue. Instead, they immediately assault the city's leaders and make plans to use the location as a secret U-boat base.

While the Nazis follow their stereotypically nefarious nature, the city's residents swiftly earn sympathy as victims. They are initially nonviolent and even a bit naive, having misunderstood the evil nature of their new guests. At length, though, they recognize their danger and begin to fight back. "These men kill human beings!" exclaims one outraged resident. "I will kill them!" (Cazeneuve, 1943b, p. 15). In short order, the city has cut off the Nazis' oxygen source and allowed them to suffocate or drown. In a telling scene at the end of the tale, the citizens destroy all of the Germans' guns and equipment, since they "are instruments of evil," belonging to those who "excell [*sic*] only at killing human beings!" (Cazeneuve, 1943b, p. 16). As with the Norwegian sailors, here is a praiseworthy victim who has resisted the Axis onslaught and eliminated the evil threat, thereby restoring a sense of peace.

Meanwhile, the allies in *War Victory Adventures* stories also benefit from consistent veneration. British characters, for instance, are uniformly friendly and supportive in their interactions with Americans—just as the average home-front reader would likely have envisioned them (see Figure 10.3). At times the British do become the target of cultural stereotypes, as when the cartoonists have royal officers wearing pith helmets, using stylish cigarette holders, and uttering phrases like "righto" and "'ol chappie" ("Desert Dynamite," 1943, p. 48). But these portrayals generally come across as good-natured fun and lack the visceral nature of the Japanese and German depictions in the series. The British, it is evident, deserve praise for their consistently supportive nature on behalf of the war effort.

Surprisingly, the most prominent ally to appear in the series was the Soviet Union. Only a few years earlier, of course, the Soviets had not been U.S. allies at all (and in fact had signed an infamous treaty with Nazi Germany). Some comic books from that earlier period even referred to the Soviets as "Mosconians," adopting virtually the same unflattering imagery that was already being used to depict evil German characters (Scott, 2007, p. 327). By 1943, however, the USSR was most certainly not in league with Hitler any longer, and so a recurring point in home-front propaganda focused on reconstructing the Soviets as faithful and stalwart allies (Chafe, 2003, p. 5).

Figure 11.3 The British as supportive ally ("Desert Dynamite," 1943, p. 47).

The story "Blitzkrieg Boomerang!" (1943) developed this reconstructive theme in detail. In it a peasant introduces her young son to Comrades Pavlikov and Olga Sotenko, relating how they saved Stalingrad from a series of secret Nazi rockets.[8] At first, the peasant recalls, the Soviet army is mystified at the nature of the German attacks on Stalingrad: bombs are exploding in the city, but no planes are visible. Lieutenants Pavlikov and Sotenko volunteer to parachute behind German lines to investigate, pretending to be a married couple to allay suspicion. Their general is quite impressed with this plan, telling them (note the flawless English) that "Russia will never fail with men and women like you" ("Blitzkrieg Boomerang!," p. 52).

On their journey to examine the secret weapon, the two Russians teach a guerilla unit how to lure German tanks into an ambush for a deadly "Russian kiss" ("Blitzkrieg Boomerang!," 1943, p. 53). The guerrillas, in turn, equip Sotenko and Pavlikov as fur traders, which allows them to gain unobtrusive access to the Nazis' secret base. The duo soon discovers that the new weapon involves radio-controlled rockets. Using their engineering skills, they manage to reprogram a rocket so that it no longer targets Stalingrad. Instead, at the story's climax, readers see that the Russians have cleverly aimed the German rocket at its own base—which then disappears in a tremendous explosion.

The ingenuity and bravery of the two Soviet soldiers in this story line is palpable, particularly given the virulent U.S. propaganda that had condemned the USSR just a few years earlier. Indeed, except for the differences in their uniforms, one could almost mistake the pair for *American* heroes. For his part, the peasant's son is so impressed with them that he exclaims, "I wish I were a soldier like you!" The pair's reply is telling, as it comments not only on the valor of the Soviet people but on the spirit of the entire Allied cast—victims, heroes, and allies—"We all do what we can, little brother! All our men, women and our children!" ("Blitzkrieg Boomerang!," 1943, p. 55).

In this way, both victims and allies in *War Victory Adventures'* metaphoric construction of the war emerged as praiseworthy for their fierce resistance to the Axis powers. By continuously valorizing these supporting character roles, the series was in effect justifying the virtue of the Allied cause as well as emphasizing the likelihood of an Allied victory. After all, if the courage and effort of Axis victims and American allies were added to the righteous might of the transformed United States, how could the forces of good fail to vanquish the forces of evil in this, the greatest war of all time? In the view of Family Comics, at least, a just end to that war must have seemed inevitable.

Conclusion

Any reader of comic books in the World War II era could tell that the booklets' essential format aimed at telling stories. It is thus no surprise to suggest that *War Victory Adventures* relied on narratives. In fact, there is a sense in which these two comic books—and the thousands of others that appeared on the home front— worked at a fairly literal level of narrativity: here is a character I like, here is one I do not like, here is some action leading to closure, here is the satisfactory end, and so on. Although such an interpretation fails to go beyond the most obvious surface meanings, it is a legitimate way to explain the appeal of a given comic book and the attraction a reader might have to it.

Yet the foregoing analysis has established, I hope, that two additional levels of meaning are present in *War Victory Adventures* and, most likely, in many additional comic books from the home-front years. The first of these levels lies in the same realm in which presidents can envision the Cold War as a poker game between well-matched players (as Harry Truman did) or imagine the first Persian Gulf War as a strategic game of baseball (as George H. W. Bush did) (Larson, 1985; Kuusisto, 1998). This is the realm of metaphoric cognition, a pseudo-reality in which individual characters are but markers that signify the characteristics of a larger group or culture, as when a brave soldier at war comes to represent in the reader's mind the best qualities of that soldier's nation.

In *War Victory Adventures*, every character interacts on the literal level of meaning. Yet when considered in the aggregate, these characters can be seen as symbolically transferring their qualities to the country they represent. This transference is metaphoric, because it uses the traditional character roles from what Lakoff (2001, p. 27) calls the "just war fairy tale" (i.e., hero, villain, victim, helper) as source material to portray specific nations in a new way. One of humanity's most basic cognitive metaphors is states as persons, and the underlying logic of that metaphor is at play here (Lakoff, 1991). It is, then, a fairly simple rhetorical process to, say, identify the United States as a heroic figure, as all that is required is for a propaganda message to transfer ideas from the domain of heroes (brave, stalwart, fights the villain, etc.) to the specific domain of the nation. Both issues in the series embraced this metaphoric process enthusiastically.

There is, however, a third level of meaning in the two comic books, one that is a logical extension of the metaphoric level. As I have suggested, the source domains in the metaphoric realm all stem from traditional war stories, so it makes sense to consider what happens when those roles are established in a reader's mind. The answer, of course, is that the reader can imagine the underlying relationships spinning into narrative action. Just as when a group of playing children knows exactly how each individual should behave when it is decided who will play the cop and who will play the robber, so too does the reader of a tale that identifies heroes, villains, victims, and allies know what to anticipate next. This is the level of narrative cognition, and it is what would have allowed readers of *War Victory Adventures* to imagine with some degree of confidence the successful outcome of the war. After all, comic book heroes (at least those from the Golden Age) nearly always gave readers "a dose of reassurance that good would triumph over evil" (Streb, 1998, p. 12). If Family Comics was right in its apportionment of the war's metaphoric roles, then, the subsequent narrative outcome would likely seem to be a foregone conclusion to many readers.

In the end, *War Victory Adventures* thus combined metaphoric and narrative appeals to adapt the classic trope of good-vanquishing-evil into the specific circumstances of World War II. In doing so, the series presented the war as a dialectical struggle between good and evil. Home-front readers, to be sure, would have had little trouble deciding which side to root for in this colorful struggle. After all, they were themselves Americans. In the world of the comic book series, this single characteristic made them heroic by default—and perhaps even made them ready to become active participants in the war effort. Even if such readers were too young to enlist in the armed forces, they could still contribute by purchasing war stamps, gathering scrap metal, or even helping out at home. As "The Death Mask Mystery" protagonist Inspector Jordan advised a colleague—and, by extension, the comic book's readers—"this is no time to be taking bows! We have to keep punching!" (1943, p. 39). For those young comic book fans who found *War Victory Adventures*' metaphoric and narrative logic compelling, this advice must have seemed wise, indeed.

Notes

1. Of the National/DC superheroes, Batman was the least involved in the war, though Streb (1998) describes a 1943 issue in which both Batman and Robin use the Batplane to help prevent an Axis invasion (pp. 10–11).

2. In the World War II era, perhaps only moving pictures offered a similar synthesis of appeals.

3. It is worth noting that the series featured very little ethnic variation among its U.S. characters; every American character except one appeared to be from a Caucasian background (the exception was a black kitchen worker who appeared in just one panel) (Epp, 1943a, p. 8). Curiously, with the possible exception of Chickie Ricks, a 17-year old U.S. marine, all of the primary characters in the continued series are adults. This is in stark contrast to issue one, which Family Comics coproduced

with the Treasury Department as a means of selling war stamps to children on the home front (U.S. Treasury, 1942). Despite the sudden absence of child characters, the advertisements in issues #2 and #3 make it clear that the series continued to see youngsters as a primary audience.

4. The only exception in the series was the adventures of Captain Red Cross, a typeset story line featured inside issue #3 ("The Story Behind," 1943). The issue's cover also offers a scene from this superhero's story, but it refers to him as "Captain Cross" (*War Victory Adventures*, 1943b, cover).

5. The difference between the two enemies here—with dehumanized Japanese and brutish, though still human, Germans—is consistent with a great deal of home-front propaganda from the time (Kimble, 2005, pp. 209–210).

6. In this sense, the fates of the series' villains are little different than those of the criminals traditionally faced by the likes of Batman and Superman.

7. Lakoff (2001, p. 23) notes that on occasion, the victim and the hero roles fall to the same nation, which gives the narrative a self-defense trajectory.

8. The story does not reveal Pavlikov's first name.

References

Arnold, M. (Ed.). (2006). *The best of the* Harveyville Fun Times! Saratoga, CA: Fun Ideas Productions.

Attack of the lone avenger! (1943). In *War victory adventures* (pp. 33–36). (Vol. 1, no. 2). St. Louis, MO: Family Comics.

Barkin, S. M. (1984). Fighting the cartoon war: Information strategies in World War II. *Journal of American Culture*, 1–2(7), 113–117.

Blitzkrieg boomerang! (1943). In *War victory adventures* (pp. 49–55). (Vol. 1, no. 2). St. Louis, MO: Family Comics.

Cazeneuve, A. (1943a). Masquerade for prey. In *War victory adventures* (pp. 21–26). (Vol. 1, no. 2). St. Louis, MO: Family Comics.

Cazeneuve, A. (1943b). Terror rides the waves. In *War victory adventures* (pp. 9–16). (Vol. 1, no. 3). St. Louis, MO: Family Comics.

Chafe, W. H. (2003). *The unfinished journey: America since World War II* (5th ed.). New York, NY: Oxford University Press.

The death mask mystery. (1943). In *War victory adventures* (pp. 32–39). (Vol. 1, no. 3). St. Louis, MO: Family Comics.

Desert dynamite. (1943). In *War victory adventures* (pp. 46–49). (Vol. 1, no. 3). St. Louis, MO: Family Comics.

Diemert, B. (2005). Uncontainable metaphor: George F. Kennan's "X" article and Cold War discourse. *Canadian Review of American Studies, 35,* 21–55.

Doherty, T. (1993). *Projections of war: Hollywood, American culture, and World War II.* New York, NY: Columbia University Press.

Dulles, A. F. (1942, December 28). A righteous faith. *Life,* 48–51.

Epp, M. (1943a). Chickie Ricks, pilot-fleet arm, U.S.M.C. In *War victory adventures* (pp. 1–8). (Vol. 1, no. 3). St. Louis, MO: Family Comics.

Epp, M. (1943b). Presenting Chickie Ricks, pilot-fleet arm, U.S.M.C. In *War victory adventures* (pp. 2–9). (Vol. 1, no. 2). St. Louis, MO: Family Comics.

Grohe, G. (1976). *He's watching you* [poster]. In A. Rhodes, *Propaganda: The art of persuasion, World War* II (p. 174). New York, NY: Chelsea House. (Original work published 1942).

Jackson, K. M., & Arnold, M. D. (2007). Baby-boom children and Harvey Comics after the code: A neighborhood of little girls and boys. *ImageTexT: Interdisciplinary Comics Studies, 3.* Retrieved from http://www.english.ufl.edu/imagetext/archives/v3_3/jackson/

Jarvis, C. S. (2004). *The male body at war: American masculinity during World War II.* DeKalb, IL: Northern Illinois University Press.

Kimble, J. J. (2005). Whither propaganda? Agonism and "the engineering of consent." *Quarterly Journal of Speech, 91,* 210–218.

Kimble, J. J., & Goodnow, T. (2009). "You boys and girls can be the Minute Men of today": Narrative possibility and normative appeal in the U.S. Treasury's 1942 *War victory comics.* In P. M. Haridakis, B. S. Hugenberg, & S. T. Wearden (Eds.), *War and the media: Essays on news reporting, propaganda and popular culture* (pp. 112–125). Jefferson, NC: McFarland.

Koehler, K., & Ancona, V. (1980). *This is the enemy* [poster]. In *Paper bullets* (p. 1). New York, NY: Chelsea House. (Original work published 1942).

Kuusisto, R. (1998). Framing the wars in the Gulf and in Bosnia: The rhetorical definitions of the Western power leaders in action. *Journal of Peace Research, 35,* 603–620.

Lakoff, G. (1991). Metaphor and war: The metaphor system used to justify war in the Gulf. *Peace Research, 23,* 25–32.

Lakoff, G. (2001). *Metaphorical thought in foreign policy: Why strategic framing matters.* Berkeley, CA: Frameworks Institute.

Lakoff, G., & Johnson, M. (1980). *Metaphors we live by.* Chicago, IL: University of Chicago Press.

Larson, D. W. (1985). *Origins of containment: A psychological explanation.* Princeton, NJ: Princeton University Press.

Legrady, G. (2000). Modular structure and image/text sequences: Comics and interactive media. In A. Magnussen & H. Christiansen (Eds.), *Comics & culture: Analytical and theoretical approaches to comics* (pp. 79–90). Copenhagen, Denmark: Museum Tusculanum Press.

McCloud, S. (1994). *Understanding comics: The invisible art.* New York, NY: HarperCollins.

Murray, C. (2011). *Champions of the oppressed? Superhero comics, popular culture, and propaganda in America during World War II.* Cresskill, NJ: Hampton.

Peril on the Pampas. (1943). In *War victory adventures* (pp. 23–30). (Vol. 1, no. 3). St. Louis, MO: Family Comics.

Pohl, F. K. (1993). *Ben Shahn.* New York, NY: Chameleon Books.

Rendezvous with revenge. (1943). In *War victory adventures* (pp. 10–20). (Vol. 1, no. 2). St. Louis, MO: Family Comics.

Scott, C. (2007). Written in red, white, and blue: A comparison of comic book propaganda from World War II and September 11. *The Journal of Popular Culture, 40,* 325–343.

The story behind the cover: Introducing Capt. Red Cross. (1943). In *War victory adventures* (pp. 40–43). (Vol. 1, no. 3). St. Louis, MO: Family Comics.

Streb, E. J. (1998, August). Truth, justice, and the American way: Propaganda and comic books in the Second World War. Paper presented at the meeting of the Comic Arts Conference, San Diego, CA.

Uncle Cal combats Axis U-boats! (1943). In *War victory adventures* (pp. 42–47). (Vol. 1, no. 2). St. Louis, MO: Family Comics.

U.S. Treasury Department. (1942, Summer). *War victory comics.* (Box 8, Folder 1). Odegard Papers, Franklin D. Roosevelt Presidential Library, Hyde Park, NY.

War victory adventures. (1943a, August). (Vol. 1, no. 2). St. Louis, MO: Family Comics.

War victory adventures. (1943b, Winter). (Vol. 1, no. 3). St. Louis, MO: Family Comics.

Waugh, C. (1947). *The comics.* New York, NY: Macmillan.

Weaver, D. (1943). Grimm, ghost spotter. In *War victory adventures* (pp. 17–22). (Vol. 1, no. 3). St. Louis, MO: Family Comics.

QUESTION TO CONSIDER

- How did comic books play a role during World War II?

PART VI

Living in the Cold War Era

A 1950s family watching television.

CHAPTER 11

Comfort and Crisis

The 1950s

By John R. Greene

Editor's Introduction

If you grew up in the 1950s, you might have spent time playing with your friends or having a night out with your parents at a drive-in movie. Possibly you watched television at home, if you had a TV set, while eating your Swanson frozen TV dinner, which was introduced in 1950. Maybe you went to see your relatives or went on a vacation with your parents. After all, it was the era of American affluence. Issues like the struggle between communism and capitalism, which dominated the 1950s, did not dominate our lives. These issues, along with domestic issues, were concerns your parents talked about between themselves or with their friends. In 1950, the average yearly income was $3,210, which would jump to $5,010 by 1959 ($31,600 and $49,300, respectively, in 2015). A new house cost $8,450 in 1950, and by the end of 1959, the cost jumped to $12,400 ($83,200 and $122,000, respectively, in 2015). The average cost of a new car was $1,510, and by the end of 1959, a car cost $2,200 ($14,900 and $21,700, respectively, in 2015), while gas cost 18 cents in 1950, only to jump to 25 cents by 1959 ($1.77 and $2.46, respectively, in 2015). Although inflation gradually grew, life in the 1950s was good for the average American. The following essay looks at the comfort and crisis one was confronted with in the 1950s.

Comfort and Crisis

The 1950s

By John Robert Greene

William Mcguire "Bill" Bryson was born in Des Moines, Iowa, in 1951. He would go on to become a prolific author, writing travel books, books on the English language, and the prize-winning *Short History of Nearly Everything.*[1] But in the 1950s he was a charter member of the post–World War II baby-boom generation, when an estimated seventy-eight million babies were born between 1946 and 1960. Like most baby boomers, Bryson looks back on growing up in the fifties with a sentimental fondness. In his hilarious and prescient memoir *The Life and Times of the Thunderbolt Kid* (named after the alter-ego Bryson took for himself after watching a few too many space-action shows on that brand new gadget, the television), Bryson waxed nostalgic for what he felt was a simpler, safer, and gentler time—what a later television show based on the 1950s would call "Happy Days":

> I can't imagine there has ever been a more gratifying time or place to be alive than America in the 1950s. ... By 1951 ... almost 90 percent of American families had refrigerators, and nearly three-quarters had washing machines, telephones, vacuum cleaners, and gas or electric stoves. ... No wonder people were happy. Suddenly they were able to have the things they never dreamed of having, and they couldn't believe their luck.

The Thunderbolt Kid and his fellow boomers were, indeed, lucky. Mired in depression and war for the better part of two decades, Americans were now, finally, comfortable. The economy was certainly booming. Average family income rose from $3,000 in 1947 to $5,200 in 1957, and the gross national product (GNP) rose from $200 billion in 1945 to $500 billion in 1960. The most rapid economic growth came in the first part of the decade, thanks to expenditures from the Korean War; the economic decline toward the end of the decade was slight, but it would prove to be ammunition for the 1960 Kennedy campaign.

As a result of the bulging economy, more and more Americans could partake of the proverbial "American Dream"—the desire, long deferred by depression and war, to advance one's social and economic status. For many, this meant a final abandonment of cities that had become overcrowded, filthy, and chaotic, and a move to the outlying suburbs. The 1950s saw a suburban revolution—by 1968, one-third of the nation's total population lived in the suburbs. Suburban growth rested on the ability of most postwar families to buy a car, a newfound ability to afford a home (Federal Home Loan policies and the GI Bill made them ultra-affordable), and the creation of superhighways that linked workplaces in the city with a home far away from that workplace.

For other Americans, the new prosperity meant the ability to fill that suburban home with stuff—stuff that most families of the 1950s could not remember being able to afford. The number-one consumer item of the 1950s was the television set—in 1947, fourteen thousand families had one; by 1957, ten million families had one. The social consequences of staring for hours at what Federal Communications Commission (FCC) chairman Newton Minow would call a "vast wasteland" of programming would not become an issue until the next decade. In the 1950s, television provided a way to spend more leisure time than middle-class families were used to having in the much more Spartan existence of the 1930s and 1940s. They also had time to acquire and enjoy a plethora of other consumer goods: electric refrigerators; washing machines; dishwashers; prepared foods (including the infamous "TV dinner"—instantly heatable and presented in a flimsy aluminum tray, which seemed to negate the need for the dishwasher, but little matter); FM radio; automatic transmissions. … America in the 1950s had indeed, in the words of the economist John Kenneth Galbraith, become an "affluent society."

But not for all Americans. Galbraith was no cheerleader for what America became in the 1950s—his 1958 book instead criticized that society, pointing out that as white, middle-class America raced to affluence, it continued an American tradition of ignoring those who by virtue of their race, gender, or economic status could not compete. Between 1945 and 1965, only 1 percent of the government-insured homes built went to blacks. That actually mattered little—local zoning laws kept blacks from even *thinking* about moving to the suburbs. And the poor did, indeed, get poorer. During the decade, more than one-fifth of the nation lived below the poverty line, and the cities, which had lost most of their wealthy residents to the suburbs, no longer had the funds to combat the problem adequately.

Many intellectuals writing in the 1950s argued, then, that the affluence found in American society had become less defensible. Sociologist David Riesman described the members of the culture of affluence as a "lonely crowd," one that had become shallower, more worried about approval, and more desirous of conforming than *thinking* about their existence. The fiction of many writers pointed out this same tendency to conform. The classic expression of this feeling in the literature of the period was J. D. Salinger's *Catcher in the Rye* (1951), whose protagonist, Holden Caulfield, came to the conclusion that the whole adult world was so phony that there was no escape—except through mental illness. The artists of those who pronounced American society "beat"—writers such as Jack Kerouac, who escaped the affluent society by going *On the Road* (1957), and poet Allen Ginsberg—began a rebellion against what would soon be termed "straight society" that would startle America in the following decade. Indeed, Ginsberg's influential 1956 poem "America" would prove to be remarkably prophetic:

> America I've given you all and now I'm nothing. ...
> America when will we end the human war? ...
> Your machinery is too much for me. ...
> There must be some other way to settle this argument. ...
> I smoke marijuana every chance I get. ...
> America you don't really want to go to war. ...
> The Russia wants to eat us alive. ...
> America this is quite serious.
> America this is the impression I get from looking in the television set.
> America is this correct? ...
> It's true I don't want to join the Army. ...

Moreover, the new affluence was stifling women. The majority of men and women in the 1950s had never known such family affluence; as children of the Great Depression, many of them had not known basic family stability. It is not surprising that they wanted for themselves a steady, traditional family environment. Women who had taken jobs in heavy industry during the war as "Rosie the Riveters" would be pressured to give up their jobs and return to the home. Not that much pressure was necessary—many women voluntarily left the workforce, seeking the same family permanence as were the men returning from war. Once a semblance of stability and affluence had been achieved, however, and once their children were of school age, middle-class women became restless. Some returned to the workforce—most in the traditionally female domains of clerical help, health care, and teaching, and all for decidedly lower wages than their nearest male counterparts.

But whether they stayed at home or worked outside the home, societal pressures—particularly mass-market advertising—were brought to bear on women to remain traditional housewives. In virtually every ad for every product, women were treated as mistresses of the kitchen and the princesses of the home. In one of the most telling photos of the 1950s, published in *Life* magazine, the viewer sees rows of automobiles waiting at a suburban train stop to pick up commuters returning home from work. The women who had driven those cars to the station have all moved over to the passenger seats—so that their men can drive them home. On television, there were few images of working women—the ever present "Mom" of *Leave It to Beaver* and *Ozzie and Harriet* reigned supreme. One exception was comedian Lucille Ball, who attempted in each week's episode of *I Love Lucy* to wheedle her way into her husband's band. It is notable that her attempts were cast as farce, and that she never succeeded. There was an equal paradox about sex. On the one hand, societal pressures to marry and have several children were overwhelming, to the point where many small all-female colleges openly billed that they taught their students the social graces needed to "catch a man." On the other hand, the statistics-laden works of psychologist Alfred Kinsey (*Sexual Behavior in the Human Male,* 1948; *Sexual Behavior in the American Female,* 1953) clearly showed that young Americans practiced various forms of sex—premarital, homosexual, and what Kinsey labeled as "perverted."

Thus, women were faced with conflicting demands. On the one hand, a male-centered society wanted women as housewives. On the other hand, they had grown out of the role during World War II and were having difficulty returning to that role in the postwar period. The majority of women resolved this tension by remaining housewives. Yet this choice left many housewives feeling unfulfilled, lonely, and guilt-ridden. These feelings of entrapment often led to real physical maladies—headaches, menstrual problems, and clinical depression. For many, alcohol and drug abuse was a socially acceptable cover for their ailments. For many others, there was a feeling that even beyond the job market there must be more. It was a yearning that they could not identify when interviewed about their lives; they were being pursued by a personal crisis that one of the most influential intellectuals of the twentieth century would soon term "the problem that has no name."

In the 1950s most Americans ignored these critics. Indeed, most of America did not question affluence and instead celebrated its escape from depression and war. However, one area of American life—the turbulent relationship between the races—refused to accept the status quo; its explosion in the South challenged some of the nation's fundamental beliefs about itself and threatened to throw the nation into a second war within.

If the hula hoop represented for many critics the nature of American society in the 1950s—moving fast, in a circle, and going nowhere—another symbol of the 1950s—the missile—might well represent the civil rights movement in the South. Explosive, surprisingly fast, soaring to unexpected heights, those who confronted the racist terrorism of the South did so in a manner that, for the first time since the Civil War, brought the issue of racial equality to a national audience. With a television now in virtually every home, those who confronted this evil tried to do so in front of a camera. As a result, white America could no longer ignore racism as an isolated, local issue—it had, by 1960, become an issue of the national conscience. This was what "movement" meant—confronting evil on a mass scale and demanding for black Americans the immediate and full protection of the law, protection that had been promised under the Fourteenth Amendment and ratified in 1868.

By the 1950s, black Americans were ready for movement. During World War II, almost one million blacks served in uniform, in both the European and Pacific Theaters of Operation. They would return home—as did all combat veterans—changed people, ready to stand up to racist demagogues as they had stood up to Hitler, Mussolini, and Tojo. The gains made by blacks on the home front ennobled their cause. Between 1940 and 1944, the number of blacks employed in manufacturing and processing had increased from 50,000 to about 1.2 million, bringing with it the rise of a black middle class that was better suited for organization and protest than any preceding generation. Established interest groups like the Congress of Racial Equality (CORE) and the National Association for the Advancement of Colored People (NAACP) began to push harder.

There were victories. The summer of 1947 saw the integration of major league baseball, albeit for largely commercial reasons, with the addition of Jackie Robinson to the Brooklyn Dodgers. There were victories in the legal battle to win integrated educational opportunities—in 1949, Ada Sipuel was granted admission to the law school at the University of Oklahoma, and the following year the Supreme Court demanded that the University of Texas open its doors to black students. In May 1954, the Supreme Court dealt what its supporters assumed to be a death blow to segregated schools when, in *Brown v. Board of Education of Topeka, Kansas,* a unanimous court concluded that "in the field of public education ... separate educational facilities are inherently unequal."

But no court could stop the random acts of racial terrorism that had long been an accepted part of southern society. On August 28, 1955, fourteen-year-old Chicagoan Emmett Till, while visiting relatives in Money, Mississippi, committed an unpardonable breach of southern racial etiquette. When leaving a dime store after buying some candy, he turned to a white girl and quipped, "Bye, Baby." That night, vigilantes kidnapped Till from his uncle's home, took the boy to a back road, shot him in the head, and brutalized him so badly that the body was disfigured beyond recognition. This was a lynching in the finest southern tradition. But the reaction to Till's murder did not follow true to form. This time, vigilantism encountered a very public resistance. Till's mother, Mamie, insisted on an open casket funeral, so that the world could see what had been done to her son, and she held many press conferences, which were replayed on the nightly television news. Till's uncle, Mose Wright, literally took his life into his hands when he took the stand, pointed to the two men charged with Till's murder, and identified them as the men who had abducted his nephew. The result was never in doubt—the defendants were acquitted. But massive resistance had been met by movement—what was to follow would be the organization of that movement.

The murder of Emmett Till—not the announcement of *Brown*—marked the beginning of the Civil Rights Movement. Martin Luther King, Jr., would be the first black leader to define the rules of engagement for that movement. Shielded from racism in his Atlanta upbringing, a moderate by both training and character, King was thought by many to be an unfortunate choice to lead in a situation that seemed to cry for immediate activism. That situation was sparked by an event later described by future Black Panther leader Eldridge Cleaver as a moment when, somewhere in the universe, a gear in the machinery shifted—the December 8, 1955, refusal of Rosa Parks to move to the back of a segregated bus in Montgomery, Alabama, and the subsequent eleven-month boycott of that city's buses by its black population. Montgomery's ministers chose King to lead the boycott because he had been in town for too short a period of time to be corrupted by city officials. He succeeded in large part because his training as both a theologian and a philosopher led him to accept the nonviolent beliefs of Mahatma Gandhi, and to adopt those views as a strategy to face down southern racism. Faced with a reaction to the boycott that included physical threats and the firebombing of both churches and his own home, King demanded that his followers turn the other cheek and quietly continue their boycott. Much like Mamie Till, who had forced the nation to look at her son's destroyed body, King forced the nation to look at its own disfigured system of racism. In the 1960s, King's strategy of nonviolence would face many challenges, as it struggled to meet the needs of a growing, more diverse movement. But in Montgomery in 1955–56, the strategy worked. After eleven months, the Supreme Court declared that Montgomery's segregated bus system was unconstitutional.

But buses were not public schools. Quite simply put, *Brown* never worked as advertised. The Court itself refused to put a deadline on integration, demanding that schools integrate not immediately, but with "all deliberate speed." This allowed southern school districts to organize what southerners called "massive resistance" and to find ways to obstruct the ruling of the Court. By 1957, less than 20 percent of the school districts in the South had complied with *Brown*. That year saw the first full-scale counterattack on desegregation when an Arkansas court issued an injunction stopping the integration plans of Central High School in Little Rock. A federal court countermanded the injunction, but the night before school was to open, Governor Orval Faubus stationed Arkansas National Guard troops around the school to stop nine black students from registering for classes. The mob that had formed outside the school chased the teens from campus, screaming racial epithets and spitting on the youngsters as they boarded escape buses. Defended by Thurgood Marshall (who had been the victorious lawyer in *Brown*), the students won affirmation of their right to attend Central High. President Dwight D. Eisenhower begrudgingly protected that right, sending federal troops to escort the students to class. They enrolled, and endured a year of unparalleled harassment. The following year, Faubus closed all the state's high schools for the entire year rather than endure the protests again. The mob violence in Little Rock, despite the Pyrrhic victory that surrounded the graduation of one black senior in June 1958, made it clear that while *Brown* might be the stated law of the nation, it was far from being the acknowledged law of the South.

Many wondered why the president of the United States refused to lend the moral power of his office to the movement. In the two decades prior to the 1950s, Americans had gotten used to having activists in the White House. Both Franklin Roosevelt and Harry Truman had been engaging public figures who relished using the various powers of the presidency to attack problems. Both men believed that if there *was* a balance of power in American government, the scales *should* tilt toward 1600 Pennsylvania Avenue.

This was *not,* however, Dwight D. Eisenhower. Hardly a political activist, Eisenhower envisioned a different, more collegial, more "businesslike" presidency. As a result, for almost a decade after the end of his presidency, no one—not contemporaries, not the press, not historians—gave Dwight D. Eisenhower credit for being anything but a kindly caretaker of the executive office. His domestic policy seemed to be a direct response to the demands of big business, while his foreign policy appeared to be the exclusive creation of his secretary of state. Treating Eisenhower as a man who relied on others but rarely initiated anything, critics dismissed the Eisenhower presidency as a passive interlude between the tenure of two boisterous activists. The contemporary press concentrated on his health, and historians concentrated on his pleasant personality. Simply put, Dwight Eisenhower received the kind of deference that one would reserve for an aged relative in a nursing home.

However, historians rejuvenated Eisenhower and his presidency with a haste that was startling even for often impetuous revisionist historians. The Eisenhower of recent history is a much younger man than the one who was written about in the 1950s and 1960s. He is no longer the doddering "Ike." He has instead become "President Eisenhower," a calculating, often shrewd politician who ruled his administration with the cunning of a career officer. To the revisionists, no one controlled Eisenhower. While these historians judge his refusal to push for the enforcement of *Brown* to be less than meritorious, they argue that Eisenhower's minimalist attitude toward civil rights kept even greater violence from breaking out in the South on his watch. Even the deception of the U-2 Affair became the badge of a tough Eisenhower. The most telling facet of the new Eisenhower is that it took *real* guts to say no in Vietnam; one could not say the same about his activist successors.

Taken on his own terms Dwight Eisenhower was indeed a success as president. It can be argued, in fact, that he has been the only true success in the White House since 1945. But this was not because he was a closet Machiavellian. Eisenhower was a success because he did not choose to push the status quo too hard. He was neither a reactionary, wishing to turn the clock back to 1928, nor a New Deal liberal, hoping to push America forward into the acceptance of a more positivist state. He went neither forward nor backward, and to his credit, he promised neither to the American public. Neither as passive as the early historians of his administration made him out to be nor as activist as the revisionists have tried to make him out to be-indeed, Eisenhower would have shunned either label—Dwight Eisenhower's gift was an innate refusal to rock the boat.

First and foremost, Eisenhower was a businessman's president, and quite in line with the economic emphasis of the decade. But he was no Warren Harding redux. Eisenhower did not undertake to rein in the spending of the New Deal and the Fair Deal. Truman left office proposing a budget of $76.6 billion—about $10 billion more than revenues. Such an imbalance bothered Eisenhower, who during the 1952 campaign had promised to balance the budget. That, however, never happened. A recession in the fall of 1953 was halted only by reducing taxes by $3 billion, thus incurring an even greater deficit. Also, Eisenhower never slashed spending as a method of budget balancing. He took some token measures—between 1954 and 1956 he cut the number of federal employees from 2.4 million to 2.2 million. But in 1955–56, the administration spent freely. Defense was the first priority, but the administration also tried to stimulate the domestic economy with spending. The minimum wage rose in 1956 from 75 cents to $1.00 an hour, and Social Security benefits were increased. The St. Lawrence Seaway, first proposed under Harding, finally began construction in 1954. The Housing Act of 1955, while not as strong as its supporters had wished, stimulated the public housing boom of the 1960s.

Perhaps the most successful venture along these lines was the Interstate Highway System. Although Eisenhower sold the program in a military fashion (arguing that a sophisticated road system would make for a more orderly retreat from cities that had suffered a nuclear attack), the plan provided for an incredible construction program and a large number of jobs.

When faced with crisis, Eisenhower responded with patience, stealth, and willingness to let his advisors play the primary public role—what political scientist Fred Greenstein called the "hidden-hand presidency." The major domestic crisis of the first term centered on the wildly flaying investigations of Joseph McCarthy. McCarthy had easily won reelection to the Senate from Wisconsin in 1952, running only a bit behind Eisenhower in the state. Yet McCarthy's national popularity, if anything, had grown during the campaign. In 1953, most Americans (53 percent) approved of the senator's crusade. That was a good thing for McCarthy because he did not plan to allow the election of a Republican president to stop his search for communists in the State Department. Indeed, the senator declared that there were still communists in the foreign service, but that he had faith that the new secretary of state, John Foster Dulles, could ferret them out.

McCarthy's role as chairman of the Committee on Government Operations, as well as the chair of the committee's most powerful subcommittee, the Permanent Subcommittee on Investigations, gave him a public platform. While remaining carefully aloof from the administration during its first days, McCarthy took his traveling fear show to Europe, where two assistants, Roy Cohn and G. David Schine, investigated the State Department and the U. S. Information Agency. Their efforts resulted in several resignations, as well as a campaign designed to purge the shelves of all overseas U.S. libraries of any books that were deemed to contain seditious material. Eisenhower largely ignored these revelations. But then McCarthy lashed out against the U.S. Army. In January 1954, McCarthy revealed that Major Irving Peress had refused to sign his loyalty certificate but had nevertheless been granted an honorable discharge from the army. Secretary of the Army Robert Stevens admitted that the Peress case had been poorly handled, but that did not satisfy McCarthy. He called several officials to testify, including Brigadier General Ralph Zwicker, who was ostensibly responsible for the decision to discharge Peress. McCarthy bellowed to Zwicker: "You are a disgrace to the uniform. ... You're not fit to be an officer. You're ignorant." Although McCarthy and Stevens worked out a compromise package, McCarthy had sown the seeds of his own destruction. Eisenhower, who just happened to be an alumnus of the Army, struck back.

Two weeks after the meeting that produced their "compromise," Stevens charged that McCarthy had used his political power to prevent Schine's induction into the army. Caught off guard by the charge, a livid McCarthy wanted revenge. It was Vice President Richard Nixon, dispatched by Eisenhower to be the broker between McCarthy and the White House, who convinced the senator to do it on television. For McCarthy, this made sense. Television had already begun to aid the careers of politicians—there was no reason for McCarthy to think that he could not control the media. He was wrong. For the first time, American *saw* both his method and his demean-or—and there was an instantaneous rejection. Glued to a TV set for thirty-six days, Americans witnessed McCarthy's thinly veiled accusations against Eisenhower ("treason that has been growing over the past twenty—twenty-*one*—years."). But it was the chief counsel for the army, Bostonian Joseph Welch, who drove the stake into McCarthy's heart. McCarthy had linked a young associate of Welch's with a communist "club." Once proclaimed on television, this disclosure meant the end of the young man's career, and that was too much for the placid Welch. Looking directly at McCarthy, Welch moaned: "Little did I dream you could be so reckless and so cruel as to do an injury to that lad. ... If it were in my power to forgive you for your reckless cruelty, I would do so. I like to think I am a gentle man, but your forgiveness will have to come from someone other than me." As McCarthy tried to go on, Welch interrupted once more: "Have you no sense of decency, sir, at long last?" As McCarthy fumbled for the next question, the Senate Caucus Room burst into applause. With that spontaneous outburst, McCarthy's career was finished.

Eisenhower had avoided a direct conflict with McCarthy, and as a result he kept the loyalty of the conservative wing of his party through 1956. Using Nixon as an intermediary was a master stroke. The vice president already had the trust of the party's right, and he sympathized with McCarthy's ends if not necessarily his means. Several historians have claimed that Nixon suggested that McCarthy televise his hearings *knowing* that the media would be his undoing. Regardless, the president had another do his bidding, stayed above the fray, and achieved the desired result—"hidden-hand" leadership.

In the area of civil rights, Eisenhower did not extend his hand, hidden or otherwise. He felt that a presidential presence in that debate was politically unwise, a violation of state's rights, and against his own personal support of southern segregation. Therefore, he did as little as possible. Although he privately referred to the 1953 appointment of Earl Warren as chief justice as the biggest mistake he had made as president, Eisenhower publicly claimed that the *Brown* decision must be enforced and did so only when faced with certain bloodshed in Little Rock. The Civil Rights Act of 1957 was a gutted affair that was largely the work of the Senate majority leader, Lyndon B. Johnson. This was hardly the stuff that moral leadership was made of. But when push came to shove, Eisenhower did not ignore his constitutional duty. What can be said of Eisenhower and civil rights can also be said of his successor—the movement dragged him along kicking and screaming.

The image of Eisenhower as a do-nothing president has been at its strongest when considering his administration's foreign policy. All too many observers have argued that Eisenhower left diplomacy up to the State Department, and Secretary of State Dulles engineered a foreign policy of boisterous, dangerous confrontation with the Soviet Union. This conclusion seems to stem from the assumption on the part of many scholars that a president and his secretary of state must be of one mind on foreign policy. However, the evidence suggests that there were *two* theories of diplomacy present in the Eisenhower White House—that of the president and that of Dulles. The fact that it was clearly Eisenhower's view that prevailed throughout the administration not only leads to a reinterpretation of his foreign policy, but can also be used to explain what many observers have seen to be the chief success of his administration—he kept the nation out of war.

John Foster Dulles mixed the small-town Presbyterian moralism he had learned as a boy in northern New York with the conservative value system he had learned while a student at Princeton. A career diplomat, Dulles came quite naturally to view the Soviet Union not only as a threat, but as morally wrong. Such a view made him an ideologically perfect choice to be Truman's token Republican in the State Department. Firsthand observation of Truman's policy of containment only hardened Dulles's anti-Soviet stance and convinced him that was not enough. He embraced the theory of liberation—that the United States should actively pursue a foreign policy that would *free* the captive nations from the yoke of communist aggression.

Eisenhower disagreed with Dulles's assessment. To him, containment—the threat of a military or a nuclear response to further Soviet aggression—had worked. It was when containment had been *abandoned* in Korea—when Truman pushed into North Korea, past the thirty-eighth parallel in an attempt to liberate that nation from the communists—that a bloody stalemate had occurred. Eisenhower believed that a reinstitution of the policy of containment would freeze the Soviets in their tracks and make another Korea unnecessary. That would particularly be so if Eisenhower threatened to use not traditional military troops against the Soviets but a nuclear strike. It was this policy, soon to be christened "massive retaliation," or "brinksmanship," that became the modus operandi of the Eisenhower foreign policy. Dulles defined the policy for *Life* magazine, arguing that "the ability to get to the verge of war is the necessary art. If you cannot master it, you eventually get into wars." Such a policy called for Eisenhower to be a bluffer with the guts of a burglar, threatening the use of military might of the United States, particularly its nuclear capability, and hoping that the threat would render unnecessary the use of such force.

The Eisenhower administration brought several key crises to peaceful conclusions using the threat of massive retaliation. Three weeks after he was elected, Eisenhower made good on his campaign promise and went to the front in Korea, an act that Truman criticized as "demagoguery." Yet there was a surprise for those who expected that the military man would be a militant president—when conferring with General Mark Clark, Eisenhower was less interested in how the war could be *won* than he was with his commander's ideas on how to get the peace talks moving. Dulles pushed for a new military initiative to break the stalemate, but Eisenhower was adamant—the war would be ended at the peace table, before it had a chance to destroy his administration, as it had Truman's. The new administration met with resistance from both the North and the South Koreans. The North refused to negotiate a wholesale release of its prisoners of war, and in the South, President Syngman Rhee was holding out for a completely unified Korea under the South's control. As the stalemate moved into mid-1953, Eisenhower took bold action. He threatened that if the talks did not move perceptibly forward, he would feel free to move decisively "without inhibition in our use of weapons"—a thinly veiled threat to use nuclear force. Whether or not Eisenhower was bluffing is impossible to gauge, but it was definitely a threat, and the threat worked. On July 27, 1953, an armistice was signed, ending the Korean War some three years after it had begun.

Eisenhower's handling of the French collapse in Indochina was equally shrewd. In April 1954, the hapless French forces, which had been fighting the Viet Minh revolutionaries since the end of World War II, had allowed themselves to be surrounded at the indefensible fortress at Dien Bien Phu. Dulles and Nixon pushed for an American intervention, on the grounds that its North Atlantic Treaty Organization (NATO) commitment to the French had to be honored. Eisenhower agreed; but with the war in Korea only recently over, he was not about to commit American forces to another Far East expedition. On April 7, Eisenhower used a press conference to proclaim that if Indochina fell to communism, the rest of the Far East was next: "You have a row of dominoes set up, you knock over the first one, and what will happen to the last one is the certainty that it will go over very quickly." However, Eisenhower and Dulles devised a way for the United States to avoid committing its troops to help the French. The strategy was put forth in a speech to the Overseas Press Club on March 29. While proclaiming that the situation in Indochina was "a grave threat to the whole free community," Eisenhower made it clear that the United States would not help the French unless *other* members of the free community, supposedly so threatened by the situation, *also* helped the French—what Eisenhower called "united action." Not surprisingly, since the rest of the free community also still had open wounds left from the Korean War, there were no takers—a fact that could have surprised neither Eisenhower nor Dulles.

Although Eisenhower's refusal to help the French was, in large part, the reason for the fall of Dien Bien Phu on May 8, that was far from the end of America's involvement in the region. On July 21, 1954, the Geneva Conference, borrowing one of the most tragic pages from the history of the Korean peninsula, temporarily divided Indochina in half along the seventeenth parallel until elections could be held. The northern portion, led by Ho Chi Minh, and more formally known as the Democratic Republic of Vietnam, received immediate promises of aid from the communist bloc; Eisenhower quickly moved to fill the power vacuum that the French had left behind in the south. Immediately following the Geneva Accord, the United States threw its support to Ngo Dinh Diem as a potential ruler in the south. Rabidly anti-French and a devout Catholic, Diem had wandered the world while the French controlled his homeland—even spending time in a Catholic seminary in New Jersey. A rigid true believer and a corrupt bureaucrat, Diem nevertheless promised the type of stability of leadership for the South that the hapless Emperor Bao Dai could never provide. In 1956, with the backing of the Americans, Diem was elected premier of the newly proclaimed Republic of Vietnam, more commonly known as South Vietnam, thus ending any hopes of an eventual political unification of the two Vietnams.

Diem, however, quickly proved to be a millstone around Eisenhower's neck. His corruption, quiet intransigence, and, most important, his complete distance from his people—as a Catholic, he showed nothing but disdain for the Buddhist majority in his nation—strained relations between Washington and Saigon almost to the breaking point. But, playing to a key theme in modern American history, the United States chose to stay with the corrupt devil they knew rather than chance a takeover by another devil they knew—Ho Chi Minh. Between 1955 and 1960, the United States gave South Vietnam almost $127 million in direct economic aid, and over $16 million in technical aid, in order to prop up the Diem government from outside pressure. Eisenhower also recognized a need to help Diem build an army, literally from scratch. During those years, the United States committed between 750 and 1,500 military advisors to assist the Diem government in establishing an effective army; the advisors were organized as the Military Assistance and Advisory Group (MAAG), Vietnam. MAAG would eventually be criticized for preparing the South Vietnamese for the wrong type of war—for not training them in the finer arts of jungle, guerilla warfare.

The need for such training would soon become apparent. Diem's heavy-handed tactics led to outcries of dissatisfaction from his own people. He proved to be incapable of controlling the protests without American help, thus playing into an anti-American sentiment in the South that was a natural outgrowth of the anti-French sentiment that the nation had experienced for decades. This gave Ho Chi Minh the opening he needed to organize an insurgency in the South. In 1960, Ho announced the existence of the National Liberation Front (NLF), an umbrella group that promised to organize all the anti-Diem revolutionaries in the South and train them in a manner that would allow them to overthrow Diem's regime. Diem proved to be a cagy adversary, however. With American assistance, particularly the covert, clandestine aid provided by Central Intelligence Agency (CIA) operative Colonel Edward Landsdale, he held the NLF at bay, derisively and inaccurately labeling the group "Vietnamese Communists"—Vietcong. At no point did Eisenhower consider putting any American ground troops in Vietnam. Financial, advisory, and covert support—support not seen by the American people until the release of the *Pentagon Papers* [...]—was all that Eisenhower had to offer, along with American participation in the Southeast Asian Treaty Organization (SEATO), giving it a symbolic presence in the region. To those few Americans who even bothered following the American role in Vietnam in 1955–60, Eisenhower had honored America's alliances and kept troops out of war.

The 1954 crisis over Quemoy and Matsu further illustrates Eisenhower's diplomatic skills. To Eisenhower, the loss of China to the communists in 1949, a loss that both he and most conservative Republicans ascribed to Truman's refusal to intercede in the Chinese Civil War, was "the greatest diplomatic defeat in this nation's history." After China had fallen to the communist army of Mao Zedong, thus creating the People's Republic of China, Chiang Kai-shek's nationalists had escaped to the tiny offshore island of Tai-wan (Formosa), soon to be dubbed the Republic of China. Chiang mixed peculiarity with patriotism; continuing to insist that he was the rightful ruler of all mainland China, his troops began every morning by firing a volley of artillery fire at the mainland, volleys that usually sputtered into the sea far short of their mark. Despite his idiosyncrasies and reports of widespread corruption in his regime, Chiang had the treaty support of the United States. For his part, Mao had threatened to invade Formosa ever since they had banished Chiang there. Both nations claimed the tiny twin islands of Quemoy and Matsu, off the Formosan shore, as their own. When Mao's troops began an artillery attack on the two islands on September 3, 1954, it was the culmination of several months of threats from both sides. Eisenhower faced the same quandary he had faced only five months before in Indochina—should he send U.S. troops to aid an ally?

The answer was once again no, despite Dulles's protests to the contrary. Despite the fact that there was a sizeable China lobby in the ranks of the Republican Party who, despite Chiang's oddities, had been consistent supporters of the Formosan government, Mao's army was a much more formidable enemy than even the Viet Minh. Consequently, Eisenhower waited the crisis out. Indeed, as historian Robert Divine has pointed out, Eisenhower was deliberately ambiguous, leaving Mao guessing as to whether or not the Americans would intervene. It was this patience, with the threat of massive retaliation lurking in the wings, that eventually cooled the crisis. By the end of April, both Chiang's and Mao's rhetoric had cooled, and the crisis passed. Despite the opinion of his detractors, Eisenhower had not taken the United States to the brink of World War III over Quemoy and Matsu; Chiang and Mao had done that for themselves. Indeed, Eisenhower had once again shown a penchant for patience in a crisis.

A key diplomatic development of the Eisenhower period was the new attention paid by both the Soviets and the Americans to the Third World, thus signaling a basic change in the temperament of the cold war. For both nations, a characteristic of this change was their renewed interest in Middle East oil. For both nations, the Suez Canal was of primary importance. Without access to the canal, the shipping of oil from the Middle East would effectively grind to a halt. No one knew this better than the flamboyant Gamel Abdul-Nasser, president of Egypt. While Nasser had reacted to American support of Israel by signing a pact with the Soviet Union, he was willing to deal with either nation to further his domestic projects. His pet project was the building of a dam on the Nile River to provide cheap power for his people. The Aswan Dam had become a symbol for Egyptian modernization, and Nasser had leveraged much of his popularity to buy support for its construction. To finance it, he borrowed money from the United States, Britain, and the World Bank.

Yet Nasser's ideology soon got in the way of his construction. After Nasser had formally recognized Communist China in May 1956, Dulles recommended to Eisenhower that the Americans withdraw their loan offer. Eisenhower ordered it to be done, and as soon as Nasser found out, he nationalized the Suez Canal, using the tolls he now collected from all shipping to pay for his dam. Despite Dulles's entreaties, Eisenhower consistently ruled out the use of the American military to force Nasser to reopen the canal. Other nations saw the situation differently. Britain and France, trying to reclaim the glory of their pre–World War II empires, and Israel, trying to solidify its claims to legitimacy in the Middle East, saw in the Suez Crisis an opportunity. On October 31, less than two weeks before the American presidential election, the three nations invaded Egypt, assuming that they would be supported by Eisenhower.

They were not. Eisenhower immediately called the British prime minister, Anthony Eden, and made his displeasure abundantly clear. The United States rammed a cease-fire resolution through the United Nations, which the Israelis immediately obeyed. As Britain and France tried to decide what to do, Eisenhower heard rumblings from the Kremlin that suggested that the Soviets were planning to enter the crisis actively. Calling the Soviet's bluff, Eisenhower put American armed forces on alert. For his part, Eden also heard the Russians coming. He continued this quest for empire for one more week, until, faced with the possibility of Soviet intervention, he too withdrew his troops. Soon after, France also withdrew.

There was a cost, however, to Eisenhower's use of brinksmanship. Eisenhower's greatest failure as president was his inability to gain a closer relationship with the Soviet Union. While the death of Joseph Stalin on March 5, 1953, seemed to offer hope for a thaw, the fact that in August of the same year the Soviets detonated their first hydrogen bomb seemed to highlight the need for a formal discussion between the two nations. Eisenhower was sincerely committed to a thaw in the cold war. But each time that he came close to his goal, he shot himself in the foot.

There had been no superpower summit since 1945, in Potsdam. It was Eisenhower who pushed for a new summit. The Soviets met his request with a surprising willingness to cooperate. Eisenhower and Soviet leaders Nikolay Bulganin and Nikita Khrushchev met in Geneva in July 1955. While they got along well enough for the press to declare a "Geneva Spirit" of good will, a serious breakthrough was scuttled by Eisenhower's absurd proposal that the Soviets open their skies for U.S. spy planes, and that the United States would do the same. The Soviets rejected the plan at face value. Indeed, Khrushchev charged Eisenhower to his face with trying to get the Soviets to accept a "very transparent espionage device." Although Khrushchev visited the United States in the fall of 1959, and the two leaders made plans for a new summit in 1960, tension continued to mount.

Evidence of this tension was Eisenhower's commitment to the U-2 program. Developed by the CIA, the U-2 was a high-altitude spy plane. Its wide wingspan and slender fuselage gave it the appearance of a pterodactyl in flight. Its powerful camera could take a picture from several miles altitude that would enable the viewer to count the number of people on the street below. Eisenhower personally approved each mission, each of which emanated from U.S. bases in Turkey. The Soviets also knew about the missions, but the U-2 planes stayed just out of the reach of Soviet interceptor missiles. That is, until May 1, 1960. In a scenario that seemed scripted for Khrushchev, the Soviets shot down a U-2 and captured its pilot, Francis Gary Powers, on May Day—the Soviet Fourth of July. Khrushchev at that point took an incredible gamble. He held back releasing the information on the fate of the plane and waited to gauge the American reaction when they found out that one of their spy planes was missing. Once the disappearance had been reported in the press, Eisenhower went with the prearranged denial—that the U-2 had been gathering information about world weather patterns. When Khrushchev released photos of both the plane and pilot, Eisenhower was seen to be a liar. In spite of Eisenhower's successes in foreign policy, the U-2 debacle would give ammunition to a young Democratic senator angling for the presidency, who would charge that in world affairs, America in the 1950s had gone soft. On January 20, 1961, in the aftermath of a snowstorm that had brought the city of Washington to a standstill, Eisenhower passed the mantle of national leadership to a young, completely untested legislator with a record of little else than name recognition. The difference between the seventy-year-old Eisenhower and his forty-four-year-old successor could not have been clearer; what remained to be seen was whether the inauguration of John F. Kennedy would also inaugurate a new era in American history.

Recommended Reading

Begin your reading on the 1950s with a laugh, and know that Bill Bryson's *Life and Times of the Thunderbolt Kid* (New York: Broadway, 2006) serves as one of the best case studies of American society during the decade. Andrew J. Dunar, *America in the Fifties* (Syracuse: Syracuse Univ. Press, 2006), is an excellent introduction to the decade. John Kenneth Galbraith, *The Affluent Society* (Boston: Houghton Mifflin, 1958) offers the most important contemporary view of the period. A recent view of the society of the 1950s is Elaine Tyler May, *Homeward Bound: American Families in the Cold War Era* (New York: Basic Books, 1999). Of the many books on the Eisenhower presidency, the one that set the stage for a revision of his place in history was Fred I. Greenstein, *The Hidden Hand Presidency: Eisenhower as a Leader* (New York: Basic Books, 1982). The most thoughtful view of Eisenhower's foreign policy continues to be Robert A. Divine, *Eisenhower and the Cold War* (New York: Oxford Univ. Press, 1981). The best concise history of the war in Vietnam is still George C. Herring, *America's Longest War: The United States and Vietnam, 1950–1975*, 3d ed. (New York: McGraw Hill, 1996).

Note

1. New York: Broadway Books, 2004.

QUESTION TO CONSIDER

- Why does Greene refer to the 1950s as a time of "comfort and crisis?"

Mercury Seven astronauts posing in front of a fighter aircraft.

Fig. 12.0: Source: https://commons.wikimedia.org/wiki/File:Mercury_Seven_astronauts_with_aircraft.jpg.

CHAPTER 12

Set and Setting

The Roots of the 1960s Era

By Timothy Miller

....

Editor's Introduction

The decade of the 1960s is best known for its radicalism and counterculture movements. It is a decade that describes the radicalism and counterculture in social norms about the way one dressed, the music one listened to, the drugs one took, sexuality, formalities, and yes, even schooling. It was a decade where one denounced the irresponsible excess, flamboyance, and decay of the social order. Norms of all kinds were broken down, especially when it came to civil rights and the endless war in Vietnam.

Tension between the United States and the Soviet Union dominated geopolitics during the 1960s. From the space race to sports, competition between the two nations was intense. The Cold War almost turned into a hot war in October 1962 during what has become known as the Cuban Missile Crisis. Thereafter, the two nations fought "proxy" wars in third-world nations hoping to set up friendly governments. The following essay by Timothy Miller looks at the problematic 1960s.

Set and Setting

The Roots of the 1960s-Era Communes

By Timothy Miller

T he communes of the 1960s era stood firmly in the American communal
tradition. To be sure, several observers have noted that many hippies and
others of their generation were not consciously interested in history, seeing
themselves as new people creating a whole new social order independent of
the past, and have hypothesized that the 1960s communes had sources entirely
apart from the dynamics that led to such earlier communal movements as those
of the Shakers, the Hutterites, and the Oneida Perfectionists. In this view, Robert
Houriet—generally one of the more perceptive contemporary observers of the
1960s-era communes—wrote: "At the outset, [the 1960s communal movement]
was the gut reaction of a generation. Hippie groups living a few country miles
apart were unaware of each other's existence and equally unaware of the other
utopian experiments in American history. They thought theirs were unique and
unprecedented."[1] However, although a sense of newness and of discontinuity
with the past did indeed characterize the 1960s outlook (particularly among
the counterculture), the people of the new generation emerged from a historical
context as surely as any other generation ever did; the communes, like the rest
of the cultural milieu, had sources in history as well as in contemporary culture.
Some individual communards may have been doing something entirely new, but
more than a few had important connections to the American communal past.

Many of the reporters and scholars who studied communes during the 1960s
accepted the notion of ahistoricity, locating the origins of the communes entirely in
the social conditions of the time. Focusing primarily on the counterculture rather
than on the other types of communes (which in fact outnumbered the hippie
settlements), these observers interpreted the 1960s communes as products of the
decay of urban hippie life in Haight-Ashbury, the East Village, and other enclaves.
The hip urban centers, so the thesis ran, were joyous centers of peace and love and
expanded consciousness only briefly (if at all), soon devolving into cesspools of
hard drugs, street crime, and official repression of dissident lifestyles. The hippies
at that point fled for the friendly precincts of the countryside, where they built

commines as new places for working out the hip vision. Voila! An entirely new social institution!

Examples of this explanation of the origins of 1960s-era (and especially hippie) communalism abound both in popular and in scholarly writings. Maren Lockwood Carden, for example, writing in 1976, says matter-of-factly that the hippies' "first communes were created within the urban areas in which they already lived" and that beginning in 1966 "and especially during 1967 and 1968, such community-oriented hippies left the city." Helen Constas and Kenneth Westhues purport to trace the history of the counterculture "from its charismatic beginnings in the old urban bohemias to its current locale in rural communes," concluding that "communes signify the routinization of hippiedom."[2]

Actually, however, the new communes began to appear before there was a clearly recognizable overall hippie culture, much less a decaying one. Catalyzed by shifts in American culture in the late 1950s and early 1960s, the new generation of communes was not initially a product of hippiedom but rather a crucible that played a major role in shaping and defining hip culture. In other words, the urban hippies did not create the first 1960s-era communes; it would be closer to the truth to say that the earliest communes helped create the hippies. Although communes were indeed founded by hippies who fled the cities, they were johnnies-come-lately to the 1960s communal scene.

To argue that the communes of the 1960s (or even just the hippie communes) were completely without historical rootedness ultimately requires that one believe the preposterous: that of the thousands or even millions of persons who lived communally, none had any knowledge of the American communal past. On the contrary, even though a great many new communards were surely without much historical knowledge about their undertaking, surprisingly many more did have such knowledge. The Diggers, for example—the communal shock troops of the early hip era—consciously named themselves after an important countercultural movement of an earlier century. The 1960s world was salted with old beatniks who understood that the venerable tradition of bohemianism embraced communities (if not always residential communes) of creative souls. The pages of the *Modern Utopian,* the trade journal of the 1960s communes, were liberally dosed with material on communes from earlier ages. Art Downing, describing his life in the 1960s commune popularly known as Kaliflower, recalled that he and his compatriots studied the nineteenth-century classic *The History of American Socialisms* by John Humphrey Noyes, founder and leader of the Oneida Community, and consciously tried to imitate Oneida in several of their communal practices, including a form of group marriage.[3] And more than few communards of the 1960s personally embodied important links to the communal and cooperative past. Before examining some of those links specifically, however, we will take a brief look at the larger context out of which the distinctive cultures of the 1960s emerged.

The Cultural Roots of the Cultural Revolution

The huge social upheaval that we generally refer to as "the sixties" was rooted in cultural developments that began to take shape over a century earlier and that were clearly taking on the distinctive contours of what would become known as 1960s culture by the mid-1950s.[4] Laurence Veysey has identified "a counter-cultural tradition, inherited from the mid-nineteenth century, burgeoning somewhat after 1900, remaining alive on the fringes, and then leaping into a new prominence after 1965 "[5] He roots that tradition in antebellum reformism (including the Transcendentalist uprising) and in the rise of anarchism and mysticism in the second half of the nineteenth century, further tracing its development through the rise of nudism, alternative healing practices, pacifism, interest in Asian and occult religions, back-to-the-land romanticism, and Depression-era socialism, as well as the ongoing presence of intentional communities.

In the 1950s that countercultural milieu started down the slippery slope that would give us the 1960s. The most important harbinger of what was to come was the emergence of the beat generation as the 1950s incarnation of the long Western tradition of bohemianism. The beats were an alienated crowd, skeptical of the pursuit of money, of traditional family life, of the American way of life itself.[6] Allen Ginsberg's "Howl," first read publicly in 1955 and published in 1956 following an obscenity suit, heralded the change of direction that the alternative culture was taking. It was a new blast of poetic wind, a stunning challenge to the formal, academic style that dominated American poetry and that even the earlier beat poets had been unable to dislodge. Other beat authors, notably Jack Kerouac and William S. Burroughs, soon began to find serious followings as well. At the same time, new and daring entertainment began to emerge; Lenny Bruce, to name one prominent performer, devastated nightclub audiences with a new type of standup comedy, a savage assault on American icons with shocking swear words never previously heard outside of private conversation.

New magazines were also pushing at the cultural boundaries. In 1958 Paul Krassner founded *The Realist*, a little newsprint journal that engaged in uninhibited social criticism and displayed freewheeling graphics—outrageous content for its time. In the early 1960s Krassner was marketing, through his magazine, such artifacts as the "Mother Poster," which consisted of the words "Fuck Communism" done up in a stars-and-stripes motif. He reached the peak of his iconoclastic renown in 1967, when he published a satire on the assassination of John F. Kennedy that included a scene in which Jacqueline Kennedy witnessed Lyndon Johnson "literally fucking my husband in the throat" (i.e., the fatal wound) just before being sworn in as president. Another new periodical, this one begun in 1962, was *Fuck Tou; A Magazine of the Arts,* put out in a mimeographed and stapled format by Ed Sanders, who had hitchhiked from Kansas City to New York in 1958. In his first issue Sanders issued a manifesto announcing that the magazine was "dedicated to pacifism, unilateral disarmament, national defense thru nonviolent resistance, multilateral indiscriminate apertural conjugation, anarchism, world federalism, civil disobedience, obstructers and submarine boarders, and all those groped by J. Edgar Hoover in the silent halls of congress." Much of the magazine's content consisted of experimental poetry and the works of leading beat literati, but Sanders also ran polemics and sexually explicit graphics; advocating the legalization of psychedelic drugs, he asked: "Why should a bunch of psychologists hog all the highs?" Sanders, like Ginsberg, would be a key figure in constructing the bridge from beat to hip. In 1964 he opened the Peace Eye bookstore in the East Village, where a good deal of hip culture was incubated, and later in the 1960s and 1970s he would gain prominence as leader of one of the farthest-out hip musical groups, the Fugs, and as a historian of the Charles Manson family.[7]

The beats, more than any other identifiable grouping, pointed alternative culture in new directions that would soon be embraced on a much wider scale. Murray Bookchin, the anarchist whose career as a public dissenter bridged beat and hip, found specific beat origins for environmental concern, the psychedelic experience, communes, the health food revolution, hip art forms, and other cultural innovations associated with the 1960s. Not every innovative idea was without antecedents.[8]

Meanwhile, other new cultural arrivals abetted the beat critique of the status quo. The seemingly innocuous *Mad* magazine, for example, which started out as a comic book, became a satirical bimonthly that had a powerful impact on children just forming their views of the world, lampooning venerable social icons and irreverently questioning authority right and left. Its contribution to the changing social milieu was no accident; as its longtime editor, Al Feldstein, said in 1996, "When Charles Wilson (Eisenhower's secretary of defense) said 'What is good for GM is good for America' we were saying 'Well, maybe not.' *Mad* was my chance to orient young people to the reality of the world—'They are lying to you.'"[9]

The list goes on: Television exposed Americans to an unprecedented range of cultures and visual images. Science fiction introduced the young to ecological issues, cultural relativity, and the ambiguities of progress;[10] indeed, one science fiction novel alone, Robert Heinlein's *Stranger in a Strange Land,* so entranced many sixties communards with its jabs at predominant social mores—especially monogamy and monotheism—that it became virtual scripture in several communes, such as Sunrise Hill in Massachusetts. New contraceptives and treatments of sexually transmitted diseases opened the door to relatively hassle-free casual sex, and a few social radicals actually began to advocate nudity and freewheeling sexuality openly. The new rock music of Chuck Berry and Elvis Presley was, compared to its immediate predecessors, primitive and sexual. Post-World War II prosperity put cash into the hands of the nonproductive young, changing their way of thinking about the relationship of work and wealth. Higher education mushroomed—with the unexpected result that a great portion of a generation was isolated from its elders, ghettoized, and given a chance to try new experiments in living.[11] In their heyday in the 1950s, liberal religious bodies (in contrast to their strait-laced predecessors) advocated loving social action and critical thinking about matters both temporal and spiritual. Even the Catholic Church was in the early stages of a modernization process that would culminate with the far-ranging reforms of the Second Vatican Council. Moreover, religions from beyond the Christian and Jewish mainstream began to creep into American culture; Zen, for example, had begun to enlarge its slender American presence as contact with Japan was expanded in the wake of World War II and as a new generation of writer-seekers, notably Alan Watts, presented the venerable tradition to English-speaking readers.[12]

The racial climate was changing as well, on campus and off. The civil rights movement, whose beginnings coincided with the rise to prominence of the beats in the mid-1950s, brought to the fore a new politics of moral passion and a new appreciation for blackness. Black radicals (notably Malcolm X) would soon emerge as cultural heroes among alienated white youth. Marijuana, that great component of the 1960s cultural upheaval, would pass from black musicians into the countercultural milieu. As Norman Mailer wrote in 1957, "the source of Hip is the Negro."[13] Civil rights—followed by antiwar political protest—would become a central, defining feature of the 1960s.

And, crucially, psychedelics, those vital shapers of the whole 1960s cultural revolution, were just beginning to show up in the 1950s. As we will see in the next chapter, the new mind-opening substances played central roles in two of the earliest 1960s communal scenes, Millbrook and the Merry Pranksters. Whatever else may be said about LSD, mescaline, psilocybin, and other related chemicals (including the milder marijuana), their use tends to break down social and intellectual conditioning and to raise in the user both a feeling of having new insights and a sense of the inadequacy of the old order. The fact that they are illegal to possess or to use creates a communal bond among those willing to take risks for the exploration of consciousness. Thus the psychedelics were powerful contributors not only to the development of an alternative culture but specifically to the formation of communes. As communard Stephen Diamond wrote, "People got stoned and they woke up."[14]

In sum, not everything—perhaps even not much—that happened in the 1960s era was *de novo*. Bennett Berger's observation on rural counter-cultural communes characterizes the 1960s generally: the period embodied a "complex mix of traditions, synthesized in fresh ways."[15]

But Why Communes?

The historical and cultural events, forces, personalities, and movements mentioned above help us understand the cultural upheaval of the 1960s, but they do not completely explain the huge wave of communal living that surged along with all the rest. After all, activists could have fought political battles, consciousness explorers could have sailed the psychedelic seas, and poets could have declaimed without living communally. Here the American communal past adds crucial tiles to the cultural mosaic in the form of the many specific individuals who embodied the transmission of the communal impulse to a new generation.

1960s Themes Long Before the 1960s

Much of what the public at large (and sometimes the communards themselves) regarded as new and sometimes shocking about 1960s communal life was not new at all, but merely a recapitulation of themes that had long danced across the American communal stage. The youth of the 1960s were not the first American communitarians to be infected with back-to-the-land romanticism; in fact that theme has been a major American communal staple. A concern for good diet and natural foods can be traced back at least as far as Fruitlands, the Massachusetts Transcendentalist commune presided over by A. Bronson Alcott from 1843 to 1845. (Indeed, had Fruitlands been founded 125 years later it would surely have been pigeonholed as a hippie commune, with its crowded housing, dedication to pacifism, idiosyncratic clothing, full economic communism, vegetarianism, high idealism, and eschewal of creature comforts.) The passion for order, for spiritual development, and for closely regulated personal behavior (including sexual behavior) that was common in the religious communes of the 1960s era was reminiscent of the Shaker colonies and of many other disciplined religious communities that reach back as far as the eighteenth century. The yearning for personal growth and fulfillment rather than for conventional social achievement that characterized the 1960s outlook reflects a central force in many historic American communes—the

Spirit Fruit Society, for example.[16] Private ownership of land was rejected by several earlier communal leaders, including Peter Armstrong, who in the 1860s deeded the land of his Pennsylvania adventist community, Celestia, to God.[17] Anarchistic communes—embracing voluntary but noncoercive cooperation and rejection of the prevailing government and culture—dotted the communal landscape of the nineteenth and early twentieth centuries. Altruistic sharing and charismatic leadership are not recent communal inventions. Nor was it novel that communes sometimes attracted loafers and deadbeats; the Shakers, for example, had a chronic problem with "Winter Shakers," persons who would arrive in the fall proclaiming their interest in joining only to leave in the spring after being nicely sheltered through the winter. Such an enumeration of prefigurations of the 1960s could be extended at great length.

The Enduring Communal Presence

It is also important to realize that earlier American communitarianism had not ground to a halt when the new generation of communes appeared so visibly on the scene. Dozens, perhaps hundreds, of intentional communities founded before 1960 were still alive when a new generation started building its experimental communities, and there was often a good deal of interaction between the newer and older communal streams. A steady stream of young idealists, for example, sought out Koinonia Farm, the interracial commune in south Georgia founded in 1942 by Clarence Jordan, whose program of building houses for the poor led to Habitat for Humanity—an organization that as we enter the twenty-first century continues to build and to rehabilitate houses for low-income persons around the world.[18] Dozens of other examples of transgenerational communal interaction could be cited; many of the communitarian groups founded prior to 1960 that are discussed in volume one of this work figured into later communal events as well.

Several of the older communities, in fact, were so compatible with the newcomers that they were virtually taken over by them, becoming indistinguishable from their newer communal siblings. East-West House in San Francisco and Quarry Hill in Vermont, for example, accommodated the new communal ethos readily. Zion's Order, a commune rooted in the Latter Day Saints tradition in southern Missouri, absorbed some of the many communal inquirers who dropped in to visit. In other cases the contact was more casual, but still formative. A few of the new communal seekers sought out the one surviving Shaker village open to new members (at Sabbathday Lake, Maine), wanting to know more about the longest-lived communal tradition in the United States. Although the highly structured Shaker life appealed to few of them and none joined as permanent members (a few stayed for a time as organic farming interns), there was some convivial interaction between the mainly aged Shakers and the young visitors, and the Shakers helped to give direction to one organized group of visitors who went on to found the Starcross Monastery in Annapolis, California.[19] Asaiah Bates, a longtime member of the WKFL Fountain of the World commune (which operated in California and Alaska for three or four decades beginning in the late 1940s), reported that when the 1960s communal surge arrived, a steady stream of commune-seekers visited the Fountain to consider joining.[20]

Heathcote Center

A case of special significance here is that of the School of Living and its Heathcote Center intentional community in Maryland. Founded by Ralph Borsodi in 1936, the School of Living promoted cooperative clusters of homesteads that would seek self-sufficiency through a combination of mutual aid and individual initiative. (Borsodi's projects are discussed in more detail in volume one of this work.) Borsodi eventually resigned from personal leadership of the project, but his work was taken up by Mildred Loomis, who started a new School of Living at her family's Lane's End Homestead near Brookville, Ohio. At Lane's End, she and her family elevated self-sufficiency to a high art, producing virtually all of their own food and living the good life with very little money. In the late 1940s Loomis began to develop what became something of a continuing-education program for rural self-sufficiency, with classes and demonstration projects carrying on the work of Borsodi and other Depression-era Decentralists, whose goal was nothing less than the overthrow of modern industrial society. A major new building was erected to house Lane's End's growing array of activities, and Loomis's thoughts turned increasingly toward developing a full-scale intentional community.

At the beginning of 1965 the School of Living acquired a thirty-seven-acre plot with five buildings, including a large old stone mill, in rural Maryland. A series of work parties effected the renovation of the mill into a group residence, and by 1966 the programs of the School of Living were operating from their new home, known as Heathcote Center. At the same time, of course, a new generation of potential communards was beginning to seek alternatives to the sterile middle-class ways of living in which they had grown up. Heathcote was within reasonably easy reach of several major East Coast population centers; more importantly, Mildred Loomis was remarkably open to the new generation of seekers who saw in Heathcote the seeds of something worthwhile, and soon the old mill was both a communal home and a conference center.[21] The physical facilities were spartan and the population rode a roller coaster, but Heathcote in effect became one of the first hippie communes. Several of the residents handbuilt their own inexpensive little dwellings to achieve a level of privacy not available in the mill building. Members paid their thirty-dollars-permonth assessments for food and other expenses in a variety of ways, often through odd-job work in the neighborhood that they located through a classified ad run periodically in the local paper: "Odd jobs by odd people. Heathcote Labor Pool."[22] Heathcote's educational mission also led to the establishment of other communes, as seekers came to Heathcote conferences and left determined to pursue the communal vision elsewhere. Some of that activity will be detailed in the next chapter.

To be sure, Heathcote was not without its shortcomings. Population turnover was considerable, and sometimes there were so few residents that it hardly deserved to be called a community. Loomis, for all her rapport with those a generation or more younger than she, was not completely comfortable with the unstructured hippie life and had trouble understanding that some of those who lived there did not want to study the ideas of the venerated Ralph Borsodi. One account by a visitor in winter (Heathcote's slow season) depicts the community as a collection of dreary persons living in squalor, in their sexual behavior as hypocritical as any of the suburbanites that they despised, claiming to be monogamous but actually having many furtive affairs.[23] Many twists and turns have ensued, but Heathcote is alive and well as of this writing, over thirty years after its founding and more than a dozen after the death of its matriarch, Loomis, in 1986. It played a critical role in shaping the communal scene of the 1960s.

The Predisposed:
New Communards with Old Communal Ties

One of the strongest arguments for connectedness between communal generations lies in individual 1960s communards. In a remarkable number of cases, those who lived communally—and especially those who had founding and leadership roles in the communes—had communitarianism, or things related to it, in their backgrounds. Many of the interviewees in the 60s Communes Project were asked if they had personal predisposing factors in their backgrounds that might have pointed them toward communal living. That is, had they had contacts with communes founded before the great 1960s communal tide? Did they have parents or other older relatives who had lived communally? Did they have relatives who engaged in other forms of organized cooperation? Did relatives or others important to their formation in some way support the common good and question the American ideal of me-first individualism? At a minimum, did they come from politically and socially progressive families that taught concern for others and questioned prevailing social values? Did their interest in community have discernible roots beyond their own 1960s experience?

Yes, came the answer in a great many cases. Rachelle Linner, who was at various times a Catholic Worker and a member of the Community for Creative Nonviolence, came from a generally progressive family; one of her cousins was a radical activist, and an aunt had supported the Abraham Lincoln Brigade in the Spanish Civil War. Cat Yronwode, who founded the Garden of Joy Blues and lived at several other communes as well, grew up in what she characterized as a bohemian left-wing environment; her mother, Lilo Glozer, had been involved in intentional communities, at one time having had some association with Ralph Borsodi of the School of Living. Tolstoy Farm, until a disastrous fire, had a communal library that included works by Borsodi and other earlier Utopians, partly because founder Huw Williams had grown up in a Christian socialist family familiar with such thinkers. Verandah Porche of Packer Corner grew up in a family of Trotskyites and union organizers. John Neumeister, who lived at Footbridge Farm in Oregon and was active in radical politics, grew up near Antioch College in Yellow Springs, Ohio, and often went with his parents to programs at that community-minded school—which was once headed by prominent communal-living advocate Arthur Morgan. (Yellow Springs is the home of Community Service, Inc., the original Fellowship of Intentional Communities, and the Vale community; thus, Antioch has one of the nation's more substantial communal archives). Judson and Marty Jerome, founders of Downhill Farm, came into contact with the communal ideal when they enrolled their handicapped daughter in a Camphill school in Pennsylvania, part of an educational network that has been serving persons with special needs in communal settings in Europe and North America since the 1930s. (Jud Jerome went on to become a scholar of 1960s-era communes). Daniel Wright, founder of Padanaram, was raised in a strongly community-minded Brethren church near Des Moines. Richard Kallweit, one of the earliest members of Drop City and the person who lived there longer than any other, had parents who had lived in the Jewish farm colonies of southern New Jersey. Peter Rabbit, another Drop City Dropper, had attended the communal Black Mountain College a decade previously. Robert Houriet, whose personal interest in the communes led to one of the most insightful contemporary books on the subject, went to Tivoli (a Catholic Worker farm in New York state) to meet Dorothy Day in his quest to find the roots of what was going on. Vivian Gotters, an early resident of Morning Star Ranch in

California, grew up in cooperative housing in Queens and had socialists in her family; of communal living she said, "It's in my blood."

And on and on. Dozens of the interviewees were red diaper babies—that is, their parents or other close relatives had been Communists or Communist sympathizers, usually in the 1930s. Lou Gottlieb, the founder of Morning Star Ranch, had himself been a Communist some years before he opened his land to a wave of community-seekers. Richard Marley, who lived communally at East-West House and then with the Diggers before becoming the principal founder of Black Bear Ranch, was a red diaper baby who became a party member himself as a young adult.

The communal predisposition of Ramón Sender, the first resident at Morning Star and a veteran communard at several locations, was remarkably broad. Born in Spain, he came to the United States at age four; his father, a famous writer who espoused anarchism and later (briefly) Communism, had been influenced by the anarchist communes of Catalonia during the Spanish Civil War. At age sixteen Sender met a great-granddaughter of John Humphrey Noyes, whose Oneida Community was one of the most notable American communes of the nineteenth century. With her he visited Oneida, where her grandparents were living in the Mansion House, the huge unitary dwelling of the community where her grandfather had been born a stirpicult—a product of a communal planned breeding experiment. After getting married the Senders enthusiastically set out to find a community in which to settle. In 1957 they visited the Bruderhof, then relatively recently established in New York state; Sender, although initially enthusiastic, did not endure beyond a trial period, but his wife remained there permanently.[24] Thus it is not entirely coincidental that Sender was the first person to live at Morning Star Ranch, or that he later lived at Wheeler's Ranch, or that he visited many other communities and still keeps up communal historiography and contacts with old communal friends today. Like Vivian Gotters, he has community in his blood.

Some 1960s-era communitarians were so interested in what had gone before that they immersed themselves in the cooperative tradition. John Curl, an early member of Drop City, went on to publish seminal historical works on cooperation and communitarianism.[25] Early East Wind members built what remains one of the more important library collections on the history of intentional community and cooperation. One bit of historical connectedness is embodied in the building names at Twin Oaks, the egalitarian commune founded in 1967 in Virginia. The original farmhouse was called Llano, after the Llano del Rio colony that operated in Texas and Louisiana from 1914 to 1937; later structures were called, among other things, Oneida, Harmony, Modern Times, Kaweah, Degania, and Tachai—all earlier communes in the United States and abroad. Twin Oakers have not been ignorant of the communal line in which they stand.

That is not to say that all of the new communitarians embodied or sought out links with the American communal past. Al Andersen, an active pre-1960s communitarian, in 1996 could not recall from his days of close association with young 1960s activists that anyone asked his advice on commune-building.[26] Much of what the 1960s communards did *was*, from their point of view at least, all new. But communal predisposition among a great many of their number was too pervasive to ignore and points to a greater continuity of the communal tradition than many have presumed to be the case.

Getting Together

The fact that some 1960s communards had some predisposition to cooperation and other progressive values does not by itself, of course, explain why so many young Americans joined the great surge of community-building. The social circumstances of the day certainly had a great deal to do with community formation, and once the migration into communes got off the ground, it became so perfectly a part of the Zeitgeist that its own momentum propelled it rapidly forward.

Even though many of the communards (especially rural ones) came to disavow overt activism, the political climate of the 1960s and the daily realities of the activist lifestyle initially had a great deal to do with making community such an attractive life option. Marty Jezer's account of his own somewhat unintentional slide into communal living—while he was working for bare subsistence wages at the radical *Win* magazine in New York in 1967—evokes an experience shared by thousands:

> Our poverty led us to share our meager resources, something we had only dabbled in before. It strikes me now how weird we were about money. In college, I had a friend named Marty Mitchell, who I turned on to jazz and who then became my constant companion. Mitchell never had any money, so whenever I wanted to go somewhere with him, we'd have to go through a standard routine.
> "Hey, Mitch, Ornette's at The Five Spot, want to go?"
> (Fingering his empty billfold) "I can't afford it."
> "How much do you need?"
> "Oh, maybe a couple of bucks for the minimum and a bite to eat later."
> "I'll lend you the money and you can pay me when you have it."

Of course, we both understood that he would never "have it." But Mitchell would open a little notebook, just the same, and record the loan in his list of debts. By graduation he owed me and his other friends hundreds of dollars. We never expected him to pay and he never intended to. Yet we kept the ritual going and he maintained an accurate list of his debts. In point of fact, we were functioning communally, but none of us were aware of the concept. ...

We took to opening our houses to the many movement people who always seemed to be passing through New York. Some stayed and so shared whatever apartment, food, bed, clothes that were available. We stopped being guests at each other's houses and no longer felt the need to entertain or be entertaining. Kitchens became liberated territory. Women still did most of the cleaning and the cooking (that would become an issue later), but we stopped thinking of our little apartments as *ours*. ... There were four or five apartments scattered throughout the city where I could spend time, eat, sleep, and feel at home.

Slowly, we were becoming a family. We weren't aware of the process, one step suggested a next step and circumstances dictated the direction. ... The world seemed to be coming apart all around us; yet in the growing hippie subculture we were experiencing an unprecedented ecstatic high. Our world, at least, was getting better all the time, and, if nothing else, we had our friends, which seemed more than enough. "With our love, we could save the world," we felt, "if they only knew" and, by God, we were more than ready to share in the good news. [We became a] family, and with thousands of other small families scattered across the nation, one big spaced-out tribe.[27]

From that kind of situation it was not hard to jump into more specifically defined communal living, as Jezer and a dozen or two of his friends did when they bought a farm in Vermont in the summer of 1968.

What in God's name had I gotten into? Here I'd invested every cent I had in a farm which we knew nothing about, with some crazy people who I hardly knew. ... But that feeling didn't last for long. Our lives, by then, had become structured on faith. If I couldn't trust my brother, who could I trust? The farm had to work out because I couldn't think of what I'd do next if it didn't.[28]

One, Two, Three, Many Communes

Once it got well started, about 1968, the communal stream became a torrent as the alienated young banded together in thousands of places, likely and unlikely, urban and rural. Media publicity had a good deal to do with it. The early coverage of the new-generation communes tended to be in specialized publications and in the underground press, which by 1968 was thriving in hundreds of American cities and towns. Soon, however, the colorful communes were featured in all the mass print media—daily newspapers, *Time* and *Newsweek* and *Life,* rural weeklies, and just about every other venue. Reporters and readers alike were fascinated with and often outraged by these strange-looking eccentrics who had suddenly taken up residence in their midst. In the smaller papers the coverage was often hostile, but more often the reportorial attitude was one of bemusement—"Here's what's going on up there on Backwater Road, I can hardly believe it either, but look at this!" Sensationalism, then as now, was the order of the day for any self-respecting news outlet; so much of the coverage focused on nudity and drug use, real or rumored—and thus helped to feed the local hostility toward communes that broke out so often. As Hugh Gardner observed, "Reporters (and to a lesser extent sociologists) were considered second only to the police as bearers of the plague."[29]

The avalanche of publicity, unsurprisingly, brought new legions of seekers swarming into communes—and often overwhelming them. One of the notable slick-magazine features was a cover story entitled "The Commune Comes to America" in the July 18, 1969, issue of *Life,* consisting mainly of exquisite color photos of a rural forty-one-member hippie clan, sometimes nude, sometimes wearing bells and beads and buckskins and granny dresses, living in tepees and bathing in the creek. The story carefully avoided naming the commune or locating it anywhere other than "somewhere in the woods," but word quickly circulated that it was actually the Family of the Mystic Arts, a rural Oregon commune, and hippies by the hundreds swarmed to and over the idyllic locale, undoubtedly hastening its decline. Such a scenario was repeated less dramatically wherever press coverage surfaced.

The mass-media coverage was supplemented by sympathetic reporting in specialized publications that were eagerly read by persons intrigued by the communes. The *Modem Utopian,* founded by Richard Fairfield while he was a student at the Unitarian theological school at Tufts University in 1966, became the flagship of the genre, featuring news coverage of as many communes as possible, interviews with key communal figures, and other coverage of interest to alternative-minded people. A variety of shortlived newsletters supplemented Fairfield's work; in the San Francisco Bay area, for example, an intercommunal periodical called *Kaliflower* was distributed to hundreds of communal houses and other places, fueling the great interest of the young in new lifestyles. Coverage in the underground press continued apace, of course. And eventually the communes movement was producing books of its own, books that in some cases got wide circulation and introduced a great many young persons to the idealized delights of intentional community. The foremost of that genre was *Living on the Earth,* a hand-lettered and whimsically illustrated paean to dropout life by Alicia Bay Laurel, written while she was living at Wheeler's Ranch, an open-land community in California. Originally published by a small press called Bookworks in Berkeley, the book was picked up by Random House and—in the wake of a surge of publicity that included three major notices in the *New York Times* in the space of six days, among them a glowing review by Raymond Mungo in the *Times Book Review*—found an enormous nationwide audience.[30] Laurel, who had resolved to live in carefree hippie poverty, gave away most of the profuse royalties that stemmed from her successful authorship.

Thus did the word spread. By the late 1960s the United States was well into the greatest epoch of commune-building in its history.

Notes

1. Robert Houriet, *Getting Back Together* (New York: Avon, 1971), 9.

2. Maren Lockwood Carden, "Communes and Protest Movements in the U.S., 1960–1974: An Analysis of Intellectual Roots," *International Review of Modern Sociology* 6 (spring 1976): 16; Helen Constas and Kenneth Westhues, "Communes: The Routinization of Hippiedom," in *Society's Shadow: Studies in the Sociology of Countercultures,* ed. Kenneth Westhues (Toronto: McGraw-Hill Ryerson, 1972), 191–94.

3. Art Downing, 60s Communes Project interview, Mar. 22, 1996.

4. Some, for that matter, would find the earliest prefigurings of hip much earlier—for example, among the second-century Adamites, who lived in isolation, worshipped in the nude, rejected marriage, and saw themselves as living in paradise. See Carl Bangs, "The Hippies: Some Historical Perspectives," *Religion in Life 37,* no. 4 (winter 1968): 498–508; J. H. Plumb, "The Secular Heretics," *Horizon* 10, no. 2 (spring 1968): 9–12.

5. Laurence Veysey, *The Communal Experience: Anarchist and Mystical Communities in Twentieth-Century America* (Chicago: Univ. of Chicago Press, 1978 [1973]), 33.

6. See John Robert Howard, "The Flowering of the Hippie Movement," *Annals of the American Academy of Political and Social Science* 382 (Mar. 1969): 43–55.

7. Paul Krassner, "The Parts That Were Left Out of the Kennedy Book," *The Realist* 74 (May 1967): 18; manifesto, *Euck You: A Magazine of the Arts* 1 [1962]; Ed Sanders, *The Family: The Story of Charles Manson's Dune Buggy Attack Battalion* (New York: Dutton, 1971). On Sanders's early years in New York see "Peace Eye: An Interview with Edward Sanders," *Mesechabe: The Journal of Surre(gion)alism* (New Orleans) 14/15 (spring 1996): 30–32.

8. Murray Bookchin, "When Everything Was Possible," *Mesechabe: The Journal of Surre(gion)alism* (New Orleans) 9/10 (winter 1991): 1–7.

9. Quoted *in Billings (Montana) Gazette* Online, Sept. 15, 1996. Feldstein was living in retirement in nearby Paradise Valley, Mont.

10. See, for example, Walt Crowley, *Rites of Passage: A Memoir of the Sixties in Seattle* (Seattle: Univ. of Washington Press, 1995), 6.

11. On these themes see D. Lawrence Wieder and Don H. Zimmerman, "Generational Experience and the Development of Freak Culture." *Journal of Social Issues* 30, no. 2 (1974): 137–61.

12. See, among many other works, Alan W. Watts, *The Way of Zen* (New York: Pantheon, 1957).

13. Norman Mailer, "The White Negro," in *Voices of Dissent* (New York: Grove, 1958), 199.

14. Stephen Diamond, *What the Trees Said: Life on a New Age Farm* (New York: Dell, 1971), 73. For an elaboration of this line of thought see Hugh Gardner, *The Children of Prosperity: Thirteen Modem American Communes* (New York: St. Martin's, 1978), 5–7.

15. Bennett M. Berger, *The Survival of a Counterculture: Ideological Work and Everyday Life Among Rural Communards* (Berkeley: Univ. of California Press, 1981), 196.

16. On this point see James L. Murphy, *The Reluctant Radicals: Jacob L. Beilhart and the Spirit Fruit Society* (Lanham, Md.: University Press of America, 1989), 226.

17. Donald Wayne Bender, *From Wilderness to Wilderness: Celestia* (Dushore, Pa.: Sullivan Review, 1980).

18. On the interaction of Koinonia with 1960s-era communitarians see, for example, William Hedgepeth and Dennis Stock, *The Alternative: Communal Life in New America* (New York: Macmillan, 1970), 175–81.

19. Brother Arnold Hadd, 60s Communes Project interview, Feb. 9, 1996.

20. Asaiah Bates, 60s Communes Project interview, Sept. 12, 1996.

21. For Loomis's account of the development of Heathcote see Richard Fairfield, *Communes USA: A Personal Tour* (Baltimore: Penguin, 1972), 32–38. Other historical tidbits were published in various issues of the School of Living's publication *Green Revolution;* see, for example, 9, no. 12 (Dec. 1971): 3–7.

22. Herb Goldstein, 60s Communes project interview, July 17, 1996.

23. Elia Katz, *Armed Love* (New York: Bantam, 1971), 37–46. The aggressively negative tone of Katz's whole book leads one to discount his impressions somewhat.

24. On Sender's early experiences with the Bruderhof see Ramón Sender Barayón, "A Bruderhof Memoir," *KIT Newsletter* 9, no. 6 (June 1997): 6–10.

25. See John Curl, *History of Work Cooperation in America: Cooperatives, Cooperative Movements, Collectivity and Communalism from Early America to the Present* (Berkeley: Homeward, 1980); John Curl, ed., *History of Collectivity in the San Francisco Bay Area* (Berkeley: Homeward, 1982).

26. Al Andersen, 60s Communes Project interview, July 12, 1996.

27. Marty Jezer, "How I Came Here," in *Home Comfort: Stories and Scenes of Life on Total Loss Farm,* ed. Richard Wizansky (New York: Saturday Review Press, 1973), 44–45.

28. Ibid., 49.

29. H. Gardner, *Children of Prosperity,* 18.

30. Raymond Mungo, "Living on the Earth," *New York Times Book Review,* Mar. 21, 1971, 6–7; Christopher Lehmann-Haupt, "A Red Fox and a Bay Laurel," *New York Times,* Mar. 25, 1971, 37; "Her Hymn to Nature Is a Guidebook for the Simplest of Lives," *New York Times,* Mar. 26, 1971, 34.

Selected Bibliography

Berger, Bennett M. *The Survival of a Counterculture: Ideological Work and Everyday Life Among Rural Communards.* Berkeley: Univ. of California Press, 1981.

Diamond, Stephen. *What the Trees Said: Life on a New Age Farm.* New York: Dell, 1971.

Fairfield, Richard [Dick]. *Communes USA: A Personal Tour.* Baltimore: Penguin, 1972.

Gardner, Hugh. *The Children of Prosperity: Thirteen Modem American Communes.* New York: St. Martin's, 1978.

Hedgepeth, William, and Dennis Stock. *The Alternative: Communal Life in New America.* New York: Macmillan, 1970.

Home Comfort: Stories and Scenes of Life on Total Loss Farm. Edited by Richard Wizansky.
New York: Saturday Review Press, 1973.

Houriet, Robert. *Getting Back Together.* New York: Avon, 1971.

Katz, Elia. *Armed Love.* New York: Bantam, 1971.

QUESTION TO CONSIDER

- What were some issues confronting the American people in the 1960s?

PART VII

The End of the Twentieth Century

West and East Germans at the Brandenburg Gate in 1989.

CHAPTER 13

The End of the 1980s

By Nina E. Serrianne

....

Editor's Introduction

Known as the Reagan era, the 1980s witnessed the collapse of communism and the end of a 45-year cold war between the United States and the Soviet Union. The 1980s were a decade of major socioeconomic change due to advances in technology. It was a time when 60 percent of Americans got cable television in their homes. The decade saw the rise of the right, which began in the 1970s and reached its height in the mid-1980s. The 1980s featured the "yuppie"—a baby boomer with a degree, "a well-paying job and expensive taste." Read the following essay by Nina E. Serrianne about the end of the 1980s.

The End of the 1980s

By Nina E. Serrianne

After decades of Cold War tensions and subsequent hot wars (military conflict with active combat) between the United States and the Soviet Union, President elect George Herbert Walker Bush confidently proclaimed, "for in a man's heart, if not in fact, the day of the dictator is over." During his 1989 inaugural address, he elucidated, "The totalitarian era is passing, its old ideas blown away like leaves from an ancient, lifeless tree. 'A new breeze is blowing.'" Before the end of his first year in office, his prophecy became a reality as the Soviet Union collapsed and the Berlin Wall fell. The year 1989 ushered in a new decade in both American and international politics. The Reagan years (1980–1988) were domestically defined by individualism and power established through personal wealth. Simultaneously, the struggle between capitalism and communism demarcated foreign relations. If Reagan brought "morning to America" in the early 1980s, Bush facilitated the "new breeze" at the end of the decade. As it happened, 1989 was the last year of both the conservative revolution and the Cold War. To the surprise of many, the Bush presidency began a new era of moderate domestic politics, and to the surprise of few, the post–Cold War era.

The conservative revolution of the 1980s was a direct backlash to the progressive social changes of the 1960s. During the 1960s, the Democratic Party gained political momentum and implemented liberal public policies. The assassination of President John F. Kennedy and the vocal student movement set the tone of the country. The American political climate now tended to abandon conservative Republican ideology and supported the new president, Lyndon B. Johnson. Because of this change, conservative Americans sought to restrategize and reclaim the White House. The strategy of the "Rockefeller Republicans" (those following the political ideology of the politician Nelson Rockefeller, often described as the liberal Republicans) focused on the elections they believed Republicans could win. In the wake of Watergate, the end of the Vietnam War, and the counterculture movement of the 1960s, the conservative lobbyists gained an opportunity to restructure the party platform. The new agenda specifically targeted their approaches to fiscal and social issues. As the GOP refocused, many of the social issues raised in the previous decades became bipartisan issues. In the years after the divide between conservative mainstream culture and counterculture, conservatives strove to be the antithesis of the liberal movement. The GOP aimed to fight the "George McGoverns" of politics (the iconic liberal Democratic candidate who lost to Richard Nixon in the 1972 general election). Supported by the evangelical movement of the 1970s, the GOP aimed to repeal the progress in abortion rights, the gay rights movement, the women's movement, gun control legislation, the death penalty, and other social issues. By 1980, the Republican Party successfully created a cohesive platform and regained control of both the Senate and the presidency.

George Bush and Ronald Reagan, then governor of California, began as political adversaries as they both sought the presidency in 1980. During the campaign, Bush tried to learn to appear more likable to the camera, but it was too late. Reagan, a former wealthy movie star, campaigned with charm, excellent communication skills, and the ability to overcome scandals. These attributes awarded him the nickname "the great communicator" and later "the Teflon president." In May 1980, after months of campaigning against each other, Bush resigned the race, leaving the Republican presidential nomination to Reagan. On July 16, 1980, while at the Republican National Convention in Detroit, Reagan selected Bush as the vice presidential nominee to appear on the ballot in November. Bush's inclusion on the ticket was contingent on his embrace of the Reagan platform. Specifically, with the intent to convince voters he was loyal to Reagan, Bush changed his political position to be against abortion. Although he worked hard to persuade voters of his trustworthiness and devotion, many Republicans remained skeptical of his political positioning throughout his career. In the end, the campaigning assuaged the fears of voters, and on November 4, 1980, Reagan-Bush defeated the incumbent Carter-Mondale by a landslide. On January 20, 1981, Bush was sworn in as the nation's vice president.

Reagan's presidency was defined by his socially and fiscally conservative agenda. Throughout both presidential terms, Reagan fulfilled his campaign promises with support from the Senate. Former President Franklin D. Roosevelt inspired Reagan to not only enter politics but also to use his political model for the conservative and Republican agenda. Ironically, the agenda itself was the inverse of FDR's liberal and Democratic agenda; Reagan reversed more New Deal policies than any previous administration. The Reagan administration's policies supported big tax cuts, small government, and were premised on the theory of a "trickle-down effect" of prosperity, which came be to known as Reaganomics. As explained by the historian Michael Schaller in *Reckoning with Reagan: America and Its President in the 1980s*, the philosophy behind Reaganomics was rooted in Reagan's status in the 90 percent income bracket and his desire to eradicate "progressive taxation." His economic plan, "America's New Beginning: A Program for Economic Recovery," was first presented to Congress in February 1981. In addition to tax changes, the plan sought to cut $41 billion from his predecessor President Jimmy Carter's budget and many social programs.

The new financial policies of the Reagan administration, combined with the recession of 1982, created an economic seesaw; consequently, class stratification grew exponentially. According to Reaganomics, theoretically, the tax cuts would create an abundance of wealth among the more affluent classes that would "trickle" down to the poor. This concentration of wealth in the top income bracket has been attributed by scholars to the making of the "1 percent" that now owns the majority of the country's wealth. Although many financial experts and advisers cautioned the president against this approach, Reagan aggressively pursued his financial agenda. As Schaller explained, Reagan met with Congress seventy times during the first four months of his administration to lobby for his tax cuts and increases to the defense budget. Ultimately, he skillfully and successfully negotiated with Congress to ensure that his financial vision was completed.

During Bush's tenure as vice president, he remained devoted to Reagan throughout an assassination attempt, the Iran-Contra affair, and Cold War and hot war negotiations. In October 1987, with the public's support, Bush announced his second bid for the presidency. His reputation with the Reagan administration gave him credibility; however, when juxtaposed with the "great communicator," Bush appeared tepid and at times uncomfortable during his own campaign for office. He was once again challenged to reveal his personality and persuasively articulate his goals to the American people. Bush's political expertise and his popularity was apparent, but he needed to prove that this was sufficient to be elected president. GOP voters were persuaded by the Reagan legacy and the vice president's fidelity. In August 1988, Bush accepted the Republican nomination at the Republican National Convention.

The 1980s was a gilded age of wealth and prosperity, specifically for the upper classes chasing the American dream. In *Sleepwalking through History: America in the Reagan Years*, the Pulitzer Prize winner Haynes Johnson described how America "was passing through a period that increasingly resembled the moral slackness of the spendthrift twenties, a new Gilded Age, and one that, like then, would extract a price for its excesses." This story of wealth and overindulgences was apparent in politics, music, and film. During the apex of the 1980s, the pop singer Madonna's song, "Material Girl," became an anthem for a decade of prosperity for the wealthy. Dressed in homage to Marilyn Monroe's performance of "Diamonds Are a Girl's Best Friend" (1953), Madonna quipped, "Living in a material world/ And I am a material girl." This song, coupled with other chart toppers such as Bruce Springsteen's rock anthem "Born in the USA," demonstrated the concurrent narcissism and fervent nationalism in American society during the 1980s. The patriotic platitudes of Springsteen's anthem reiterated the height of American pride under the Reagan-Bush administration.

The national obsession with the lucrative lifestyle of the 1980s was a result of a Machiavellian Wall Street culture and pursuits of the American dream. In *The Presidency of George Bush*, the historian John Robert Greene analyzes how the 1987 movie *Wall Street* captured the essence of the 1980s. The young stockbroker Bud Fox's ambition was to take the fast track to the top by any means necessary and as quickly as possible. Fox found a mentor in the high-powered and opportunistic stockbroker Gordon Gekko—the quintessential Wall Street yuppie. Throughout the movie, Gekko, the antihero, preaches his life and business philosophy: "greed is good." As he infamously proclaims during a stockbroker's meeting: "Greed is right, greed works. Greed clarifies, cuts through, and captures the essence of the evolutionary spirit. Greed, in all of its forms—greed for life, for money, for love, knowledge—has marked the upward surge of mankind." Gekko's soliloquy captured the sentiments of the material motivations of the 1980s.

The preoccupation with wealth and affluence was in part a result of the long-term obsession with the American dream, but more important was a symptom of the Cold War culture. The fixation on capitalism and the free market perpetuated American investment in a capitalist society. Regardless of the rise and fall of the stock market, Wall Street firms maintained an authority in the 1980s that represented copious amounts of wealth and power. Throughout the 1980s, access to wealth continued to increase, but in 1987 the economy reached its pinnacle before crashing. As discontentment rose during Bush's term in office, he took the fall for the inevitable decline of the economy.

Across society, the 1980s were a backlash to the counterculture movement and to the progressive legislative changes of the 1960s and 1970s; the free love and drug-dominated counterculture gave way to the decade of conservativism. The 1980s followed on the heels of the sexual liberation movement and the rise of second-wave feminism. The social agenda of the country was more conservative and puritanical. In the early part of the 1980s, there were still moments that were reminiscent of the sexual liberation movement, such as Madonna's or Pat Benatar's music videos aired on the cable television station MTV. As the culture became more conservative and the Republican revolution pushed for traditional values, specifically around gender and marriage, the representation of women in music and movies drifted back to conventional roles.

Additionally, during the 1980s, the glamorous side of sex faded as a new virus took lives. The first cases of Human Immunodeficiency Virus (HIV) and Acquired

Immune Deficiency Syndrome (AIDS) were identified in 1981. The quick-spreading and misunderstood virus plagued communities across the United States and the globe, disproportionately impacting minority communities. Since the first five cases were discovered, approximately thirty-four million people have been infected with HIV. This includes more than one million cases in the United States and an estimated half a million deaths; of these, two hundred thousand occurred before the 1990s. In *AIDS in America*, the medical anthropologist Susan Hunter explained that New York City has more HIV infections due to drug use than many developing countries combined. Every thirteen minutes someone in America becomes infected. During the 1980s, views on this rapidly growing disease were commonly rooted in discrimination, homophobia, and confusion. The response from the government was highly intolerant and inactive in preventing or curing the virus. Reagan was supported by religious extremists such as the Reverend Jerry Falwell, who attributed the epidemic to the "wrath of God upon homosexuals." The Reagan administration evaded the issue in a way that the presidents of the 1990s were unable to, as by then the virus was too consuming. As described by Greene in *The Presidency of George Bush*, AIDS was no longer an issue the Reagan administration, or Americans, could ignore. "Because of AIDS, the morality of Reaganism had to confront the very real possibility that one could die from having sex." Unlike during the sexual revolution, casual sex now had a fatal consequence and the epidemic was sweeping the country.

When Bush took office as president in January 1989, the conservative revolution and the rapacious stockbrokers of Wall Street had been dominating America for nearly a decade. As heir to the Reagan legacy, voters anticipated that the vice president would follow in his predecessor's footsteps and continue the trend of conservativism. The popularity of the Reagan administration secured Bush's place as the next president against the Democratic Party challenger Michael Dukakis. Since Bush's days as a young politico, many of his critics denounced him as a RINO—Republican in name only. As a conservative who voted for the Voting Right Act of 1964 and changed his position on abortion, many believed that he was a weak politician or more liberal than he stated. A cover of *Newsweek* magazine hit the stands during the presidential campaign that charged Bush with "fighting the wimp factor." Although the admiration of the Reagan administration was enough to maintain his voting base, Republican voters worried about his presidential style. During his 1988 campaign, Bush was afraid to "go negative" and only adopted a more aggressive campaign style when pushed by his aides. Speaking to his character, he wanted his moral ideology and résumé to speak for itself.

The softer side of Bush that worried voters during the campaign appeared in his first moments in office. His inaugural speech began as an ode to the Reagan years. Considerable portions of his discourse reiterated his support for the policies of the Reagan administration, including criticisms of welfare, support of family values and the anti-abortion movement, and a call to action for activism on the part of the youth and the elderly. However, a glimpse of the forthcoming Bush presidency and departure from his campaign strategy was captured when he called on Americans "to make kinder the face of the nation and gentler the face of the world." Although Bush proved to be a hawkish president on the international front, his domestic policies led to much criticism and eventually debased his career.

The first two years in office, Bush disassociated himself from the Reagan legacy and established his own prestige. Although Reagan left office with the highest approval rating since FDR, the factions of the Democratic and Republican government needed bipartisan collaboration. This was integral to moving forward with new legislation and to address the impending financial crisis. Bush reflected in *All the Best, George Bush: My Life in Letters and Other Writings* that he knew success would require him to work closely with the Democratic-controlled Congress. During Bush's inauguration speech, he set the tone for bipartisan partnership when he labeled the incoming era "the age of the offered hand" and extended his hand to those across the aisle in a gesture to create a bipartisan movement. Although Bush ran an aggressive election campaign, once elected, he returned to his imperturbable political style.

When Bush transitioned to the White House in January 1989, he broke from the Reagan administration by appointing new members to his cabinet. During Bush's campaign, he established his right-hand men in the Republican Party and trusted them to guide him through his presidency. Reagan loyalists and appointed staff viewed this as Bush's first step to abandon the Republican Party. Greene described this political decision as an "ideological house cleaning." He elaborated, "Reagan appointees were shown the door in a way that made it look like a Democrat was coming into office." Among Bush's transition team was his most influential appointee, John Sununu, his chief of staff. Whereas Bush was known for being diplomatic and soft, Sununu was aggressive and relentless. In *The Modern Presidency*, the political scientist James Pfiffner described him as "Bush's pit bull." Despite being saturated in politics from a young age, Bush was inclined to take a soft approach to policymaking. Sununu's antagonistic approach to politics allowed both the president and his staff to play into the "good cop/bad cop" dynamic that was inherent in the administration. Pfiffner expounded that Sununu's more conservative politics also helped retain the Republican voting base during the early years of the Bush presidency. Although Sununu pushed Bush to the Right politically, the president's commitment to his own agenda, not the Reagan agenda, set him up for immense criticism. As his term progressed, almost fulfilling the critical prediction, Bush became the "soft" version of himself for which he was berated.

The economic calamity of the Bush administration was inevitable. During Reagan's time in office, the federal debt more than tripled; by January 1989, the debt amounted to over $2.7 trillion dollars. Although the rich continued to profit and to gain prosperity, Reaganomics created instability in the economy. Greene noted Reagan's impact on the Bush administration: "In his seemingly sincere attempt to turn the clock back to a time when values were simpler and America's place in the world was strong and secure, Reagan unleashed a host of demons that plagued his successor." Reagan believed that "high taxes and excess spending" needed to be fixed. However, his economic plan backfired when the deficit grew under Reaganomics. Additionally, the interest on the debt increased from $69 billion when Reagan took office to $169 billion when Bush took office eight years later. Unfortunately, the consequences of Reagan administration policies came at the worst time for the new president. Johnson wrote that in the first weeks of Bush's term in office, "the unpaid bills of the eighties were coming due" and the new president was faced with the consequences. The tax cuts and fiscal policies of the Reagan administration created a volatile economy that resulted in the economic recession, which beleaguered the Bush administration. The recession specifically burdened Bush during the 1992 campaign.

Bush's succession was impacted by international politics. As a result of the animosity with the Soviet Union and Communist countries, the foreign policy agenda of the Reagan administration concentrated on the Cold War and subsequent hot wars. The administration took an aggressive stance on both the Cold War and the Berlin Wall. Throughout the 1980s, Reagan accelerated a heavily anticommunist agenda and spoke at length about bringing capitalism to Soviet countries and the world. The Cold War caused Americans to feel fear and hostility for decades. For the duration of the Cold War, America and the Soviet Union engaged in "us versus them" rhetoric, which perpetuated a malevolent relationship between the two super powers.

The cultural and political divisions of the Cold War were literally embodied in the Berlin Wall. The guarded wall was erected in 1961 to cut off East Germany from West Germany, obstructing emigration and separating pro- and anti-Soviet states. Countries around the world had been pushing for a unified Germany. The United States and England were apprehensive about what unification meant for international relations, but Mikhail Gorbachev, General Secretary of the

Communist Party of the Soviet Union (1985–1991), ultimately decided it was best for his country and the Pan-European vision to tear down the tangible barrier. As Bush predicted in his inaugural speech, the Cold War was coming to an end. After forty years, the symbolic end of the war came on November 9, 1989, when Gorbachev gave the order to tear the wall down. Overnight, international relations changed. At home and in Washington politics, the collapse was viewed as triumph for the United States and capitalism abroad.

As the Wall fell, Bush's popularity among the American people soared. Bush was criticized for not partaking in a more aggressive stance against the end of the Cold War. Consistent with his character, he was publically humble; he famously stated that he would not "dance on the wall" as it fell. He was slighted for his lack of enthusiasm during this historic moment. A reporter asked him, "you do not seem elated. … I am wondering if you are thinking of the problems." The president candidly responded, "I am not an emotional kind of guy." Bush's public hesitation was in part due to concern about what an overly patriotic and bellicose reaction from the United States might spark. At the time, it was uncertain what would unfold globally as the Wall crumbled. The muted response from Bush was intentional in an effort to appear diplomatic and to not incite backlash against the United States. With the fall of the Berlin Wall, the United States and capitalism led in an era of new global politics.

The Reagan administration and the events of the 1980s determined the context of the 1990s. Bush was affected by the decisions of his predecessor. On the domestic front he continued to negotiate the economic calamity as the recession continued. During the 1980s, as an extension of the Cold War, the United States became involved in hot wars across the globe. Additionally and unbeknownst to the American people, during the Iraq-Iran War from 1980 to 1988, the United States government supported Iraq and its leader Saddam Hussein. The Reagan administration was plagued with the scandal of illegally shipping arms to Iran during the conflict. Simultaneously, the United States also sent confidential information and arms to Iraq. As the *New York Times* reported on January 26, 1992, "In the end, officials acknowledged, American arms, technology and intelligence helped Iraq avert defeat and eventually grow, with much help from the Soviet Union later, into the regional power that invaded Kuwait in August 1990." The support of Hussein from the Reagan-Bush administration only precipitated the dictatorship; the strengthened power of the Iraqi leader became problematic during Bush's first year in office. The challenges and successes of the Bush administration were rooted in the policy decisions of the Reagan administration. The conflict in Iraq and the faltering economy provided Bush with both his legacy and the albatross of his career.

Recommended Reading

A great and lengthy introduction to the 1980s can be found in Haynes Johnson's *Sleepwalking through History: America in the Reagan Years* (New York: W. W. Norton, 2003). The recent editions are not only a national best-seller but also connect the Reagan years to the current and consequential issues of the twenty-first century. For more on the Reagan administration, see the Reagan scholar Michael Schaller's *Reckoning with Reagan: America and Its President in the 1980s* (Oxford: Oxford University Press, 1994). Addressing the AIDS crisis in America is the internationally acclaimed book by Randy Shilts, *And the Band Played On: Politics, People, and the AIDS Epidemic, 20th Anniversary Edition* (New York: St. Martin's Press, 2007). Tony Kushner's play and TV miniseries *Angels in America* provides a look into the early struggles with the virus.

QUESTION TO CONSIDER

- According to Serrianne, what were some issues confronting the American people in the 1980s?

CHAPTER 14

Americans Not Drinking Milk as Often as Their Parents

By Hayden Stewart and Diansheng Dong

Editor's Introduction

According to the USDA, the average person drinks 18 gallons of milk a year, which is a drop from 30 gallons a year back in 1970. It seems that those born in the 1980s and 1990s drink less milk in their adulthood than those born in the 1970s. One reason is culture change: Americans now have more choices. Read the essay by Stewart and Dong on why Americans drink less milk.

Americans Not Drinking Milk as Often as Their Parents

By Hayden Stewart and Diansheng Dong

Fig 14.1

Fluid milk has long been a staple of the American diet. However, as dietary habits change, Americans of all ages are drinking less milk, on average. Since 1970, per capita consumption of fluid milk has fallen from almost 1 cup (8 fl. oz.) to 0.6 cups per day. Contributing to the trend are differences in the eating and drinking habits of newer and older generations. Americans born in the 1970s, for example, drank less milk in their teens, twenties, and thirties than did Americans born in the 1960s at the same age points. Those born in the 1980s and 1990s, in turn, appear poised to drink even less milk in their adulthood than those born in the 1970s.

To study milk drinking by Americans over time and across generations, ERS researchers analyzed data from food consumption surveys conducted in 1977–78, 1989–91, 1994–96, 2003–04, and 2007–08. Individuals participating in these USDA-sponsored surveys reported their food and beverage consumption over a 24-hour period. The surveys reveal that portion size has been fairly steady over this time. Americans—on the occasions when they drink fluid milk—continue to consume about 1 cup.

Changes are instead occurring in the frequency of fluid milk consumption. As teenagers in 1977–78, Americans born in the early 1960s drank milk 1.5 times per day. As they grew older, they drank milk less often, consuming it on 0.7 occasions per day as young adults (in 1994–96) and 0.6 occasions per day in middle age (in 2007–08). By contrast, Americans born in the early 1980s entered their teenage years

Hayden Stewart & Diansheng Dong, "Americans Not Drinking Milk as Often as Their Parents," *Amber Waves*, vol. 9, 2013.

drinking milk just 1.2 times per day (in 1994–96) and, by the time they were young adults, had already reduced that frequency to 0.5 occasions per day (in 2007–08).

These generational differences in the frequency of milk drinking are contributing to decreases in per capita consumption. Between the 1977–78 and 2007–08 surveys, children's consumption of fluid milk declined from an average of 1.7 cups to 1.2 cups per day, and milk consumption by American teenagers and adults fell from 0.8 cups to 0.6 cups per day.

Several factors may account for variations in milk drinking habits across generations, including the food environment in which people come of age and a generation's unique experiences as children. Every decade brings a wider selection of beverage choices at supermarkets, restaurants, and other food outlets. Soft drinks, sports drinks, bottled water, juice boxes, and other products increasingly compete with fluid milk to quench consumers' thirst.

Fluid milk consumption is decreasing in all age groups

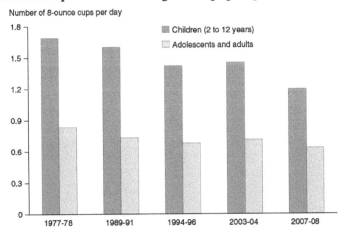

Number of 8-ounce cups per day

Source: USDA, Economic Research Service using data from the 1977–78 Nationwide Food Consumption Survey, 1989–91 Continuing Survey of Food Intakes by Individuals (CSFII), 1994–96 CSFII, 2003–04 National Health and Nutrition Examination Survey (NHANES), and 2007–08 NHANES.

This article is drawn from ...
Why Are Americans Consuming Less Fluid Milk? A Look at Generational Differences in Intake Frequency.
by Hayden Stewart, Diansheng Dong, and Andrea Carlson, USDA, Economic Research Service, May 2013

"Is Generational Change Contributing to the Decline in Fluid Milk Consumption?", by Hayden Stewart, Diansheng Dong, and Andrea Carlson, Journal of Agricultural and Resource Economics, Vol. 37: 435–454, December 2012

QUESTION TO CONSIDER

- According to Stewart and Dong, why are Americans drinking less milk than their parents?

PART VIII

The New Cold War

Presidents v. Putin and D. Trump at the 2017 G-20 Hamburg Summit.

CHAPTER 15

Managing the New Cold War

What Moscow and Washington Can Learn from the Last One

By Robert Legvold

Editor's Introduction

From the end of the Cold War in 1991 to 2014, American–Russian relations can be viewed as neither friendly nor adversarial. By 2015, this view began to change with the presence of NATO forces at the Russian border, the events in Syria, and the events in Ukraine. These major events would spark a dramatic change and bring the relationship between the two nations to an all-time low. There was talk of a new cold war or even World War III between the two major nuclear powers. However, with the election of Donald Trump as president, there was talk of cooperation with Russia. However, this was not the case. In fact, relations between the two nations are worse than they have ever been. It will not be business as usual between the United States and Russia. In the following essay, Robert Legvold gives his views on what Moscow and Washington can learn from the last cold war.

Managing the New Cold War

What Moscow and Washington Can Learn from the Last One

By Robert Legvold

N o one should casually label the current confrontation between Russia and the West a "new Cold War." After all, the current crisis hardly matches the depth and scale of the contest that dominated the international system in the second half of the twentieth century. And accepting the premise that Russia and the West are locked in such a conflict could lead policymakers to pursue the wrong, even dangerous strategies. Using such a label is thus a serious matter.

Yet it is important to call things by their names, and the collapse in relations between Russia and the West does indeed deserve to be called a new Cold War. The hard reality is that whatever the outcome of the crisis in Ukraine, Russia's relations with the United States and Europe won't return to business as usual, as they did after the 2008 Russian–Georgian war.

The Obama administration enjoyed some success in lifting the U.S.–Russian relationship from its 2008 nadir, as the two sides forged the New Strategic Arms Reduction Treaty (New START), agreed on tougher sanctions against Iran, cooperated on supply routes for NATO's war in Afghanistan, and worked together on President Barack Obama's plan to secure nuclear materials around the world. Relations never really moved to the next phase, as further progress was waylaid by frictions over missile defense, NATO's war in Libya, the civil war in Syria, and a host of repressive measures that Russian President Vladimir Putin's regime directed at its own citizens. But even those obstacles never completely dashed the hope that Moscow and Washington might find common ground on a number of critical issues.

That hope is now gone. The crisis in Ukraine has pushed the two sides over a cliff and into a new relationship, one not softened by the ambiguity that defined the last decade of the post–Cold War period, when each party viewed the other as neither friend nor foe. Russia and the West are now adversaries.

Although this new Cold War will be fundamentally different from the original, it will still be immensely damaging. Unlike the original, the new one won't encompass the entire global system. The world is no longer bipolar, and significant regions and key players, such as China and India, will avoid being drawn in. In addition, the new conflict will not pit one "ism" against another, nor will it likely unfold under the permanent threat of nuclear Armageddon. Yet the new Cold War will affect nearly every important dimension of the international system, and Putin's emphasis on Russia's alienation from contemporary Western cultural values will add to the estrangement. Finally, were a security crisis in the center of Europe to escalate, the danger of nuclear war could quickly return.

For both Moscow and Washington, then, the top priority must be to contain the conflict, ensuring that it ends up being as short and as shallow as possible. To achieve that goal, both sides must carefully study the lessons of the original Cold War. During that conflict, the two sides, despite their bitter rivalry, were eventually able to develop a variety of mechanisms for reducing tensions and containing risks. By the 1970s, U.S. and Russian leaders had come to see managing the contest and focusing on areas of cooperation, especially nuclear arms control, as their principal tasks. Without discounting the fundamental differences that set them at odds, leaders on both sides embraced the wisdom of engaging, rather than isolating, the other. Toward the end of the original Cold War, the earnest, albeit fumbling, efforts of U.S. President Ronald Reagan and Soviet Premier Mikhail Gorbachev to understand what drove each other greatly influenced the final outcome. Today, as leaders in Moscow and Washington move in the other direction, they might pause and reflect on how the wisest among their predecessors approached the original Cold War.

The Big Chill

For all the differences between the two periods, the new Cold War will share many of its predecessor's features. First, Russian and Western leaders have already begun framing the standoff in unforgiving terms—much as their predecessors did at the start of the first Cold War, most famously with Soviet Premier Joseph Stalin's February 1946 preelection speech and British Prime Minister Winston Churchill's Iron Curtain speech a month later. This past March, for example, Putin defended Russia's annexation of Crimea by saying that Washington and its European allies were guided by "the rule of the gun" rather than international law and were convinced that their "exceptionalism" allowed them to unlawfully use force against sovereign states, "building coalitions based on the principle, 'If you are not with us, you are against us.'" In May, Alexander Vershbow, the deputy secretary-general of NATO, asserted that Russia should now be considered "more of an adversary than a partner."

Second, as in the early phases of the original Cold War, each side sees the conflict as a result solely of the actions—or even the nature—of the other. Neither pays attention to the complicated interactions that brought relations to their present low. This preoccupation with pinning fault on the other side recalls attitudes during the late 1950s and early 1960s, when each side viewed the other as inherently alien. Only after surviving the perils of the Berlin crisis of 1958–61 and the Cuban missile crisis in 1962 did the Americans and the Soviets step back and consider where their interests converged. Over the next ten years, they negotiated three major arms control agreements: the Limited Test Ban Treaty, the Nuclear Nonproliferation Treaty, and the first Strategic Arms Limitation Talks (SALT I).

Third, as during much of the original Cold War, neither side now expects much from the relationship. Isolated moments of cooperation might emerge when the two sides' interests on specific issues happen to coincide. But neither believes it feasible to pursue cooperation across a broad front with the aim of changing the nature of the relationship overall. Nor does either camp seem willing to take the first step in that direction.

Fourth, to punish Moscow and to signal the price it will pay for further aggression, Washington has resorted to a series of Cold War–style reprisals. Beginning in March, it put military-to-military activities with Russia on hold and ended missile defense negotiations. The Obama administration has also banned the export to Russia of civilian technology with potential military applications, suspended cooperation with Russia on civilian nuclear energy projects, cut off NASA's contacts with its Russian counterpart, and denied Russian specialists access to the laboratories of the U.S. Department of Energy. Many of these measures will likely remain in place after the Ukraine crisis ends. And even those that are lifted will leave a corrosive residue.

Fifth, and most serious, just as the confrontation over security in the heart of Europe constituted the epicenter of the original Cold War, renewed uncertainty over central and eastern Europe's stability will drive this one as well. Beginning in the 1990s, NATO's expansion into much of eastern Europe, including the Baltic states, moved Europe's political-military border to the edges of the former Soviet Union. NATO enlargement also transformed Belarus, Moldova, and Ukraine into the new "lands in between," successors to Poland and the parts of the Austro-Hungarian Empire that the great powers fought over, with tragic results, in the nineteenth and twentieth centuries. Today, as Moscow fortifies its Western Military District, a key military command, and NATO refocuses on Russia, the military standoff over continental Europe, which took two decades to dismantle, will swiftly be reconstituted on Europe's eastern edge.

Red Zone

Some might assume that the new Cold War, although undesirable, won't matter nearly as much as the last one did, especially since modern Russia presents a mere shadow of the threat once posed by the Soviet Union. It is true, of course, that the United States enjoys massive material advantages over its adversary: its economy is around eight times as large as Russia's, and its military budget is seven times as large. Moreover, the magnitude of the other challenges Washington faces, from turbulence in the Middle East to rising tensions in the Asia-Pacific, might make a collapse of Russia's relations with the United States and most of Europe seem relatively unimportant.

> Whatever the outcome of the Ukraine crisis, Russia and the West won't return to business as usual.

But to doubt the likelihood or significance of a prolonged confrontation would be deeply misguided. In truth, if Russia and the United States approach each other in starkly adversarial terms, the conflict will badly warp the foreign policies of both countries, damage virtually every important dimension of international politics, and divert attention and resources from the major security challenges of the new century.

Consider Washington's position in the Asia-Pacific, toward which it has for several years now intended to rebalance its diplomatic and military resources. Recent events in Ukraine have already caused Tokyo to fear that Washington's new focus on Europe will diminish its commitment to Asia—and, more specifically, its commitment to helping Japan ward off a rising China. Japanese leaders even worry that Obama's relatively mild response to Moscow's annexation of Crimea foreshadows how Washington would react if Beijing seized the disputed Senkaku Islands (known in China as the Diaoyu Islands), in the East China Sea. Moreover, a belligerent Russia will have every incentive to hinder, rather than help, the United States' efforts to manage the delicate task of deterring Chinese aggression while widening the sphere of U.S.–Chinese cooperation. Similarly, at a time when Washington needs Russian cooperation to address new sources of global disorder, Moscow will instead step aside, impairing U.S. efforts to deal with terrorism, climate change, nuclear proliferation, and cyberwarfare.

The pressure to reorient U.S. defense planning to meet what many members of the U.S. Congress and many of Washington's eastern European allies see as a revived Russian military threat will complicate the Pentagon's effort to save money by modernizing and downsizing. The U.S. military, which is currently focused on counterterrorism and securing access to the seas surrounding China, will now have to beef up its capabilities to fight a ground war in Europe.

The new Cold War with the United States and Europe will hurt Russia even more, especially because Moscow is much more dependent on the West than vice versa, in at least one critical respect. To diversify its resource-dependent economy and modernize its aging, Soviet-era infrastructure, Russia has counted on an inflow of Western capital and technology. To the degree that this option is lost, Moscow will be forced to become vastly more dependent either on its relationship with Beijing—in which it is a distinctly junior partner—or on scattered partnerships with countries that do not offer anything resembling the resources of the United States and Europe.

Only four years ago, after the global financial crisis had laid bare the weakness of the Russian economy, then Russian President Dmitry Medvedev argued that the country sorely needed "special alliances for modernization" with the United States and the countries of the EU. But now, as the crisis in Russia's relations with those countries deepens, Russia is already feeling the crunch, as capital is fleeing the country, its credit markets are shrinking, and its economy will soon enter a recession.

Such economic hardship may prompt Russian leaders to preemptively clamp down on domestic dissent even harder than they already have to avert potential social unrest at home, which would mean a level of repression that could backfire and at some point produce the very kind of widespread opposition the Kremlin fears. Meanwhile, Russia's poisoned relations with the United States and its European allies might well lead such Russian partners as Armenia, Belarus, and Kazakhstan—all of which are crucial to Russia's plans for a Eurasian economic union and a stronger Collective Security Treaty Organization—to subtly distance themselves from Moscow for fear of tainting their own relationships with the Western powers.

The new confrontation with the West will also force Russia to stretch its military resources thin. That will leave Moscow poorly equipped to handle a host of other security challenges, such as violence in the northern Caucasus and instability in Central Asia, the latter of which is compounded by the unpredictable futures facing Afghanistan and Pakistan. Russia must also defend its vast border with China and prepare for a potential conflict between North and South Korea.

Pressure Points

The collapse of Russia's relations with the West will not only distort U.S., European, and Russian foreign policy but also inflict serious harm on a broad array of international issues. What still remains of the arms control regime that took Russia and the United States years to build will now largely come undone. The new

Cold War has eliminated any chance that Moscow and Washington will resolve their differences over missile defense, a Russian precondition for further strategic arms control agreements. Instead, the two sides will likely start developing new and potentially destabilizing technologies, including advanced precision-guided conventional weapons and cyberwarfare tools.

Meanwhile, the European component of the U.S. missile defense program will now likely take on a specifically anti-Russian character, particularly because the Obama administration reportedly believes that Russia has violated the 1987 Intermediate-Range Nuclear Forces Treaty. And it is unlikely that Moscow and Washington will be able to agree on how to place limits on the deployment of major weapons systems in Europe. The new Cold War has also dashed any hopes of strengthening other basic agreements, such as the 1992 Treaty on Open Skies, which regulates unarmed aerial surveillance flights.

Geostrategic calculations will now also assume a far more dominant role in U.S.–Russian energy relations. Each side will attempt to use the oil and gas trade to gain leverage over the other and minimize its own vulnerability. In the Arctic, the chances for U.S.–Russian cooperation in developing that region's vast hydrocarbon reserves will surely shrink. More broadly, the new Cold War will set back international efforts to deal with the impact of climate change on the Arctic—an issue on which U.S.–Russian relations have been surprisingly cooperative.

One of the most successful but underappreciated aspects of recent U.S.–Russian relations has been the progress made by the 20 working groups of the U.S.–Russia Bilateral Presidential Commission, which was established in 2009 to facilitate high-level cooperation on a range of policies, from prison reform and military education to civilian emergencies and counterterrorism. It seems unlikely that such cooperation will continue, much less improve, during the new Cold War. Moscow and Washington will also struggle to align their positions on key matters of global governance, including the much-needed reforms of the un, the International Monetary Fund, and the Organization for Security and Cooperation in Europe. Washington is now focused on excluding Russia where possible (from the G-8, for example) and circumscribing Russia's role elsewhere. Meanwhile, Moscow will work harder than before to supplant U.S. and European influence in these institutions.

Finally, should one or more of the long-simmering conflicts in the post-Soviet region again explode, the chances that Russia and the United States would act together to contain the violence seem close to zero. Instead, were Nagorno-Karabakh, in Azerbaijan, or Transnistria, in Moldova, to blow up, Moscow and Washington would both be far more likely to focus on counteracting what they each saw as the malevolent role of the other.

Damage Control

The immediate crisis in Ukraine, even if momentarily muffled, has scarcely ended. The presidential election in May could not settle the crisis of legitimacy facing Ukraine's leadership, which lacks the trust of the eastern part of the country. Nor will the modest aid packages currently being cobbled together by the International Monetary Fund and other Western donors resolve the deep structural problems eating away at Ukraine's economy, namely unconstrained corruption and the power exerted by a small number of oligarchic clans. In short, the country has a long slog ahead, filled with political and economic uncertainty.

Yet Ukraine forms only part of a larger and more ominous picture. Europe's stability, which only recently seemed assured, now appears more tenuous. A new fault line has opened up in the heart of the continent, and instability anywhere within it—not only in Ukraine but in Belarus or Moldova as well—will likely lead to an escalating confrontation between the East and the West. Leaders in Moscow and Washington need to face up to this reality and to the price they will pay if they blind themselves to the larger consequences of the new Cold War. Understating both the risks and the costs will only lead to underestimating how much effort will be required to surmount them. The overarching goal of both Moscow and Washington must therefore be to make the new Cold War as quick and as shallow as possible.

This goal can be achieved only if leaders on both sides embrace damage control as their first-order objective. So far, they have not. Rather than understanding the Ukraine crisis in this larger perspective, Russian and Western leaders seem fixated on prevailing in the crisis itself. For Russia, that means toughing it out: taking the pain the West means to inflict through sanctions and forcing Washington and U.S. allies to accept what Russian leaders see as their country's legitimate interests in Ukraine and beyond. For the United States and Europe, winning in Ukraine means stymieing Russia's aggressive behavior and forcing Moscow back onto a more cooperative path. (In some Western circles, winning also entails weakening Putin enough to hasten the end of his regime.)

Committing to limiting the damage done by the new Cold War does not mean that the West should tolerate Russian attempts to control events in Europe's new lands in between by abetting political instability or using military force. If the United States and its European allies cannot find a way to thwart this Russian temptation—through credible military threats, if necessary—the new Cold War will only deepen. At the same time, a policy to deal with conflicts over Europe's unsettled center needs to be guided by a larger goal. Everything that Western leaders do to induce Russian restraint must be paired with a compelling vision of an alternative path that, if taken, would lead in a more constructive direction. Both halves of this approach need to be clear and concrete: the redlines must be self-evident and backed by the threat of credible military force, and the opportunities for cooperation must be specific and significant.

Anger Management

Minimizing the damage done by the new Cold War will require managing it with the intention of gradually overcoming it. To this end, leaders in Moscow, Washington, and European capitals should heed three lessons from the original Cold War.

First, they need to recognize that during the Cold War, mistrust often distorted each side's perceptions of the other's intentions. As one among many examples, consider Washington's incorrect belief that the Soviet invasion of Afghanistan in 1979 was an attempt to gain control over the oil in the Persian Gulf—a misperception rooted in the deep-seated mistrust of Soviet territorial ambitions that U.S. leaders had harbored ever since Stalin seized much of eastern Europe after World War II and then sought to expand Soviet influence in such places as Iran and Korea.

Ever since the first Cold War ended, misperceptions have continued to plague relations between the two sides, constantly disrupting Moscow's and Washington's efforts to build a new partnership and allowing a potentially functional relationship to devolve into an adversarial one. NATO enlargement and U.S. plans for a European missile defense system fed a preexisting Russian disposition to believe such moves were directed against Moscow. And Russia's heavy-handed treatment of its neighbors—particularly Ukraine—created a Western perception that Moscow wants not merely influence but also control over old Soviet territory.

> Moscow and Washington must focus on making the new Cold War as short and as shallow as possible.

Peeling away such mistrust won't be easy. It will require great effort on the part of U.S. and Russian officials and a willingness to take real risks. Leaders on both sides know that their domestic political opponents will characterize any attempts to overcome hostility as weakness. They also worry that any overtures will look feckless if they are not immediately reciprocated—or, worse, that such efforts will look like appeasement if the other side responds with further aggression.

Still, it is each side's distorted notions of the other's aims that represent the largest barriers to cooperation. The way to begin unwinding this tangle is for the two sides to talk directly to each other, quietly, at the highest levels, and without preconditions. They must meet with an understanding that every issue is on the table, including the most contentious ones. Such dialogue, of course, is the most difficult precisely when it is also the most necessary, but neither government need abandon its current positions before it starts talking. Probing the sources of each side's deeper concerns, however, is only the first step. Next, talk must lead to action. Each side should specify a modest step or series of steps that, if taken, would convince it to begin rethinking its assumptions about the other.

The two sides should also stop blaming the other side and instead step back and consider what in their own behavior has contributed to the derailment. The original Cold War's second lesson is that it was the interaction between the two sides, rather than the actions of only one side, that created the spiral in tensions. In the Ukraine crisis, at least, there is enough blame to go around. The EU was tone-deaf in dismissing legitimate Russian concerns over the failed association agreement with Ukraine. During the unrest in Kiev in February, the United States too quickly abandoned an agreement reached by diplomats on all sides that offered a potential way out of the crisis, promising new presidential elections and constitutional reform. And throughout, Russia has been all too ready to exploit Ukraine's instability to further its objectives.

The original Cold War's third lesson might be the most important. Events, and not predetermined plans and policies, usually determined U.S. and Soviet behavior. In the current crisis over Ukraine and in others to follow, the United States and its European allies should therefore focus on influencing Russian choices by shaping events rather than by trying to change the way the Kremlin sees things. In practical terms, this means that Washington, alongside the EU, should commit to giving Ukraine the economic assistance it desperately needs (provided that real steps are taken to fix its corrupt political system), insist that Ukrainian leaders establish a government that can regain legitimacy in the eastern part of the country, and strive to create an environment in which Ukraine can cooperate with Europe and Russia without having to choose between the two. If U.S. policy moves in this direction, Russian choices are likely to be more constructive.

At the moment, emotions are running high in Moscow, Washington, and the capitals of Europe, and the confrontation over Ukraine seems to have taken on a momentum of its own. If somehow the Ukraine crisis fades, the intensity of the new Cold War will weaken, but not end. If the crisis in Ukraine deepens (or a crisis elsewhere arises), so will the new Cold War. In other words, Ukraine is central to the direction the confrontation will take, but not everything depends on what happens there. Just like the original Cold War, the new Cold War will play out on many stages, and it will not even begin to be resolved until both sides recognize the high costs of the course they are on and decide to tackle the difficult steps leading to a different path.

QUESTION TO CONSIDER

- In Legvold's opinion, what can Washington and Moscow learn from the last Cold War?

CHAPTER 16

Why This Cold War Is More Dangerous than the One We Survived

By Stephen F. Cohen

Editor's Introduction

Stephen F. Cohen gives a different view on US–Russian relations. Cohen believes that we are already in a new cold war, which was started by the West. Some say his views have made him an apologist for Putin, while others say that Cohen is a highly informed critic of US–Russian relations. Read Cohen's essay and decide for yourself.

Why This Cold War Is More Dangerous than the One We Survived

By Stephen F. Cohen

A formal meeting between Presidents Trump and Putin is being seriously discussed in Washington and Moscow. Ritualized but substantive "summits," as they were termed, were frequently used during the 40-year US–Soviet Cold War to reduce conflicts and increase cooperation between the two superpowers. They were most important when tensions were highest. Some were very successful, some less so, others were deemed failures.

Given today's extraordinary political circumstances, we may wonder if anything positive would come from a Trump–Putin summit. But it is necessary, even imperative, that Washington and Moscow try because this Cold War is more dangerous than was its predecessor. By now, the reasons should be clear, but it is time to recall and update them. There are at least ten:

1. The political epicenter of the new Cold War is not in far-away Berlin, as it was from the late 1940s on, but directly on Russia's borders, from the Baltic states and Ukraine to another former Soviet republic, Georgia. Each of these new Cold War fronts is fraught with the possibility of hot war. US–Russian military relations are especially tense today in the Baltic region, where a large-scale NATO buildup is under way, and in Ukraine, where a US–Russian proxy war is intensifying.

    The "Soviet Bloc" that once served as a buffer between NATO and Russia no longer exists. And many imaginable incidents on the West's new Eastern Front, intentional or unintentional, could easily trigger actual war between the United States and Russia. What brought about this situation on Russia's borders—unprecedented at least since the Nazi German invasion in 1941— was, of course, Washihgton's exceedingly unwise decision, in the late 1990s, to expand NATO eastward. Done in the name of "security," it has made all the states involved only more insecure.

2. Proxy wars were a feature of the old Cold War, but usually small ones in what was called the "Third World," in Africa, for example. They rarely involved

many, if any, Soviet of American personnel, mostly only money and weapons. Today's US–Russian proxy wars are different, located in the center of geopolitics and accompanied by too many American and Russian trainers, minders, and possibly fighters. Two have already erupted: in Georgia in 2008, where Russian forces fought a Georgian army financed, trained, and minded by American funds and personnel; and in Syria, where in February scores of Russians were killed by US-backed anti-Assad forces. Moscow did not retaliate, but it has pledged to do so if there is "a next time," as there very well might be.

If so, this would in effect be war directly between Russia and America. The risk of a direct conflict also continues to grow in Ukraine. The country's US-backed but politically failing President Petro Poroshenko seems periodically tempted to launch another all-out military assault on rebel-controlled Donbass, which is backed by Moscow. If he does so, and the assault does not quickly fail as previous ones did, Russia will certainly intervene in eastern Ukraine with a truly tangible "invasion."

Washington will then have to make a fateful war-or-peace decision. Having already reneged on its commitments to the Minsk Accords, the best hope for ending the four-year Ukrainian crisis peacefully, Kiev seems to have an unrelenting impulse to be a tail wagging the dog of US–Russian war. Its capacity for provocations and disinformation seem second to none, as evidenced again recently by the faked "assassination and resurrection" of journalist Arkady Babchenko.

3. Years-long Western, especially American, demonization of the Kremlin leader, Putin, is also unprecedented. Too obvious to spell out again here, no Soviet Communist leader, at least since Stalin, was ever subjected to such prolonged, baseless, crudely derogatory personal vilification. Whereas Soviet leaders were regarded as acceptable negotiating partners for American presidents, including at major summits, Putin has been made to seem to be an illegitimate national leader—at best "a KGB thug" or murderous "mafia boss."

4. Still more, demonizing Putin has generated widespread Russophobic vilification of Russia itself, or what the *New York Times* and other mainstream-media outlets have taken to calling "Vladimir Putin's Russia." Yesterday's enemy was Soviet Communism. Today it is increasingly Russia, thereby also delegitimizing Russia as a great power with legitimate national interests. "The Parity Principle," as I termed it during the preceding Cold War—the principle that both sides had legitimate interests at home and abroad, which was the basis for diplomacy and negotiations, and symbolized by leadership summits—no longer exists, at least on the American side.

Nor does the acknowledgment that both sides were to blame to some extent for the previous Cold War. Among influential American observers who even recognize the new Cold War, "Putin's Russia" alone is to blame. When there is no recognized parity and shared responsibility, there is ever-shrinking space for diplomacy, but more and more for increasingly militarized relations, as we are witnessing today.

5. Meanwhile, most of the Cold War safeguards—cooperative mechanisms and mutually observed rules of conduct that evolved over decades in order to prevent superpower hot war—have been vaporized or badly frayed since the Ukrainian crisis in 2014, as the UN General Secretary António Guterres, almost alone, has recognized: "The Cold War is back—with a vengeance but with a difference. The mechanisms and the safeguards to manage the risks of escalation that existed in the past no longer seem to be present."[1] Trump's recent missile strike on Syria carefully avoided killing any Russians, but Moscow has vowed to retaliate against the US if there is a "next time," as there may be.

   Even the decades-long process of arms control may, an expert warns, be coming to an "end."[2] It would mean an unfettered new nuclear-arms race as well as the termination of an ongoing diplomatic process that buffered US–Soviet relations during very bad political times.

   In short, if there actually are any new Cold War rules of conduct, they are yet to be formulated and mutually accepted. Nor does this semi-anarchy take into account the new warfare technology of cyber-attacks. What are its implications for the secure functioning of existential Russian and American nuclear command-and-control and early-warning systems that guard against an accidental launching of missiles still on high alert?

6. Russiagate allegations that the American president has been compromised by—or is even an agent of—the Kremlin are also without precedent. These allegations, as we have seen, have already had profoundly dangerous consequences. They include the nonsensical, mantra-like declaration that "Russia attacked America" during the 2016 presidential election; crippling assaults on President Trump every time he speaks with Putin in person or by phone; and making both Trump and Putin so toxic that most American politicians, journalists, and intellectuals who understand the present-day dangers are reluctant to speak out against US contributions to the new Cold War.

7. Mainstream media outlets have, we know, played a woeful role in all of this. Unlike in the past, when pro-détente advocates had roughly equal access to influential media, today's new Cold War media continue to enforce their orthodox narrative that Russia is solely to blame. They offer not diversity of opinion and reporting but "confirmation bias." Alternative voices (with, yes, "alternative" or opposing facts) rarely appear any longer in the most influential newspapers or on national television or radio.

One alarming result is that "disinformation" generated by or pleasing to Washington and its allies has consequences before it can be corrected. The Ukrainian fake Babchenko assassination (allegedly ordered by Putin, of course) was quickly exposed, but not the official version of the Skripal assassination attempt in the UK, which led to the largest US expulsion of Russian diplomats in history before London's initial account could be thoroughly examined. This too—Cold War without debate—is unprecedented, precluding the frequent rethinking and revising of US policy that characterized the preceding 40-year Cold War.

8. Equally lamentable, and very much unlike during the 40-year Cold War, there still is virtually no significant opposition in the American mainstream to the US role in the new Cold War—not in the media, not in Congress, not in the two major political parties, not in think tanks, not in the universities, not at grassroots levels. This continues to be unprecedented, dangerous, and contrary to real democracy.

Consider again the still thunderous silence of scores of large US corporations that have been doing profitable business in post-Soviet Russia for years, from fast-food chains and automobile manufacturers to pharmaceutical and energy giants. Contrast their behavior to that of CEOs of PepsiCo, Control Data, IBM, and other major American corporations seeking entry to the Soviet market in the 1970s and 1980s, when they publicly supported and even funded pro-détente organizations and politicians. How to explain the continuing silence of their counterparts today, who are usually so profit-motivated? Are they also fearful of being labeled "pro-Putin" or possibly "pro-Trump"?

9. And then there remains the widespread escalatory myth that today's Russia, unlike the Soviet Union, is too weak—its economy too small and fragile, its leader too "isolated in international affairs"—to wage a sustained Cold War, and that eventually Putin, who is "punching above his weight," as the cliché has it, will capitulate. This too is a dangerous delusion—one that cannot be attributed to President Trump. It was, we saw earlier, President Obama who, in 2014, as approvingly reported by the *New York Times,* set out to make Putin's Russia "a pariah state."

Washington and some of its allies certainly tried to isolate Russia. How else to interpret fully the political scandals and media campaigns that erupted on the eve of the Sochi Olympics and again on the eve of the World Cup championship in Russia? Or the tantrum-like, mostly ineffective, even counter-productive cascade of economic sanctions on Moscow?

But Russia is hardly isolated in world affairs, not even in Europe, where five or more governments are tilting away from the anti-Russian line of Washington, London, and Brussels. Despite sanctions, Russia's energy industry and agricultural exports are flourishing. Moreover, geopolitically, Moscow has many military and related advantages in regions where the new Cold War has unfolded. And no state with Russia's modern nuclear and other weapons is "punching above its weight." Contrary to Washington's expectations, the great majority of Russians have rallied behind Putin because they believe their country is under attack by the US-led West. Anyone with a rudimentary knowledge of Russia's history understands it is highly unlikely to capitulate under any circumstances.

10. Finally (at least as of now), there is the growing warlike "hysteria" fueled both in Washington and Moscow. It is driven by various factors, but television talk "news" broadcasts, as common in Russia as in the United States, play a major role. Only an extensive quantitative study could discern which plays a more lamentable role in promoting this frenzy—MSNBC and CNN or their Russian counterparts. The Russian dark witticism seems apt: "Both are worst" (*Oba khuzhe*). Again, some of this American broadcast extremism existed during the preceding Cold War, but almost always balanced, even offset, by informed, wiser opinions, which are now largely excluded.

Is my analysis of the graver dangers inherent in the new Cold War itself extremist or alarmist? Some usually reticent specialists would seem to agree with my general assessment. As I reported earlier, experts gathered by a centrist Washington think tank thought that on a scale of 1 to 10, there is a 5 to 7 chance of actual war with Russia. There are other such opinions. A former head of British M16 is reported as saying that "for the first time in living memory, there's a realistic chance of a superpower conflict." And a respected retired Russian general tells the same Washington think tank that any military confrontation "will end up with the use of nuclear weapons between the United States and Russia."[3, 4]

A single Trump-Putin summit cannot eliminate these new Cold War dangers. But US-Soviet summits traditionally served three corollary purposes. They created a kind of security partnership—not a conspiracy—that involved each leader's limited political capital at home, which the other should recognize and not heedlessly jeopardize. They sent a clear message to the two leaders' respective national-security bureaucracies, which often did not favor détente-like cooperation, that the "boss" was determined and they must end their foot-dragging, even sabotage. And summits, with their exalted rituals and intense coverage, usually improved the media-political environment needed to enhance cooperation amid Cold War conflicts.

If a Trump–Putin summit achieves even some of those purposes, it might pull us back from the precipice.

Notes

1. un.org, April 13, 2018

2. Eugene Rumer, carnegieendowment.org, April 17, 2018

3. Quoted by Gerald F. Seib, *wsj.com,* April 16, 2018

4. nationalinterest.org, April 4, 2018

QUESTION TO CONSIDER

- Why does Cohen consider the "new" Cold War to be more dangerous than the last Cold War?